BALOCHISTAN

A Saga of Insurgency, Freedom, and Injustice

BALOCHISTAN

A Saga of Insurgency, Freedom, and Injustice

Dr. Anas Mir

HOW
ACADEMICS
an imprint of Highlyy Publishing LLP

ISBN: 978-93-95522-56-4
First Published : 2023

Published by : HOW ACADEMICS
an imprint of Highlyy Publishing LLP

Correspondence Address :
4/30 A II Floor, Double Storey Buildings
Vijay Nagar, Delhi-110009
Editorial: +91 9811026449
Sales : +91 9999953412
Email: info@howacademics.com
Website: www.howacademics.com

Printed in India

Preface

In the turbulent landscapes of South Asia, where history, insurgency, politics, and human rights converge, there exists a region that has remained enigmatic and underexplored - Balochistan. Nestled amidst the rugged terrain, Balochistan, straddling the borders of Iran, Afghanistan, and Pakistan, has long been a subject of fascination and intrigue. This book, "Balochistan: Unveiling the Veiled Truth," delves deep into the heart of this region to unravel its complex past and present, shedding light on the multifaceted aspects that make Balochistan a region of utmost significance in contemporary global affairs. Our journey begins with "Tracing the Historical Pathway of Balochistan." In this chapter, we take you on a voyage through time, exploring the rich tapestry of Balochistan's history, its ancient civilizations, and the forces that have shaped its destiny. From the ancient Silk Road to the modern geopolitics of the region, we lay the foundation for understanding the intricate web of influences that have left an indelible mark on Balochistan. Moving forward, "Gaining Insight into Balochistan's Insurgency" peels back the layers of conflict and resistance that have defined Balochistan's contemporary history. This chapter delves into the roots of insurgency, examining the grievances, aspirations, and challenges faced by the Baloch people as they struggle for autonomy and justice in the face of formidable odds. "Balochis of Pakistan" provides a comprehensive examination of the Baloch population in Pakistan, exploring their culture, traditions, and socio-economic conditions. We shed light on their rich heritage while also discussing the complex relationship between the Baloch people and the Pakistani state. As we venture deeper into Balochistan's complexities, "Security Situation in Pakistani Balochistan" offers an in-depth analysis of the security dynamics within the Pakistani province of Balochistan. This chapter dissects the various actors involved and their interests, painting a vivid picture of the challenges and opportunities that define this region. In "Champions of Human Rights in Balochistan," we pay homage to the brave individuals and organizations who have taken up the mantle of advocating for human rights in Balochistan. Their tireless efforts to bring attention to the plight of the Baloch people in the face of oppression and violence are both inspiring and commendable. The chapter "Government Apathy and State Collaboration" explores the delicate balance between governance and resistance in Balochistan. We examine the role of the state, its policies, and the impact of its actions on the Baloch people. The chapter underscores the urgent need for a more inclusive and equitable approach. "Unexplained Vanishings in Balochistan" is a sobering exploration of the disturbing phenomenon of enforced disappearances that have plagued the region. We shed light on the stories of those who have disappeared and the anguished families who continue to seek answers and justice. Finally, "CPEC - Future Scenarios and Complexities for Balochistan and Pakistan" delves into the ambitious China-Pakistan Economic Corridor (CPEC) project and its implications for Balochistan and the wider region. We analyze the potential benefits and challenges while considering the diverse perspectives on this transformative initiative.

This book is a culmination of extensive research, interviews, and on-the-ground reporting, aiming to provide readers with a nuanced understanding of Balochistan's multifaceted reality. As you embark on this journey through the pages, may you gain not only knowledge but also empathy for the people who call Balochistan their home. Our hope is that this book contributes to a more informed and compassionate discourse surrounding the region, ultimately paving the way for a brighter future for Balochistan and its people.

Contents

Chapter 1
Tracing the Historical Pathway of Balochistan

About the Region

Balochistan is in the southeast of the Iranian plains, which is in the south. On a map, the area that is now the Pakistani state of Balochistan looks like a lozenge with an odd shape. Its shorter diagonal runs north-west from Cape Monze to Koh-i-Malik Shah, which is where Iran, Pakistan, and Afghanistan meet. This is a distance of 475 miles. Its longest stretch is 625 miles long and runs north-east from the point where the coast of Iran meets the coast of Pakistan to the mountains of Southern Waziristan. The land is some of the least friendly in the world, with a lot of sandy areas and mountain ranges full of rocks. With only 3 to 12 inches of rain a year and temperatures that go from very hot to very cold, the vegetation is mostly good for raising sheep and goats in the north-east and camels and horses in the south-west. Some of the few natural waterways dry up completely, but meltwater from the winter snow feeds springs and wells in areas that are good for farming. This makes it possible to grow grain and other foods for people to eat and pasture for cattle. Irrigation ditches and karezes, which are deep channels that are covered to keep water from evaporating, can bring water from miles away, but they only work if they are cleaned regularly, which can be hard to do when there is trouble. Where water rights are as important as land rights, semi-nomadic shepherds move their flocks between typical grazing grounds.

In the few fertile valleys, there are towns and villages with churches, bazaars, government offices, and the fortified homes of local magnates. In places that get enough water but aren't farmed, plants grow tall enough to become jangal, which means "forest" or "thicket." This gives wild animals and possible thieves a place to hide. Flat desert areas are sometimes hit by violent sandstorms that make it very dark, even at noon, and simoom winds, which are short-lived but very hot and are thought to be caused by Satan opening the doors of Hell and can kill both people and animals by causing heatstroke. When it rains far away, as it does in other desert areas, dry ravines can quickly fill with raging floods that can drown travelers who are sleeping in their camps.

Kachhi, a large triangle plain that stretches north from Upper Sind and is about 2,000 square miles in size, is a good example of how the desert and the sown are different. Away from water, the land is a dry, desert-like place. It grows well where there is water. During the time period covered by this book, the government's share of the crop was taken from the land revenue. This was a standard practice all over central and southern Asia. Balochistan's main product, wool from its large flocks of sheep, was not taxed. Instead, the country made money by charging transit tolls or customs duties on all things that went through the country. Kachhi was especially valuable as a source of this kind of income because it was the main route for traffic going through the Bolan Pass. The Bolan Pass is a defile that goes for more than 44 miles and rises from 500 feet above sea level in Kachhi's northernmost town, Dadhar, to 6,000 feet above sea level in Quetta, the first town above the pass.

For safety, traders and other people usually traveled in groups called kafilas (Arabic: qafila). Each kafila was led by a professional qafila-bash, or Master of the Caravan, whose job was similar to that of a wagonmaster in the early American West. Each kafila was a separate group that came together for the length of the trip. It could change its route or destination if it heard that there was danger ahead or a better market had been found. Because it is higher up, the district of Shal above the Bolan Pass, which is often called Quetta (or, in early spellings, Kwatta after the name of its main town), is cooler than Kachhi. It is the second most valuable land area in Balochistan, and its strategic value comes from the fact that it controls the approaches to the Bolan. The much shorter Khojak Pass connects southern Afghanistan to Balochistan about 50 miles from Quetta.

Before modern times, most of the roads that went to the Bolan were only good for carrying packs, and wheeled vehicles had a hard time getting there. As they did everywhere else, kind or religious people sometimes built "semis," which were like service stops where travelers and their animals could stay the night. Depending on how hard each stretch was, distances were measured in terms of how many days it would take to walk that distance. In the driest areas, kafilas might have had extra pack animals to carry food and water for the people moving the commercial payload, just like current convoys that take the same route can have their own fuel bowsers. A pack animal or a car with a motor can only go so far into a desert before it has used up all the water, food, or fuel it can take. Movement stays pretty much limited to areas where these things can be bought locally or from pre-stocked depots, which themselves need to be restocked often. But raiders may be interested in these stores, so they need to be guarded on their own.

Under Sharia law, customs fees were equal to 2.5% of the value of the goods being transported. In reality, transit fees were set as high as the traffic would allow. This was a legal way to protect travelers, as local chiefs hired a few "token riders" to follow each kafila through their area and show potential thieves that the fee for safe passage had been paid. This was accepted as a form of insurance because if a kafila was robbed, the people who had been paid to guard it were expected to pay for the goods and animals that were stolen and for any injuries the travelers got.

Ethnicity

Balochistan is named after the Baloch or Baluchis, who are an agricultural, semi-nomadic group of people with Indo-European roots. During the regional movement of people in the 14th and 15th centuries, they left their homes south of the Caspian Sea to find new pastures in or beyond Sistan, according to their own stories. This idea is supported by the fact that there are still large Baloch people in eastern Iran and southern Central Asia. The Brahuis, who were also herders, were the most important people in Balochistan. Even though these people are Indo-European in their culture, they speak a language that is linked to the Dravidian languages of southern India. Different ideas have been put forward to explain this linguistic oddity, such as a link to the ancient Indus Valley Civilization, evidence of which can still be found in Balochistan, but the subject is still controversial.

The Brahui core is in the middle of the country. It includes the hill city of Kalat and the provinces of Sarawan and Jhalawan, which are also called the Upper and Lower Highlands. To the west of this area, the Baloch took over Makran, which goes all the way to the Arabian Sea, and Kharan, which is mostly desert and is to the north of Makran. In the east, between Kachhi on one side and Sind on the other, Baloch tribes lived in the impressive but barren Suleiman Mountains and their foothills. The Marris and Bugtis were among the most warlike of these groups.

At the beginning of the 18th century, the Kalhora kings who ruled Sind gave land to the Taipur clan of Marris in exchange for military service. Eventually, the soldiers who came to Sind killed their bosses, and in 1783, the Taipurs took control of Sind for themselves. The country stayed a single unit in theory, just like it had been when it was part of the Mughal Empire before the Kalhora period. However, in reality, it split into three almost-independent states whose princes or amirs (commanders) stayed close to each other through family ties. The amirs gave land to their Baloch followers, who then became the most powerful armed class in the country. This hurt the regular Sindi people and made the Baloch diaspora even bigger.

Baloch and Brahuis had a social system that was mostly the same. Bands of pastoralists were part of clans and tribes that were often thousands of people strong. Both groups wore clothes that were mostly the same. The men wore their hair in long, oiled ringlets, and the women didn't cover their faces. The eastern Baloch called their tribal leaders "tomandar," which is made up of the suffix "dar," which means "the holder of a post or appointment," and the Turkish word for "ten thousand." The title, like all mili, was different between these societies, but the sardars of Balochistan were a lot like medieval European noblemen in that they would not stand for any insult to their honor or threat to their political power.

Sardars were supposed to dole out justice based on local customs and the advice of people who knew the Holy Law. There was a written method for how people who did something bad to property or people were supposed to pay compensation to the people who were hurt. This did a lot to stop the blood feuds that were popular among their Pashtun neighbors. The Pashtunwali, their code or set of rules, said that killing a male relative or seducing a female relative was a stain on the family's honor that could only be cleaned up with blood. In Balochistan, feuds could still happen if the right compensation wasn't made (especially for a murder). These feuds could last for years and often happened between sardars or against their rulers, which was bad for the whole country.

Sardars were powerful in politics because they could get their clansmen to form armed units. The post of sardar was usually given to the most respected member of the tribe's leading family. It was not passed down through the family. Respect was earned and kept by a sardar's ability to care for the well-being of his people, especially by giving them money or jobs in the military or grazing rights or land ownership. To do this and pay for the feasts and gifts that came with his social position, a sardar needed a lot of money. He usually got this money by selling his own crops and flocks, taking money from his clansmen from time to time, getting money from the ruler of the country in exchange for military or political support, and raiding neighboring areas. This is a sad fact about many pastoral societies, where most of the property is mobile animals.

Military Structure

Balochistan was run by the military for hundreds of years, just like many medieval countries in Europe and Asia. Great men were given jagirs, which were liens on the income (usually the government's share of the crop) of certain places in exchange for sending troops when the ruler asked. In theory, the king could give jagirs to anyone who could raise the number of troops needed. In real life, where society was built on tribes, the jagirdar or assignee was usually a local chief who hired troops from his own clansmen, for whom this was an important source of income. Over time, jagirs became a way to pass on land from generation to generation, and the British didn't see much difference between how a jagirdar collected money and how a big owner in their own country collected rent.

In more advanced cultures, like those of medieval Europe, Iran, and South Asia, the need to make troops was turned into money. This was easier for both the government, which could use the money to hire their own, more reliable troops, and the people who were supposed to serve but didn't want to. In Balochistan, these changes were not welcomed by the sardars, who chose to raise their own armies to improve their reputations as leaders and employers. If a contingent was called up for more than a short time, the central government was responsible for paying and providing it. Because this put a strain on their finances, poor rulers were often hesitant to call for these fees. When they did, campaigns were usually short and finished through talks rather than a victory on the battlefield.

When they weren't needed for farming, many Brahui and Baloch moved to the south for seasonal farm work. Most of them seemed willing to trade honest work for raiding, which was more exciting and less hard work, especially since their chief took care of them while they were attacking. Young men in many societies love being put to the test in war and earning respect from their peers through brave acts. After a successful raid, everyone got their share of the money and could take any private property they wanted. Not only did people steal animals or grain during these raids. Men, women, and children could be taken away, at best for a fee and at worst to sell in the slave markets of Herat and Central Asia. Most of the time, the Jats or farmers were hurt the most by these attacks. The free-spirited Baloch and Brahui stockmen looked down on farmers and only worked in the fields when they had to.

Most men owned the traditional weapons of the country, which were long spears, knives, curved Indo-Saracenic swords, small round shields made of tough hide and strengthened with metal bosses, and jezails, which were long-barreled smoothbore matchlock muskets. Men who didn't have their own weapons would get them from their wealthier friends or clan leaders. Those who could afford them wore mail coats and the conical steel helmets that were common in battle in the East. Some people used the thick folds of their turbans to protect their heads. In addition to the tribal levies, who were called up when needed, there were also a few sepoys, or professional fighters. These were used as home troops or artillerymen. However, because regular soldiers were both inefficient and expensive, only the richest chiefs could afford to keep them around all the time. If long-term conventional operations were planned, mercenaries could be hired for the duration of the war or until the money to pay them ran out, which was usually the same thing. As part of their normal business, neighborhood contractors and merchants helped out with logistics. Hakims were educated men who lived in the homes of every great chief and worked as doctors and priests. The bard (raizwar) was also a very important part of the war band. He or she kept the soldiers' spirits up by singing about their ancestors' wins and writing down their own deeds as they happened. Loris were armourers who went with the fighting men and had mobile workshops to fix broken weapons and equipment.

Balochistan was not the only place where robber bands preyed on farmers and travelers going about their business. It was and still is common in countries with weak governments that can't protect people who can't protect themselves. In Balochistan, the problem was worse because the country was organized in a quasi-feudal way. This meant that the sardars had the military means needed to stop raids, punish raiders, and get back stolen property if deterrence didn't work. As a group, they didn't have much reason to pay the cost of calling up their guards unless it was to protect their own land or steal from other people's. When they did go out into the streets, they were often just as likely to fight against the government as they were to back it. Armed robberies happened all the time, and there was always a chance that someone from outside the country would step in. Balochistan was a political backwater, and many of its neighbors saw it as a place where thieves harassed travelers and stole from settlements regardless of international lines. When the British took control of the area, they had to deal with the possibility of another power using Balochistan as a way to invade India. They also had to protect their border areas from Baloch raiders.

History and Roots

The name Kalat comes from a misspelling of the Arabic word Qila, which means "fort." Kalat is the most important city in the country of the Brahui. Like the English words "Chester" and "Borough," which mean almost the same thing, "Kalat" (also spelled "Khelat," "Qalat," "Qala," "Killa," etc.) is a common part of place names in parts of the world where there are many forts, often with the name of a local ruler or group.

At the beginning of the sixteenth century, Kalat city, which was part of the Mughal province of Kandahar, became the center of local government. A hundred years later, a Brahui prince named Ahmad Khan came to power in the area that went from Kalat to Mastung to Quetta to the north-east. In exchange for money from local farms, he protected them from raiders and got rich enough that other Brahui sardars agreed to follow him as their leader. He called himself

Khan (Lord) of Kalat in 1666. His family kept the name Kambarani, which came from an early Brahui chief named Kambar. His line was called the Ahmadzai, which means "the children of Ahmad." At the head of an alliance of Brahui tribes, Ahmad Khan I led a revolt against the weakening Mughal rule and grew his new khanate to include areas where Baloch tribes lived. He then took the name Khan-i-Baloch, which his descendants and successors have kept to this day.

In addition to the jagirs that the khans gave them, the Brahui and Baloch sardars kept their family holdings, called inam lands, that were there before the khanate was set up. Most of the most strong chiefs saw the khan more as the leader of a group of equals than as an absolute ruler. Even though traditional jurists (both Brahuis and Balochis were Sunnis) taught that a king is God's representative on earth and that sharing power is the same as giving God a partner, which is the sin of polytheism, they did it anyway. Since this doctrine says that all legal power comes from God, Sunni law-makers were always arguing about whether or when it was okay to stand up to a tyrant. In Balochistan, the sardars knew the answer and, using tyranny as an excuse, were always ready to fight against the khan when it was in their best interests to do so. When a khan made a decision about a disagreement between sardars, the losing side often questioned his authority by appealing to nearby rulers in Sind or Kandahar. Both Sind and Kandahar had vague claims to being in charge of Balochistan. Still, the khan and the sardars had enough in common for Kalat to keep going as a sort of independent state, at least as long as civil wars in neighboring countries kept them from claiming it. Successive khans, whose troops were made up of military units from the sardars, used the Machiavellian strategy of "divide and rule" to keep their power.

The wazir was in charge of the khanate's central government. His main job was to run the treasury, which made him the top minister. The daroga, a minister whose title, like constable or marshal, could mean either a high officer of the state or a local cop, but here was similar to Home Secretary or Minister of the Interior, was almost as powerful. These were helped by a small number of royal officials, called shaghasis, which is often translated as "chamberlain" and is the same as a high-level government worker. Most of the time, they were high-status slaves in the ruler's personal home who were part of the khanazad class. At the provincial level, the Khan's power was applied by his naibs, who were often minor sardars who could find paid work for their own clansmen by making sure local laws were followed. The most important part of a naib's job was to collect taxes, which were often paid in kind, especially in grain. This grain was then sold to local laborers for cash. Because of this, most local government centers had their own treasuries and stores, which made them easy targets for thieves when things went wrong. The naibs gathered customs fees and transit tolls, which they used to pay their own salaries and those of their men. They also shared some of this money with the sardars who helped protect the caravans. Any money left over was sent to the national bank. People often thought that naibs added to their public income by doing things that weren't allowed, but naibs often complained that they didn't have enough money. In towns, the qadi, a government official who knew the Holy Law, was in charge of arrests, trials, and punishments.

Balochistan and Nadir Shah

The great warrior Nadir Shah chased his Afghan enemies into the Mughal provinces of Ghazni and Kabul in 1738. He had just put Iran back in charge of eastern Afghanistan. When he saw that the Mughals were weaker because of their own wars, he attacked India and, after winning at Karnal on February 13, 1739, marched into Delhi as a victor. Muhammad Shah, the Mughal ruler, was forced to give Nadir all of the old Mughal lands west of the Indus River. This included Kalat, where successive khans had kept gathering Baloch lands.

Mir Abdulla Khan, the fourth Khan of Kalat, took the throne in 1714 and became known as the Mountain Hawk or, more poetically, the Royal Eagle of Kohistan. He was a brave fighter and a smart leader. In 1740, he agreed to let Nadir Shah be his new leader. He also agreed to send 500 soldiers and gave Muhabat and Nasir as prisoners. According to the rules of the time, these kings joined Nadir Shah's family and fought with him in battles, including ones in north-west India. Nadir Shah gave Abdulla Khan the title Beglarbeg, which means "chief of chiefs" and is the same as "GovernorGeneral" in the West.

In 1730, the king of Upper Sind, Nur Muhammad Kalhora, made Abdulla Khan give up his claim on Kachhi and marry off two of his daughters to two of Nur Muhammad Kalhora's sons. Five years later, Abdulla Khan tried to take back the province, but he lost and was killed along with about 300 of his men. His son Muhabat Khan took over as ruler of Kalat. Nur Muhammad Kalhora tried to stop Nadir Shah from taking over the former Mughal lands in Sind in 1739, but he failed and was taken prisoner. Then, Abdulla Khan's widow, the Bibi (Lady) Maryam, convinced Nadir Shah to give Nur Muhammad to her son Muhabat Khan to get revenge for Abdulla Khan's death. Muhabat said he would rather have the land his father died for than his enemy's blood. Muhabat Khan was in charge of the Kalat group when Nadir Shah took Kandahar. As a gift for his service and to make up for Abdulla Khan's death, Nadir Shah gave Muhabat Khan Kachhi. So, this province became part of the state of Kalat, and the Brahui sardars, whose troops had fought for it, were given a lot of land as jagir.

Balochistan and Ahmad Shah of Afghanistan

Nadir Shah went on to become one of the best rulers in Iran's history. He brought back a lot of the power and respect that had been lost in the country's civil wars and took back land from the Russian and Ottoman Empires. Still, many of his people came to see him as an abuser, so much so that he feared there were plans to kill him. He had Afghans in his army for a long time and came to depend on them more and more. This was partly because, as Sunnis, he knew they wouldn't work with the mostly Shia Iranians against him. In 1747, when he was fighting rebels in Kurdistan, he told Ahmad Khan, a 35-year-old prince of the Abdali tribe of Pashtuns and leader of his household men, to arrest some Iranian generals he thought were plotting against him. Someone told the generals about Nadir Shah, so they killed him before he could kill them. Ahmad Khan and his men got away, and he led them back to their home country of Afghanistan.

On the way to Kandahar, they met a kafila that was bringing a lot of the stolen goods from Delhi eight years before. Its protection, which was made up of another group of Nadir Shah's trusted Afghan guards, went to Ahmad Khan. This gave Ahmad Khan a trained army and the money to pay for it right away. By 1748, most Afghans accepted him as their king. He changed his name to Ahmad Shah and took the title Dur-i-Durran, which means "Pearl of the Pearls." This was a clever play on the Persian words for "age" and "pearls," which he and his followers often wore. His tribe, the Abdalis, changed their name to the Durranis, which means "Pearlies." His family, the Sadozai, took the name of their ancestor prince, Sado, and became the ruling dynasty of the new Afghan country.

Before, Ahmad Shah had helped Nadir Shah invade India. During that time, he had seen both how rich the country was and how weak its defenses were. In 1748, he followed Nadir's lead and led his army down the Khyber in the first of a series of battles against the Mughal Emperor Shah Alam. After a series of losses, Shah Alam was forced to give Ahmad Shah all of the Mughal provinces (including Kalat) that he had given to Nadir Shah. He also had to marry both Ahmad and his oldest son, Timur Mirza, to imperial women. At its largest, Ahmad Shah's Durrani Empire reached from the Oxus to the Indus and from Kashmir to the Arabian Sea. He died in 1773, when he was fifty years old and had been king for twenty-six years. At the time, he was one of the best Muslim kings.

Near the end of his rule, Nadir Shah told Mir Nasir Khan Ahmadzai in public that his half-brother Muhabat Khan was a bad leader and that Mir Nasir Khan Ahmadzai should get rid of him and return Kalat to the wealth it had under their father, the brave Abdulla Khan. Mir Nasir Khan fought with Nadir Shah in India, and Nadir Shah was surprised by how hard Mir Nasir Khan worked and how smart he was. Before Mir Nasir Khan could act on this advice, Nadir Shah was killed by his generals. Later that same year, Muhabat Khan was also stabbed to death in his own castle, either by his palace guards or by Mir Nasir Khan himself. A less exciting account of what happened is that Nasir Khan stayed outside until his stepbrother was killed in a palace coup. He then rode in as the long-awaited savior from Muhabat Khan's rule.

Even though Nasir Khan agreed that Ahmad Shah Durrani was the rightful king of Afghanistan, he thought that any outside power over Kalat had ended with Nadir Shah. After being in charge for ten years, when Ahmad Shah was busy fighting in other places, he officially declared his independence. The Durrani governor of Kandahar led an army to restore Ahmad Shah's power, but Nasir called out his tribe forces and beat the Durranis near Mas-tung, about 70 miles north of Kalat. Ahmad Shah came in person with a stronger army, and after another fight, Nasir Khan ran back to Kalat, where he had set up defenses. Ahmad Shah went after him and put the city under attack. After three failed tries at the walls, Nasir Khan pointed a gun at Ahmad Shah's tent. The ball hit the prayer rug where Ahmad Shah had just finished praying.

Ahmad Shah had other things to do with his army and time, so he praised his opponent for how good he was at putting up guns and raised the siege in exchange for Nasir Khans agreeing to the same terms as when Nadir Shah was in charge. Ahmad Shah's only compromise was that his group of 500 soldiers would not have to fight in a civil war. A daughter of Hajji Khan (son of the late Muhabat Khan) was married to Ahmad Shah. He then went back to Kandahar with his new wife, accompanied by Hajji Khan, her brother Bahram Khan, and Hajji Khan's mother, a princess who never forgave Nasir Khan for killing her husband and taking the throne she thought was rightfully her son's. This deal was good for both Ahmad Shah and Nasir Khan. It gave Ahmad Shah a steady reminder to Nasir Khan that there was another claimant to the throne of Kalat, and it got the other claimant out of Kalat.

Balochistan during the rule of Nasir Khan *the Great of Kalat*

Nasir Khan did what he said he would do and fought with Ahmad Shah when the Afghans crushed the Marathas at Panipat (12 January 1761). In 1769, he led 3,000 soldiers for Ahmad Shah's son Timur Mirza against an Iranian attempt to take the western Afghan city of Herat. He was given the jagirs of Shal (now called Quetta) and Harrand on the south-western edge of the Punjab as a prize for his work. He added the Baloch hill tracts between Kachhi and Harrand on his eastern border and the deserts of Makran, Kech, Panjgur, and Kharan in the west to his previous territories of Kachhi, Sarawan, and Jhalawan. Las Bela, which is on the coast between Karachi and Makran, was left to its own leader, the Jam, as long as he paid tribute and accepted Nasir Khan as ruler.

Under Nasir Khan, the state of Kalat was at its largest, including Karachi and parts of Sind that were close by. In the far west, in 1783, he gave Oman's exiled king, Sultan Said, refuge and gave him the port of Gwadar, which at the time was just a roadstead surrounded by date groves and deserts. Sultan Said promised to stop attacks by nearby Baloch groups and to fight any Iranian invasions. He kept this promise when he took back the throne of Oman a decade later. Gwadar stayed under Omani control until 1955, when Pakistan bought it with the condition that Oman could still hire Baloch troops.

Nasir Khan's accomplishments at home were just as good as those he made abroad. He split Sarawan and Jhalawan into two separate provinces. He put a top sardar in charge of each province and gave them each a place on his right and left in his council, or darbar. He fixed and improved Kalat city's defenses, paid for orchards and gardens to be planted, and urged craftsmen and merchants to move there. Regular cash payments to the village sardars helped keep the kafilas safe as they went through the Bolan and Kachhi. He became known for being brave in fight, not caring about how he looked, giving gifts (but not money, because he thought that made people lazy), being fair, kind, and true to his word. He was liked by his people, and he was the only Khan of Kalat to be called "The Great." In later reigns, when there were disagreements about how the country should be run, both sides pointed to how things were during his reign as the right way things should be. This is similar to how English people relied on Magna Carta, even though few knew what it was. In June 1794, he died at a very old age. He left behind five daughters and three boys. Mir Mahmud, who was only seven years old at the time, became the next khan.

The Downfall of the Durrani Empire

In Afghanistan, Ahmad Shah was replaced by his son Timur, who had been a soldier with Nasir Khan in the past. Timur Shah died a year before Nasir Khan, likely from poison. Most of his twenty-three kids met in Kabul to choose who would take over after him. There, Timur Shah's fifth son from his first wife, Zaman Mirza, put them in jail until they decided to call him Zaman Shah. Mahmud Mirza, one of the two brothers who didn't go to Kabul, went to Herat instead. There, he resisted Zaman Shah and took over as Mahmud Shah. Zaman Shah took control of Balochistan, Sind, and Peshawar, as well as the rest of the Durrani country.

Zaman Shah wanted to be less reliant on the Afghan tribal sardars, so he tried to set up a reserve army that would be paid by the central government. This made people dislike the new national army, especially since their jagirs, which were no longer needed for their original purpose, would be taken back to pay for it. In 1801 a group of important sardars planned to get rid of him and put his brother Shuja-ul-Mulk in his place. The plan didn't work, and the people who were behind it were killed in front of Zaman. Painda Khan, who was the leader of the Durrani family Barakzai (which means "children of Barak"), was one of those who died. Mahmud Shah gave refuge to Painda Khan's son, Fatah Khan, in Herat. Fatah Khan then convinced Mahmud Shah to lead the Barakzais in a revolt. Zaman Shah was defeated, caught, and blinded, which, according to orthodox Islamic law, made him unfit to be king. He was then sent to prison in Kabul, and his brother Mahmud Shah took over as king. Soon after, in 1802, another group of rebels got rid of Mahmud Shah and put Shah Shuja-ul-Mulk in his place. Mahmud Shah then ran away to Herat.

Shah Shuja-ul-Mulk's claim to the Durrani throne was not accepted by either Mahmud Shah or Fatah Khan. In 1809, Mahmud Shah went back to Kabul from where he had been in Herat. Shah Shuja-ul-Mulk took over the war from Peshawur, and Mahmud Shah gathered more troops to fight against him. Mahmud Khan of Kalat, however, refused to join because he didn't think he had to fight in a civil war. In 1810, Mahmud Shah took over Peshawar and went to Rawalpindi to meet Maharaja Ranjit Singh, who was now his neighbor.

This Sikh prince was once Zaman Shah's viceroy of the western Punjab. He turned the area he was in charge of into the separate kingdom of Lahore, which he kept expanding. In July 1813, Shah Shuja-ul-Mulk, who had fled to Ranjit Singh's camp, gave him the Koh-i-Nur diamond, which Ahmad Shah Durrani had taken from the Mughals. In exchange, Ranjit Singh promised to help him get back on the throne. The gem was added to Ranjit's treasure, but no soldiers were sent. In 1816, Shah Shuja-ul-Mulk fled across the Satlej to the state of Ludhiana, which was ruled by the British. The British gave him refuge and money, partly because he had promised, when he was in charge, to fight any European army that tried to attack India through Afghanistan and partly to make sure he would be grateful if he ever got his kingdom back.

After years of fighting between Sadozais and Barakzais and even between brothers in each family, Ahmad Shah's kingdom fell apart in 1818. Kalat and Sind were almost like two separate countries. Mahmud Shah still ruled in Herat, but the rest of Afghanistan was now run by the Barakzai brothers: Dost Muhammad in Kabul and Ghazni, Kohan Dil Khan and Rahim Dil Khan in Kandahar, and Sultan Muhammad Khan in Peshawar. In 1818, Shah Shuja-ul-Mulk put together a new army and marched against Peshawar with Ranjit Singh's help. He hoped to take advantage of fighting between the Barakzais. At the same time, Mahmud Shah got to the edge of Kabul before turning around and going back to Herat. Shah Shuja-ul-Mulk took control of parts of Upper Sind and the province of Peshawar for a short time, but the Barakzais beat him, and by 1822 he was back living on a British income in Ludhiana.

Balochistan during the reign of Mahmud Khan of Kalat

At the same time, in Kalat, a series of feuds had led to the same result: the loss of provinces on the edges and a shrinking of the center. The Muhabatzai pretender Hajji Khan and his son Bahram Khan tried to take the throne of Kalat while Nasir Khan the Great was still alive, but they were beaten in battle and had to go back to Kandahar. When Nasir Khan died, they started another uprising with the help of sardars who agreed with them and took over Kalat. Mahmud Khan's officials went to Zaman Shah and asked for his help in fighting the rebels. Khoda Baksh, the chief sardar of Jhalawan, had offered both Hajji Khan and Mahmud Khan his help. He then led his men to join Mahmud. When accused of lying, he said that he had sworn by the Koran when he gave it to Hajji, but by his beard when he gave it to Mahmud. Hajji Khan was beaten, and he was sent back to Kandahar as a prisoner of the state. He later died there. In exchange for letting Mahmud Khan run the rest of Kalat, Bahram Khan was given Kachhi.

With the money he got from Kachhi, Bahram Khan put together an army of Baloch people in Sind and asked that he be made khan for as long as he lived, with the young Mahmud Khan as his chosen successor. Mahmud Khan's side again asked Zaman Shah to help, but Bahram Khan turned him down. This led to a war over who would be the next king, in which Bahram was hurt and lost. He went south to Sind, but the amir of Hyderabad, Mir Ghulam Ali Talpur, didn't want to upset Zaman Shah, so he wouldn't let him stay there. Bahram Khan and his two sons then went north-east, trying to find refuge with the ruler of Bahawalpur, Nawab Sadiq Muhammad Khan II. Instead, they became Mahmud Khan's prisoners at Kalat, where Bahram Khan died.

Mahmud Khan's half-sister took up Bahram Khan's cause. In 1801, she set up a marriage between Bahram Khan's only daughter and Mir Ghulam Ali Talpur. In exchange, Mir Ghulam Ali Talpur promised to help get rid of Mahmud Khan and restore the Muhabatzai line. After the wedding, Mir Ghulam Ali said that he had no plans to get involved in Kalat's internal matters. This didn't make Mahmud Khan happy. He took it as a personal insult that a Brahui girl was getting married to a member of the Talpur family, who he saw as nothing more than a group of usurping Baloch mercenaries. He couldn't stop the marriage without starting a fight with the Taipurs, so he had to settle for telling Zaman Shah that he would get his own back later. He found that Zaman Shah could no longer help because his brother Mahmud Shah was going to win and get rid of him.

After Bahram Khan was finally defeated, one of Mahmud Khan's two older half-brothers, Mir Mustafa Khan, took over as ruler of Kachhi. He kept an army of 800 regular Afghan soldiers. He paid them out of his own money, so they weren't tied to the tribe sardars. He also sent them on a number of punitive missions against Baloch hill raiders. Their tribes were fined a lot, and any thieves caught living were put on spikes as a warning to others. To stop the practice of Hindu travelers paying Muslims for security, he fined any Hindu who did it and killed any Muslim who took it. When he went down a road, he would drop rolls of cloth on the ground and expect them to stay there until he came back. This showed that people respected his power.

Mir Mustafa Khan gave cultivators and kafilas a rare time of safety, and he was praised for the traditional virtues of being brave in battle, fair in government, and kind to his friends and supporters. It was said that he and Nawab Sadiq Muhammad Khan II of Bahawalpur had made a deal to split Sind between them. All of Sind west of the Indus River, including Karachi, which the amirs of Sind took back during Kalat's wars of succession, was to be taken by Kalat, and the rest of Sind on the east side was to be taken by Bahawalpur. He did get the Taipurs to agree to give the money from Karachi back to Kalat, but he died before he could carry out his bigger plans.

Mir Mustafa Khan was killed as he came back from a shooting trip. He had gone on the trip instead of going to the funeral of his half-brother Rahim Khan's mother. Rahim Khan was angered by this insult, so he set up a trap, shot Mir Mustafa Khan, and hurt him. Mir Mustafa Khan lived up to his image as a brave man by shouting, "O Rahim, don't kill me from far away; if you're a man, get close to me and fight hand-to-hand." Mir Mustafa Khan was killed in the fight that followed, and Rahim Khan ran away to Sind. There, he gathered a force and took control of Harrand, ignoring his other half-brother Mahmud Khan and refusing to accept his offer of forgiveness. In November 1812, he went to Kachhi with a group of fifty men, probably to make peace with Mahmud Khan. He then headed toward the town of Gandava, even though he had been warned that his half-sister, the sister of the late Mir Mustafa Khan, was there and planning to get revenge for her brother's death. Rahim Khan said he wouldn't stop because a woman scared him, but the woman convinced a local sardar, Qadir Baksh, to call out Mahmud Khan's men. Then, Rahim Khan and most of his followers were killed in a fight.

Mahmud Khan was in charge of Kalat for about 35 years. He was too busy with family fights and didn't want to go to war, so he let the amirs of Sind take back Karachi, the Jam of Las Bela declare independence again, and the sardars of Makran and Kharan refuse to pay their due payment. Mir Mustafa Khan died, and when he did, the Baloch tribes went back to raiding in his eastern lands.

Harrand was left with almost no defenses, and it was pillaged so much that farming stopped, the irrigation ditches filled up, and most of the people left. Ranjit Singh took it over in 1819. He gave it to Nawab Sadiq Muhammad Khan II of Baha-walpur at first, but in 1830 he gave it to the nearby province of Multan, which was part of his own kingdom of Lahore. Some people thought Daud Muhammad Ghilzai, the disliked wazir of Mahmud Khan's son Mahrab Khan II, was a traitor because he let Multan take over Harrand. Later, when it was part of the Punjab region of Dera Ghazi Khan, it made it very hard for the British to help with things in Kalat.

Mahmud Khan died in 1831. He was still in his early 40s at the time. In his country, men usually didn't die of natural causes until they were twice his age. Some people said that he died because he drank too much wine. His late half-brother, the brave Mir Mustafa Khan, was also known to have done this. Others said it was because he was too kind to a group of dancing girls from Sind that he had brought to India, putting his government, his women, and his own health last. In the bazaar, people said that one of his ignored wives had poisoned him. However, in Balochistan, it was common for people to think this way when a great man died in a way other than in battle. Mahmud Khan's son, Mir Mahrab, who is thought to have been poisoned by his mother, took over after him. By that time, the khanate didn't cover much more than Kalat city, the two original Brahui provinces of Sarawan and Jhalawan, and the plain of Kachhi.

Balochistan during the rule of Mahrab Khan II of Kalat

Mahrab Khan II chose, with all the energy of a new ruler, to re-establish his power over the tribal sardars and get back the khanate's lost lands. He started by firing his late father's wazir and replacing him with Daud Muhammad, a Ghilzai Pashtun. This action in and of itself angered many sardars, because the wazirship had always been passed down through the same royal Tajik family, and each khan had always gotten the sardars' approval before appointing a new wazir, even if it was just for political reasons. Still, the rule started off well because Makran was brought back under control and raiders were stopped elsewhere. Then, Ahmad Yar Khan Muhabatzai, the son of the late Bahram Khan, led a series of uprisings with the help of Brahui and Baloch sardars to question Mahrab Khan II's right to rule. Ahmad Yar Khan lost each time. The first three times, he was given a second chance, but the last time, he was taken as a prisoner to Kalat, where he died or was killed on Wazir Daud Khan's advice. It was said that the wazir also wanted to kill Shah Nawaz Khan and Mir Fatah Khan, two of Ahmad Yar's sons who had been taken with him, but Mahrab Khan II stopped him. But about two dozen other Brahui chiefs and important people died in these rebellions, which made their families and Mahrab Khan II's enemies.

A group of rebel Sardars got their men together and marched to Kalat, where they chose the religious leader Muhammad Sadiq as their new khan. Mahrab Khan II's daroga, Ghul Muhammad, held the city for him, but Mahrab Khan II himself was trapped in his camp outside the city walls. The rebels then decided to let Mahrab Khan II back into the city through one gate, while Daroga Ghul Muhammad let the wives and children of the Akhunds leave through another. As soon as this was done, the daroga told the citadel's guns to fire on the rebel camp, which caused the rebels to run away in a panic.

Mahrab Khan II was able to regain control of most of the country, but there were still times when different sardars fought against each other and against him. Sometimes they would ask Rahim Dil Khan, the Barakzai king of Kandahar, for help. Shah Nawaz Khan and his brother Mir Fatah ran away from Kalat in 1832 and, with help from the Sarawans, took over Kachhi. The Magsis were a Baloch group that lived in the southeast corner of Kachhi. They helped Mahrab Khan II beat the Muhabatzais. Shah Nawaz Khan was given refuge in Kandahar, and Mir Fatah ran away to Sind. Khan Mahrab Us wazir Daud Muhammad, who was becoming less and less popular and was long thought to be a traitor, was then killed (possibly with Mahrab Khan H's approval) by Naib Mulla Hasan, the son of the previous wazir, whose death many people blamed on Daud Muhammad. Naib Mulla Hasan took Daud Muhammad's place as wazir, but he still didn't like Mahrab Khan II because he had fired (and probably killed) his father. Akhund Muhammad Sadiq was forgiven for being a rogue, and the Khan put him on his council.

Shah Shuja-ul-Mulk went to Kalat to try again to get his own throne back as soon as Mahrab Khan II was done with Shah Nawaz Khan. In exchange for giving up Peshawar, Maharaja Ranjit Singh offered to help Shah Shuja-ul-Mulk by going into Afghanistan through the Khyber Pass. Shah Shuja-ul-Mulk was happy to agree, even though he didn't own this region (it was ruled by the Barakzai at the time). He planned to lead his own army through Sind, Kachhi, and the Bolan into southern Afghanistan. Shah Shuja-ul-Mulk also asked Lord William Bentinck, the British governor-general in India, for help. Lord Bentinck told him that British policy was not to get involved in the problems of neighboring states and told him not to start another war. When it became clear that Shah Shuja-ul-Mulk would not listen to this advice, Bentinck gave him a large part of his yearly pension early. This allowed him to lead an army of mercenaries from Ludhiana to Shikarpur in Upper Sind in January 1833.

Shah Shuja-ul-Mulk was at first accepted by the amirs of Sind, who were growing more worried about the British and Ranjit Singh's interest in their country. They thought that if they accepted Shah Shuja-ul-Mulk, who said Sind was part of Ahmad Shah's Durrani kingdom, it would make them stronger against these other powers. They soon learned that, with an army to keep up, he wanted more than just a show of respect. After a fight at Rohri on January 1, 1834, the amirs decided to pay their back taxes and send a group of troops to join his army. In exchange, he gave up all rights to their country. This deal was sworn to by everyone involved and written down in two Korans that were given to the amirs.

Shah Shuja-ul-Mulk then moved into Mahrab Khan II's territory. Mahrab Khan II told his people to treat him with respect and help. He got to Kandahar and held the city for a few months until Dost Muhammad came to help the Barakzai cause. Shah Shuja-ul-Mulk's mercenaries left him, so he went west to Herat, where his nephew Kamran Shah had taken over as king five years before. As a rival dynasty, he was given refuge but not any other help, so he went south through the wastes of Sistan. Rahim Dil Khan Barakzai went after them after taking back Kandahar. Shah Shuja-ul-Mulk went to Kalat, where Mahrab Khan II gave him a place to stay. It was a local rule that a guest must be protected at all costs, so Mahrab Khan II wouldn't give him up to the Barakzais who were after him. Kohan Dil Khan, Rahim Dil Khan's brother, wanted to attack the city, but Rahim Dil Khan said Mahrab Khan II had shown himself to be an honorable man and praised his actions. As a settlement, the Barakzais stopped chasing Shah Shuja-ul-Mulk, and Mahrab Khan II made him go back through Sind to Ludhiana, where he was once again a British pensioner. In March 1835, Bentinck told people in London what had happened and said that Mahrab Khan II had shown the kindness and hospitality for which the Baloch people were known.

Dost Muhammad took the title Amir after beating Shah Shuja-ul-Mulk. Ranjit Singh took over Peshawur in the east. He said that because Shah Shuja-ul-Mulk had given him the land, he was now the rightful master of Peshawur. In April 1837, Amir Dost Muhammad sent forces under the command of Muhammad Akbar Khan, his eldest son and best general, to take back the city, which had been the summer capital of the Durranis. At the end of that month, they attacked Jamrud, which was protecting the lower end of the Khyber. Ranjit Singh's field army was defeated, but Jamrud fort held out. After a few days, Akbar Khan retired to Jalalabad on the Afghan side of the pass. The British continued to be interested in the places that Shah Shuja-ul-Mulk used to rule. British politicians were getting more and more worried that Russia or, more likely, Iran under pressure from Russia wanted to take over the land north of the Indus. The Great Game was already going on outside of Balochistan.

Uncovering Balochistan's Historical Narrative

Nearly 3,000 years ago, many groups left their homes in Central Asia and moved toward the west, south, and southeast. Some of these people became known as Indo-Iranic groups. They were called Aryans. Some of the Indo-Iranian tribes moved to the Balashakan area in the northwest of Iran. Circumstances caused this group of nomadic pastoralist tribes, called Balashchik at the time, to move as a whole and leave their original home. After wandering and suffering for many centuries, these pastoralist nomads finally settled in the south and east of the Iranian plains. Here, they stopped being Balashchik and started being Baloch. The area where they finally settled became known as Balochistan, which means "the country of the Baloch." They spread their language and culture throughout the area and made a nation-state that lasted for nearly 300 years as an independent or semi-independent country. Throughout its history, the Baloch state went through many ups and downs. It finally disappeared from the map of the world when Pakistan took it over in 1948.

Baloch past is hard to track down. Rarely do old historical records talk about the Baloch people. From old historical accounts, we can piece together some parts of Baloch history, but only in a very rough and general way. Ancient writers don't seem to have said much about the Baloch. Most likely, it's because the Baloch were a group of nomadic tribes who raised livestock and didn't have much to do with the government changes of the time. History doesn't say much about the Baloch, just like it doesn't say much about many other pastoralist nomads of ancient Iran who came from Central Asia. However, some of these ethnic groups disappeared and stopped being a separate entity, while the Baloch became a separate language and culture during the Middle Ages.

Because there aren't many specific stories about the Baloch, it's still hard to say where they came from and where their original home was on the Iranian plateau. No history records show what really happened when they moved or were kicked out of where they lived before. In some old reports of Iranian history, there are only a few brief mentions. Only on some rock carvings from the time of the Sassanids can you find a place called Balasagan, Balashakan, or Balashagan, as well as a description of a group of people called Balashchik. At times, the Baloch were called warriors in the armies of the Median, Achaemenid, and Sassanid rulers. At other times, they were called brigands and wild barbarians. There are also some short stories about how some of these kings met the Baloch and how many other emperors of Persian dynasties said they got rid of the Baloch.

There is proof from the past that the Baloch served in the armies of Emperor Cyrus, Xerxes, and Cambyses of the Achaemenid Dynasty. In his "Book of Kings"

(Shahnama), Firdausi said that the Baloch were part of the army of Cambyses (Siahwash), who was the son of Kai Kaous and ruled during the Achaemenid Dynasty. The second time the Baloch are mentioned in the "Book of Kings" is when Chosroes I (Anosharvan) was king from AD 531 to AD 579. From the time of Kai Kaous to Anosharvan, which is about a thousand years, there is nothing written in history books about the Baloch. It is not clear what happened to this ethnic group during this time. In the Middle Ages, Iranian historians wrote in detail about how this group served in the armies of different Achaemenid rulers.

Because there wasn't much known about the Baloch's history and culture, there were many theories about where they came from. People have had different ideas and theories about where the Baloch come from. Researchers who tried to figure out where the Baloch came from in the past came up with different ideas and tried to connect them to different groups of people in the area. Most of the speculation was about whether the Baloch were Aryan, Semitic, or Turkmen. Pottinger (1976) thought they were Turkmen, Rawlinson (1873) thought they were Chaldean (Jewish), Bellew (1874) thought they were from the Indian Rajput tribes, and Dames (1904) thought they were from the Aryan tribes.

In the last part of the 20th century, thorough and reliable study on the languages of the Iranian plateau showed that the Baloch have clear ties to other ethnic groups in the area. Based on these studies of the origins of Balochi and other languages, it became clear that ideas that the Baloch are descended from Chaldeans, Arabs, or the people who lived in Balochistan before them were neither logical nor scientific. The Baloch are from the Iranian branch of the Indo-Iranian groups. This is a well-known fact in the academic world. People now think that the Kurds and the Baloch are part of the Median group of tribes because of their language and culture. Studying where the Balochi language came from has been a very important piece of evidence for this point of view.

From what we know about their language and culture, we can figure out that the Baloch and other Indo-Iranian tribes moved from Central Asia to the area around the Caspian Sea on the Iranian plateau, possibly around 1200 BC. This is thought to be related to the Aryan movements of that time in history as a whole. It has also been proven that they first lived in northern Persia, near the Caspian Sea and the Elborz Mountain. Their home area was called Balashakan (or Balashagan). The Baloch and tribes from other ethnic groups lived here for a long time, making agreements and ties with many different groups. From a cultural and language point of view, it seems that the Baloch and the Kurds were two large tribes that came from the same place and lived in the same area. No one really knows why the Baloch moved from their original home in Balashakan to where they live now in Balochistan while the Kurds stayed where they were from the beginning. But some Kurdish tribes, or parts of some Kurdish tribes, chose to move east with the Baloch, and they are now a full part of the Baloch national identity as a whole.

History has mostly been written from the point of view of the dominant or winning power, and the accounts of the Baloch may have been "infected" by Persian-centric and Islam-centric "viruses." These writers were focused on writing about the great deeds of their own ethnic or national groups, and they didn't care much about their "barbarian" neighbors like the Baloch, who they thought were beyond the pale.

The Baloch were shepherds who took care of sheep and goats. Like other nomad shepherds in the area, they moved around a lot and lived in tribal groups rather than political entities. As there was a clear gap between them and the settled communities, there were sometimes misunderstandings in which the wandering Baloch were blamed for bothering the settled communities. Nomadic, seminomadic, and settled people in different Persian realms have always had different levels of power, rivalries, wars, and alliances based on different reasons. These changing ties caused a lot of trouble for the Baloch tribes and made it hard for them to find their own identity as a separate ethnic group. As the historical accounts were written by people who lived in settled communities and were also from the winning or dominating power, there are many differences in how the Baloch were described.

Over the last two thousand years, strong and organized religions have been persecuting the Baloch. This has made the Baloch less interested in religion in their social or community matters. In ancient times, Persians and Arabs wrote about the Baloch as being wild, dangerous, and highway robbers. They said that the Baloch were the least interested in their religious duties, whether they were Zoroastrian or Muslim. Even though they tell the history of the Baloch from an indirect point of view, their stories are very important because we can learn a lot by reading between the lines. As the Baloch were facing genocide at the hands of the Sassanid and the Arabs, one cannot expect neutral accounts of the events from the historians of these conquering nations, even though they tell us about meeting a hostile "ethnic group." However, these writers do offer at least a macrohistorical version of the events involving the Baloch (the version of the winning side). So, each of these stories must be reviewed on its own to see how true it is.

It has been looked into where the Brahui group of the Baloch tribes came from so that they can have a very different identity than the Baloch national identity. When the British took over Balochistan, the idea that Brahui-speaking tribes were different from Balochi-speaking tribes began to spread. It was clear that this was done to make the Baloch split up, which was in line with the time-tested "divide and rule" strategy of colonial powers. But based on the little study that Dr. Gershevitch, a big part of the picture of where the Brahui tribes came from became clear. He found that Bashkardi dialects came from the Central Persian Bradazhui group during the Achaemenid Dynasty. Based on what Dr. Gershevitch found in 1962a and 1962b, it is safe to say that the Brahui were part of the group of Baloch people in Kerman. They were part of a Baloch group that lived in

Barez Mountains. Most likely, they changed their name to Brahui after being called Barezui when they came down from their mountain homes and started moving as a group toward the east in the Middle Ages. They used to be called Barezui, but when they moved to where they live now in Jhalawan and Sarawan (Turn) areas of Baluchistan, they changed their name to Brahui. Based on Dr. Gershevitch's work, more study needs to be done on the Brahui language. This research shouldn't be limited by the fact that it was once thought to have come from the Dravidian language family.

Since the Arab tribes invaded Iran in the seventh century, the Baloch have been persecuted, deported, and forced to move. At first, some Baloch tribes sided with the Arabs, but soon after, the Arabs started to persecute the Baloch for many different reasons. After the Arabs lost some of their power, Iran was ruled for a long time by strong local dynasties. During this time, the Baloch also got some of the worst treatment. Some of the major political forces and dynasties that did bad things to the Baloch were the Saffarids, Buyids, Samanids, Ghaznavids, Seljuqs, and Mongols. Some of these horrible things were acts of genocide, which finally drove the Baloch out of Kerman and the northern parts of Sistan and into the southern parts of Sistan, Makuran, and Turan. With so many Baloch groups moving into the area, the social and political situation in the area changed a lot. During this time, a lot of Baloch people moved to the area, and the area started to take on the traits of the Baloch people. The Baloch groups moved around, and their language, "Balochi," became the common language of the area. This area became known as "Balochistan."

Balochistan is the area of land that stretches from the southeast of Iran to the east bank of the River Sindh in Punjab and from the lower parts of Helmand in Afghanistan to the Indian Ocean. Spooner (1983) said that Balochistan is a half-circle of historically important towns and farming areas that goes from Bandar Abbas on the Persian Gulf to Kerman, the Delta of the Helmand River in Sistan, Kandahar, and Sindh. It is on the edge of India and Iran and connects the Iranian plateau to the Arabian Peninsula. In terms of geography, it is separated from Persia Proper by the Dasht-e-Lut, Dasht-e-Kavir, and Kerman Mountains in the west, and from Sindh by the Hub River and the Kirther line of Mountains in the southeast. In the northeast, it is separated from Pashtunistan and Punjab by the right bank of the Indus. In the north, the natural borders of Helmand and the mountain range north of Quetta split Balochistan from Afghanistan. Balochistan and the Sultanate of Oman are on opposite sides of the Indian Ocean in the south.

Archeological digs have shown that Balochistan was a link between the cultures of Mesopotamia and the Iranian highlands on one side and the cultures of the Indus lowlands on the other. Archaeological evidence shows that the early civilizations in the Indus valley and Mesopotamia were linked by land routes that went through Balochistan. From the middle of the first millennium, the area was split into many provinces of the Achaemenid Empire, such as Maka (Makuran) and Zaranka (Sistan). During Alexander the Great's wars, the Greeks called the southern parts of Balochistan Gedrosia. During the Sassanid time, the areas that make up modern-day Balochistan were called Turan (Tugran, Turgestan), which corresponds to modern-day Sarhad, Sarawan, and Jhalawan, Pradhan (probably modern-day Kharan and Chagai), Makuran, and Sakastan (modern-day Sistan).

In the Middle Ages, when a lot of Baloch groups moved to Balochistan, the region's population and government changed in ways that helped the Baloch. It was the start of a time when the Baloch ruled the area. Baloch tribes joined together to form strong confederacies, and one of these, the Khanate of Kalat, became the first Baloch state in the middle of the 17th century. The Khanate was a loose grouping of Baloch groups that stayed independent or semi-independent for almost 300 years, until it was taken over by Pakistan in 1948.

There are different times in the past of the Baloch. The first time period is when they moved to the Iranian plateau with other Indo-Iranian groups and settled in Balashakan or Balashagan. Because there isn't much information about how they moved into the northwestern Caspian region, settled in Balashakan, and were persecuted by different royal powers at the time, it's hard to get a clear picture of who the Baloch were at that time. But there is no question that they were pastoralists who herded sheep and goats and that, like other pastoralists in Central Asia, they were highly mobile, if not completely nomadic, and lived in tribal communities. It was during this time that the Baloch stood out as a different ethnic group from other nomadic pastoralist tribes in the northwestern part of the Caspian Sea. During this time, they were called Balashchik, and the area where they lived was called Balashakan. At that time, the Balochi language probably started to develop some of the things that make it different from other Iranian languages. During the same time period, they looked like they were part of the armies of the Median, Achaemenid, Parthian, and maybe even Sassanid powers. During this same time, however, the Baloch were persecuted for different reasons, and many of them moved or were sent to other parts of the Iranian plains. At the end of this time, the Balashchik and Balashagan were no longer mentioned in history.

The second part of Baloch history starts when the Balashchik of Balashagan showed up in Kerman, Sistan, Makuran, and Turan as nomadic shepherds with a new name, the Baloch. In Arab and Persian records of history from that time, they were called Koch and Baloch. Almost all of the stories from this time in Baloch history are about oppression, genocide, migration, and wandering. This could easily be called the worst time for the Baloch as a group of people. During this time, the Baloch were always fighting with different regional forces that wanted to take control of Iran after the Arab Caliphate in Baghdad fell apart in the 10th century. During this time, a lot of Kok and Baloch people moved from Kerman and the northern parts of Sistan. This might have been the time when the Brahui (Barezui) group of Baloch tribes left almost all of eastern Kerman and started to live in Thran.

During the Middle Ages, as Baloch tribes moved into Makuran, southern Sistan, Turan, and Kachchi, they started to have a cultural, political, and military impact on these areas, either on their own or as part of clan confederacies. During this time, even though people were suffering and moving around, the Baloch culture started to take over the area. Balochi became the common language of the area, and different native tribes started to merge with Baloch tribes or join forces with Baloch tribal confederacies. During this time, the name Balochistan was given to the whole area.

During their long and difficult journeys from different parts of the Iranian plateau, the Baloch took on large parts of the cultures and languages of other ethnic groups. From this point of view, it looks like being a Baloch is, in many ways, a choice. A Baloch is someone who calls himself Baloch, and no one who is not a Baloch would do this. In traditional Baloch thought, a person is a Baloch not because of where they were born, but because they follow a certain set of rules. A person is a high-status Baloch if they follow the basic rules of their society. If they don't follow any of these rules, they are a low-status Baloch.

The third time period in Baloch history is seen as their best age. During this time, the Baloch were able to create a nation-state by taking advantage of the chaos of the 17th century. In the east, the Mughal Empire was falling apart, and in the west, the Safavid Dynasty was starting to fall apart. The Baloch state of Kalat was the first sign of Baloch political power in the area, and it was also the last. Even though Kalat State was a weak alliance of different tribes and often gave in to the wishes of other powers in the area, it gave the Baloch a sense of being part of a country. The Baloch's golden age ended in the year 1839, when the Baloch state was attacked and taken over by the British. At the time, the British were trying to strengthen their position in Central Asia against a new Russian push toward their valuable Indian colonies.

The history of how the Baloch fought back against the occupation and splitting of Balochistan is the fourth stage. During this time, Balochistan was slowly strangled by new Persian kingdoms and the newly formed buffer state of Afghanistan, as well as by different administrative steps taken by the government of British India in the area. Heroes fought against foreign rule on an individual, clan, and national level during this time. This time can be seen as the second time the Baloch suffered after their terrible defeats in the Middle Ages. However, this time they did so as an occupied country instead of as a group of tribes.

In 1948, Pakistan took over the Baloch territory, which marked the beginning of the fifth time period in their history.

Beginning when Aryan groups moved out of Central Asia a thousand years before Christ, different things happened at different times in Baloch history. The Baloch people got their ethnic name, Balashchik, when they moved to Balashakan. At different times and for different reasons, the major powers attacked them, and they faced genocide, forced exile, or migration. In the Middle Ages, they left signs of their presence on a part of the Iranian Plateau that came to be called Balochistan. They set up a number of clan confederacies, and one of these, the Khanate of Kalat, became the first Baloch state in 1666. They were unable to keep their country's freedom, and on April 1, 1948, after almost 300 years of being independent or almost independent, the Baloch state was no longer on the map.

Chapter 2
Gaining Insight into Balochistan's Insurgency

Introduction

Balochistan has had a lot of trouble with how to deal with and include different ethnic and national groups in Pakistan. The state was added to the federation, making it the biggest province with the fewest people. Over the last 60 years, it has been the site of resistance and open conflict. After the military killed Akbar Bugti in 2006, the province became more politically divided and started a new cycle of bombs, kidnappings, and killings. This has sparked new calls for independence, pushed most of the Baloch political leadership away from the center, and led to a revolt that has led to a large security operation that raises serious questions about human rights. Putting the security forces against the Baloch people could stop big projects from moving forward and make the country more unstable as a whole. The insurgency is different from other rebellions in the province, like those in the 1970s, which started when the National Awami Party-led alliance of different ethnic groups was thrown out of power. Even though the Baloch were at the center of the conflict, which was mostly led by the Marri tribe, the main fight was between the rebels and the government. This time, the Baloch uprising is bigger and is happening all over the province. Residents of the Pukhtun and Punjabi groups are becoming more hostile, and sectarian violence is also a factor.

Akbar Bugti often got into fights with Islamabad over issues like provincial authority, the building of Gwadar Port, and the way that Balochistan's natural resources, especially gas, were taken out of the ground. The Bugti tribes are very important because they live in an area with the largest gas fields in Pakistan. These fields are in the harsh, hilly, and uninhabitable Bugti district, which is also home to the Sui Gas plant, which supplies nearly 40% of Pakistan's gas output. Even though the area has a lot of minerals, the Bugti district is the poorest place in Pakistan. With these tensions in the background, the ruling party has been trying to talk to the Baloch leadership since 2000. Pervez Musharraf, who was President of Pakistan from June 2001 to August 2008, finally gave in and sent senior members of the Pakistan Muslim League to talk to Akbar Bugti. So, Senator Mushahid Hussain, who was in charge of the Senate Sub-Committee on Balochistan , was able to come up with a number of suggestions about different controversial problems in the province.

But what happened on the ground took priority over what the Senate Subcommittee said should be done. In December 2005, rockets were fired at security troops several times. Major General Shujaat Zamir Dar, the Inspector General of the Frontier Corps, and Brigadier Salim Nawaz, the Divisional Inspector General, were both hurt in Kohlu. Musharraf was also a target. Musharraf took the attack personally and went to Military Intelligence for advice. They told him to get rid of the opposition. On August 27, 2006, Akbar Bugti and 60 other people were killed in his hideout in the Bambore Mountains. At first, Musharraf said that his satellite phone was used to track him and that he was bombed from the air. Later, the story was changed to say that soldiers from the Special Services Group pounded a cave where he was hiding, killing the 79-year-old disabled man who was killed by falling rocks. The body was placed in a sealed coffin, and no one in the family was allowed to see the body or check that it was the right person at the funeral. In the name of the "War on Terror," the army could use force, and Musharraf's Western supporters didn't care because he was using the same targeted killings and "renditions" that they did. Many people who fight for human rights saw this as an execution without a trial, which made the Pakistani ruling class very angry. They all opposed the killing, which caused a huge uproar in Balochistan and fueled the rebellion, which grew from attacks on government buildings and pipelines to attacks on Punjabi settlers and the security forces.

Again, a political problem in Balochistan was solved with the help of the troops. In the Marri Bugti area, the army did a lot of work to keep people safe. As a result, 200,000 people were forced to leave their homes, and 20–30,000 of them went to Afghanistan. The security establishment, which was led by Military Intelligence, Inter-Services Intelligence, and the Intelligence Bureau and helped by the Frontier Corps, police, levies, and death squads, tried to crush the insurgency violently and ran a campaign of kidnappings, detentions, torture, and executions outside of the court system. The way things seem to work is that security services round up people and hold them in secret detention centers on cantonments. In a sense, they "disappear," and their dead bodies are sometimes found on the side of the road. There were militia groups that worked with the security forces. The 'disappearances' and 'kill and dump' cases hurt the intelligence agencies' reputations. As an alternative, they formed armed militias to kidnap and kill dissidents who wanted independence. People say that the Tehreek-e-Nefaz-e-Aman Balochistan is the armed side of the United Front of Balochistan, which is a political party led by Siraj Raisani's brother.

There is disagreement about how many people the security forces in the area have taken away, and exact numbers are not known. Baloch nationalists say that the number is in the thousands, but the Balochistan regional government has said more than once that 1,000 people have been taken away by force. During General Musharraf's rule, which ended in August 2008, 1102 Baloch were taken and never seen again, according to the Federal Interior Ministry. From 2005 to January 2011, the Human Rights Commission of Pakistan looked into 169 cases, and between 2009 and 2010, Human Rights Watch found 49 cases. The Centre for Research and Security Studies in Islamabad, which is an independent, non-profit think tank, looked at data from different sources, put it all together in a longitudinal way, and came to the conclusion that there had been a big rise in disappearances since 2010 and a big jump in 2011. The places where most people went missing were Quetta, Dera Bugti, Gwadar, and Karachi. There have been reports, though, of Baloch people going missing in places where there are a lot of Baloch people, like northern Sindh and Dera Ghazi Khan in the Punjab.

Many of the people who were taken into prison have been killed, and their bodies have been found with signs of torture and killings that didn't follow the law. Ghulam Mohammad Baloch, Chairman of the Baloch Nationalist Movement and General Secretary of the Baloch National Front, Lala Munir Baloch, also a member of the Baloch National Movement, and Sher Mohammad Baloch, a member of the Baloch Republican Party, were the people whose disappearances and killings without a trial got the most attention. Their bodies were found a few days after they were taken from their lawyer's office in a Turbat courthouse. They had been hooded, abused, and shot. Students are important in Balochistan politics because the Baloch middle class is not very well formed. Student leaders and allies, especially members of the Baloch Students Organization, have been targeted by the security forces, who have either arrested them on campus and then made them disappear or just taken them away. Since the middle of 2010, Human Rights Watch has found the bodies of 70 people who had gone missing. Between December 2010 and January 2011, 22 more bodies of Baloch people who had been taken were found. From October 2010 to September 2011, Amnesty International found that 249 Baloch activists were killed or went missing. Many of them were killed in 'kill and dump' operations.

Different government agencies or government-supported groups are operating a 'kill and dump' policy with impunity. As one official stated to an abductee:

> Even if the president or chief justice tells us to release you, we won't. We can torture you, or kill you, or keep you for years at our will. It is only the Army chief and the [intelligence] chief that we obey.

In 2009, the Supreme Court reopened cases about people who went missing. In May 2010, it set up a Commission of Inquiry on Forced Disappearances, which is led by a retired Supreme Court judge. The Commission was told to make a complete list of all the people who had gone missing, collect proof and testimonies about missing people, suggest ways to find missing people, and pay victims. But it didn't have the power to bring criminal charges. Baloch activists didn't go to the Commission because it wouldn't record most of the missing people. The Commission gave its report to the Supreme Court, but the Court hasn't made the report public yet. But it said that 290 people who had gone missing had been found, and 78 of them had been found in the custody of different intelligence services. In March 2011, the Federal Ministry of the Interior set up a new Commission of Inquiry to find the last 136 missing people, find out who was responsible for them going missing, and file First Information Reports against those people. Families have told the Commission about their problems, but they did not know what the Commission did about them. Justice Fayyaz Ahmed, who is in charge of the Commission, said that the government seems weak in the face of the spy agencies. Aslam Raisani, the Chief Minister of Balochistan, seemed to confirm these claims when he told the Human Rights Commission that the provincial government didn't have control over the security agencies and that the intelligence agencies and Frontier Corps were running a parallel government in the province. Even the President at the time, Asif Zardari, is said to have told Baloch leaders that he had no power over how the army worked in the province.

The story shows that the war has been violent, bloody, and has had no regard for human rights. Several points of view have been used to try to explain the conflict: The Pakistani "Establishment," which includes the government and military, has been quick to say that this is because of outside interference and the resistance of tribe leaders to social change. But there are other points to think about, like the resource-driven conflict theory, the role of transnationalism and exile, and the failure to deal with differences by not letting federalism work well. This piece will take a look at each of the different approaches and try to figure out which one is the main reason for the current conflict. This isn't to say that there aren't multiple causes of the current strife; rather, it's to figure out which one is the most important.

Pushback against Social Change

From the point of view of the Establishment, the main cause of the problem in Balochistan is the sardari (tribal) system and culture, which is a way of life. Shah (2007) and Hasnat agree with this and say that the major cause of the problems in Balochistan is the politics of the sardari system. They think that separatism is caused by the sardars' high opinion of themselves and their opposition to more education and development, which they see as a threat to their power as clan leaders, along with outside interference. Dunne also looks at how the Baloch chiefs are related to their political problems and how the difference in culture between the Baloch and the Punjabis has been used by the sardars to get the Baloch to blame someone else.

In this argument, there are a few main points to think about. The first is how the Pakistani government has handled the sardari system, the second is how the system is changing, and the third is how rivalries between tribes relate to pro-government and anti-government views. Balochistan is split into 'A' areas and 'B' areas. The Army, the Coast Guard, the Navy, the police, and the Frontier Corps are in charge of the "A" zones, which are the cities and towns. This kind of direct control is used in other parts of Pakistan as well, except that the Army and paramilitary forces play a bigger role in Balochistan because of its past of violence. The remote areas are called "B" areas, and the local sardar is in charge of keeping them safe with the help of the local Levies. Levies are a way for the community to police itself within the rules of the tribes' customs and practices. The fact that the community helps them find and stop crime is one of their strengths. But they can also become the center from which sardars rule the area, a source of conflict between tribes, or, in the worst case, the center from which to start an uprising. So, there have been efforts to get rid of the "B" areas by putting them under direct state rule and reducing the sardars' power. For example, Zulfikhar Bhutto's Pakistan People's Party government passed the Sardari Abolition Ordinance in 1976, and General Musharraf held the Qaumi Bugti Jirga in 2006 to get rid of the Bugti tribe's sardari system and replace it with a District Commissioner structure. Recently, the Balochistan package has been trying to get rid of 'B' places.

But the Establishment's attitude has been based on politics and has been all over the place. During the revolt of the 1970s, Akbar Bugti sided with the government and was governor of the region for a short time. Meanwhile, Ghous Bux Bizenjo, Ataullah Khan Mengal, and Khair Bux Marri were locked up. The sardari system was only taken away from people who were against the government. Those who were for the regime were left alone. Musharraf's reform was also only meant to punish Bugti tribesmen who supported the revolt. It did not apply to Bugti tribesmen who supported the government or to other areas where sardars stayed loyal to the regime. This shows how political this approach is and how it has been applied in different ways.

The tribal system in Balochistan, where it appears, is different from the system among Pukhtuns. The Pukhtun system is more decentralized, while the Balochistan system is more hierarchical, with the tribal chief at the top. Also, the sardari system has different effects in different parts of Balochistan and is changing as a result. Several anthropology studies look at cultural and social norms, tribal systems, and how they interact with modern life. Scholz's study looks at the link between nomadism and colonialism in the 1800s. It also looks at how social change affected tribal societies as they came into contact with modern life. Matheson looked into a similar idea when he looked at how the Bugti tribe was affected by modernization after natural gas was found in Sui. Titus has been studying how tribal systems have changed and adapted in response to modernization. He shows how urbanization is creating a middle class, how tribal identities and structures are changing, and how all of this affects relationships between different groups of people in Balochistan. Tribal systems are changing quickly. This is especially true in places where they were weak to begin with, like on the Makran coast. The Human Rights Commission of Pakistan says that limiting the political process and not giving provinces more freedom slows down social change and makes the tribal system stronger, even though people don't like it.

There is a complicated link between tribal structures and the current conflict, which can be traced back to rivalries between tribes and between tribes and the government. Balochistan has about 60 tribes, but the insurgency is mostly made up of three of the bigger groups: the Bugti, the Marri, and the Mengal. The rebellion is important in the Marri-Bugti area, where the tribal system is strong and led by tribesmen, the cities of Quetta and Khuzdar, the Lasbela District in the southeast of Balochistan, Lyari Town in Karachi, and the Makran coast, where the sardari system is weaker and an emerging middle class is in charge.

When Balochistan's political groups are looked at, there is no link between tribal structures and separatists. All Baloch political parties are led by sardars. They range from mainstream Pakistani parties like the Muslim League and the PPP to parties that want more autonomy, like the Balochistan National Party (Mengal), the National Party, the Jamhoori Wattan Party, and the Baloch National Front, which is an alliance of eight political parties that want independence. Baloch National Movement, Balochistan Student Organization-Azad, and Balochistan Republican Party are all part of the partnership. Sardars are involved in all kinds of politics. The former chief minister, Muhammad Aslam Khan Raisani, and the governor, Zulfikar Ali Magsi, both of whom were removed from office in 2013 because they were members of the PPP, are tribal chiefs, as are most of the elected members of the Balochistan Provincial Assembly. Tribal chiefs run the governments of the provinces and work with the Federal government. Also, they are part of the militia groups that are thought to be responsible for many of the unjust killings of Baloch nationalists. For example, the Tehreek-e-Nefaz-e-Aman Balochistan is said to be the armed wing of the United Front of Balochistan, which is a political party led by Siraj Raisani's brother. Shafiq Mengal is in charge of the Baloch Musla Defai Tanzeem, which has been linked to attacks on Hazara Shias because of their religion. Both groups have ties to vigilante groups that kidnap and kill activists who fight for freedom. So, even though they are still part of the Sardar tribe, they have different political views that are based on pragmatism rather than theory. In conclusion, blaming the rebellion on the tribal system is not a good reason, but it is clear that it plays a minor role because sardars are a common part of Baloch culture.

Foreign Intervention

The realist view, which looks at the international system through the lens of nation states, is the most common one in the security establishment. This view says that outside forces are helping the rebellion. Usually, this is said along with the first idea about the role of the tribal structure. There are a number of people who could be involved from the outside. India is the main suspect, but Afghanistan, Iran, and the USA are also being looked at. Pakistan and Afghanistan have different ways of running their governments in a number of ways. For example, Kabul doesn't recognize the Durand Line as the border between the two countries. When Pakistan got its independence in 1947, it brought up the Pukhtunistan issue, in which it was suggested that all the Pukhtun tribes on both sides of the Durand Line should be united in an independent state called Pukhtunistan. Kabul was a friend of Pakistan's worst enemy, India, and during the Baloch uprising in the 1970s, militant Balochs trained in Afghanistan.

During the current insurgency, Bugti and Marri refugees have sought safety in Afghanistan, and insurgents start attacks across the porous border from Afghanistan. President Musharraf asked the US for help by saying that 200 Bugtis wanted by Islamabad were in Afghanistan. Brahamdagh Bugti, the grandson of Akbar Bugti, was said to be the most important of these people. Brahamdagh Bugti is the leader of the separatist Baloch Republican Party and what is said to be its militant wing, the Baloch Republican Army. He stayed in Kabul for four years starting in 2006, even though the Pakistani government said he was behind attacks on Punjabi settlers in Balochistan, government buildings, and the Pakistani military. The fact that Brahamdagh Bugti was in Kabul made things hard between Afghanistan and the United States, so the USA and its friends had to step in. The President of Afghanistan, Hamid Karzai, talked with Washington about finding an alternative safe haven in the West. In general, Islamabad agreed with this plan. Late in October 2010, Brahamdagh Bugti finally left Afghanistan for exile in Switzerland, supposedly on an Indian visa. However, the Pakistani government is fighting his request for asylum. In March 2012, in an effort to make peace, the Government of Balochistan dropped 28 cases against Brahamdagh Bugti in Dera Bugti and Sui for working against Pakistan from Afghanistan with the help of India. Similar charges were dropped against Hyrbyair Marri, who was said to be the head of the Balochistan Liberation Army, and others. But the nationalists won't talk to the government until the people who have gone missing are found and extrajudicial killings are looked into.

Before the Soviet attack of Afghanistan on Christmas Eve 1979, Delhi had a lot of power there. Islamabad's help for the Afghan resistance led to the fall of the Soviet Union, but it also ended Delhi's power in the country, even if only for a short time. During the intervention, Pakistan made a plan called "strategic depth." This plan said that if Pakistan supported the intervention against the Soviets, it would get a friendly government in Kabul. Operation Enduring Freedom, which was led by the US in October 2001, was based on a plan called "light footprint." This meant that the Northern Alliance troops and US air power were needed to beat the Taliban. The Northern Alliance's takeover of Kabul, on the other hand, meant that Indian influence was back in Afghanistan. This was a big change in Pakistan's strategy. From this point of view, the Pakistan Army sees its own interests as closely linked to those of the Pukhtun groups that are against the Karzai government. These groups include the Taliban, Hekmatyar's, and Haqqani's. They see these groups as important partners who can help them stop Delhi from having more power in their own area.

Even though Pakistan didn't like it, New Delhi has become one of the biggest donors to Afghanistan. It has given US$1.2 billion in reconstruction aid for a wide range of projects, such as building roads, schools, dams, power lines, and the parliament building, where 3000 Indian workers are working. This was followed by an Indo-Afghanistan security agreement that said India would increase the limited training program for Afghani Army and police officers. Right away, 150 army officers were sent to India to get training at an Indian military establishment. India has been working with Iran to build the Chabahar port, which is a direct rival to Gwadar Port. It has also built a Delram-Zanraj link road that connects the Iranian border to the main road between the cities of Herat, Kandahar, and Kabul. Both of these things are very important for Pakistan. On the Iranian side, it connects to a road that goes to the port of Chabahar. This way, Afghanistan can get to the Persian Gulf without going through Pakistan. The road was built by the Borders Road Organisation, which is made up of both Border Roads Engineering Service officers from the Ministry of Surface Transport's work force, the General Reserve Engineer Force, and Indian Army Corps of Engineers officers. The Indo-Tibetan police force was hidden inside the Borders Road Organisation to protect against strikes by the Taliban.

Pakistan has directly accused India of meddling in Balochistan's issues more than once. At the meeting between Indian Prime Minister Manmohan Singh and Pakistani Prime Minister Yousaf Reza Gilani in Sharm el-Sheik in 2009, it was said that a dossier was shown with photos of Brahamdagh Bugti meeting Indian agents in Kabul and Indian officials in India. It was also said that the Indian consulate in Kandahar was organizing and funding the Baloch Republican Army and the Balochistan Liberation Army. Alok Banasal says that if India gives the Baloch rebels as little as US$2 million per month, they can hold up three to five Pakistani army divisions. This is an attractive idea for India. Pakistan also said it would tell the media about three Indian citizens who had been caught for helping Baloch militants. The Tehreek-e-Taliban, which is led by Baitullah Mehsud, was also accused of getting help from camps in Afghanistan. But these claims have not been proven in public, and the report has not been made public. Balochistan was added to the agenda of the Sharm el-Sheik meeting only after Manmohan Singh agreed to it. US State Department documents show that India only put Balochistan on the agenda at the meeting because of US pressure. This made it easier for Islamabad and New Delhi to talk about terrorism, which kept the dialogue between the two countries going. It let them compare Pakistan's ISI to India's RAW, or Research and Analysis Wing, which is India's foreign intelligence agency. It also let them counter India's worries about Mumbai with Pakistan's worries about Balochistan. So, India's political posturing was easy to get around for Pakistan without Pakistan having to show any proof. Recently, when Akhtar Mengal of the Balochistan National Party (Mengal) came back from self-imposed exile to run in the 2013 elections, he said again that foreign forces are involved in the conflict in Balochistan. This brought the debate about foreign participation back into the spotlight. This shows that the military establishment still thinks that India is to blame for the violence in the province because it gives money to the Baloch fighters at least.

Pakistan has said that both the United States and the United Kingdom are meddling in Balochistan's business. Abdul Basit, a spokesman for the Foreign Ministry, said there was proof that the weapons used by Baloch insurgents came from NATO. This is not surprising, though, because the Taliban also use NATO weapons that they bought on the black market. The other proof is that Baloch leaders in flight have been given asylum instead of being prosecuted. But President Musharraf was able to get the UK and US governments to say that the Baloch Liberation Front was a terrorist group. In 2007, his government also tried to send Mehran Baloch, who was the Baloch representative on the UN Human Rights Council, but failed. It also accused Hyrbyair Marri and Faiz Baloch of terrorism. Hyrbyair Marri and Faiz Baloch were finally brought to trial in the UK in 2008, but they were later cleared of all charges. The UK government gave them refugee status only after the Commonwealth & Comparative Politics 303 verdict .

Some experts say that the United States backs the rebels. People say that US defense contractors are "moving a lot of money from Afghanistan to Balochistan" with the help of Afghan guides and translators. The US is upset that China will be able to get into the Gulf through Gwadar, which is too close to where the US Naval Forces Central Command and US Fifth Fleet are based in Bahrain. There is some proof that the US is helping militants in Iranian Balochistan, but this is not being looked at seriously in the Balochistan conflict in Pakistan. Instead, conspiracy theories say that the rebellion is part of a grand US plan to break up Muslim countries. Modern worries about the crisis in Balochistan overlap and get mixed up with the world's fixation on Al Qaeda and the Taliban and the idea that Pakistan, a nuclear state, is unstable.

When the argument for outside intervention is looked at, there is circumstantial proof of Afghan (by giving them a place to stay) and Indian (by giving them money) involvement in Balochistan. This isn't really a surprise, since Pakistan backs the Taliban and militants in Kashmir and has bad ties with both of those countries. But it would be too much to say that this is the main reason for the problem in the province. At most, these powers are just taking advantage of a chance made by the Pakistani security establishment's poor handling of the situation. As for the part of the UK and US, this is an even weaker theory, which could be a result of helping Iranian Baloch dissidents.

Resource Exploration

Collier and Hoeffler's detailed study of civil wars shows that a high percentage of basic commodities in a country's exports makes the risk of a civil war much higher. A lot of resources can cause conflict and affect when and how long it lasts. Balochistan has always contributed the same amount to Pakistan's economy, which is about 4% of GDP. However, the province provides about 40% of the country's energy needs. Grare, Wirsing, and Niazi focus on the resource-driven conflict method. They say that taking away natural resources, being left out, and being kicked out are all important factors. Baloch hostility toward the center was made worse by the fact that natural resources like Sui natural gas were not used to help the local people. Sui, which was found in the 1950s, is where most of the gas in Balochistan is made. In fact, 38% of the country's gas comes from Balochistan. But in terms of spread, only 6% of Balochistan has access to gas, and the town closest to the Sui gas fields, Sibi, doesn't have it. Also, it was a terrible irony that Balochistan only got a tiny amount of the money that was made.

The government has put a lot of effort into using the big copper reserves in Balochistan. As a result, copper production has gone from 10,000 tonnes in 2002-2003 to almost 4 million tonnes in 2004-2005. The Saindak Copper Gold Project in Chagai, the largest district in Pakistan, which is in northern Balochistan, is the largest copper and gold mining project in Balochistan. The Federal Ministry of Petroleum and Natural Resources is in charge of the project. It is being led by Saindak Metals Limited. In 2002, the SML and the Chinese Metallurgical Construction Company agreed to work together for 10 years. In the Rekodiq area, which is also in the Chagai district, there is a second large copper-gold mining project. This is a 25:37.5:37.5 agreement between the government of Balochistan, Chile's Antofagasta, and Canada's Barrick Gold. The goal of this project is to use Balochistan's estimated 2 billion tons of copper and 20 million ounces of gold. The local people are angry about the whole project because they don't see how it will help them. Since the Balochistan provincial government challenged the company's original license and the Supreme Court ruled that the Rekodiq deal was invalid in January 2013, mineral extraction has been stuck in the courts.

Gas pipes also go through Balochistan to get to other places. The planned US$4 billion Iran-Pakistan-India gas pipeline will go through Balochistan. It will be about 3000 km long and can move between 1.1 and 3.4 billion cubic feet of gas per day. The Turkmenistan-Pakistan gas pipeline, which is planned to be 1700 km long, and the Qatar-Pakistan gas pipeline, which is 1650 km long, both go through Balochistan. So, not only does the state produce energy, but it is also in a good spot to send energy to the power-hungry cities of Pakistan. Even though the US is against it, the gas pipeline between Iran and Pakistan will still be built. However, India will no longer be a part of it. The pipeline from Iran would go through Balochistan, join Punjab at Multan, and then go to Lahore and Karachi. Iran will also give Pakistan power, which is very important because Pakistan needs energy badly. But Pakistan's financial problems make it hard to finish this project, and it also depends on the security situation in Balochistan and on how serious Washington is about enforcing the ban against Tehran. The Turkmenistan pipeline, which the White House wants, would go through Afghanistan, enter Balochistan, cross the Punjab from Multan to Lahore, and then join India. This route, on the other hand, depends on both Balochistan and Afghanistan being stable. Without peace in these two places, it will always be a pipe dream in more ways than one.

The port of Gwadar is also a factor because it gives China access to the Persian Gulf and makes it easier for Islamabad to depend less on Karachi, which is a geopolitical weak spot. Poor infrastructure development, on the other hand, means that the port can't meet the needs of either Afghanistan or China.

In China's case, a link between Karakorum and Gwadar would only be worth it if Pakistan was a gateway to the bigger and more lucrative Indian market. The Pak-Qatari pipeline is expected to reach Gwadar, which is on the coast of Balochistan. Beijing has already put a lot of money into building a port and a military base there. The Chinese want to move the gas along the Indus River by land across the Karakorum Highway using a "white oil pipeline" to feed their energy grid. After losing interest in joining the Iran-Pakistan-India gas pipeline and the Turkmenistan-Afghanistan-Pakistan (TAP) gas pipeline, China has stepped up its efforts in this area. Even though the first pipeline is stuck because of international politics, Beijing is not too interested in the TAP line because of security concerns.

Unlike other wars, like those over blood diamonds in Liberia or oil in the Niger delta, resources are not a direct cause of this one. Resources are not a reason for and a chance for violence. But they are a big reason why the Baloch are unhappy. At the moment, resources are mostly just ideas because they haven't been taken out of the ground yet. The Baloch are worried that outsiders will get the benefits at the cost of the locals, as happened with the Sui gas. Energy, access to it, and mineral wealth fuel discontent, help explain why there is an insurgency, and could become an important variable if international rivalry and domestic discontent can mix. This would give the conflict a regional and global dimension. Resources could be a big factor in the war, but there doesn't seem to be any evidence to back this up right now. These ideas are more hypothetical. If and when mining happens, this could change.

Global Migration and Dispersion

There are two academic ideas about how people move: ***transnationalism*** and ***migration***. These ideas have different paths, but they also overlap. There are a lot of parallels between the groups, but there are also some big differences. The two have something in common: communication and the way it changes the world and makes it into a "global village." Transnationalism is when people talk and interact over long distances as if it were normal and routine for groups of people working in globally integrated fields. Interpersonal connections between transnational people are merged with or maybe even replaced by connections and networks between communities and organizations across countries. Theories of transnationalism focus on how people talk to each other, how much pressure comes from their home country, and how much money they send back home. Diasporas are groups, not people like transnationals, who have used new technologies to move around the world. Classical examples from the literature, like the Jews and Armenians, have become very similar to each other. Their differences may only be symbolic, but they can still use them to rally for a common cause, which helps diasporas function as a way for long-distance nationalism to take place.

A low estimate says that there are about nine million Baloch people in the world, with about seven million of them living in Pakistan. There are just over a million in Iran, less than half a million in Afghanistan and Oman, and about 36,000 in Turkmenistan. Because the borders between Iran, Pakistan, and Afghanistan are not solid, many Baloch can move easily between them, and many of them have Pakistani ID cards. A large number of people live in Oman and make up just over 20% of the country's settled population. This number does not include casual workers. In Bahrain and Dubai, there are smaller groups. Baloch people have lived in the Gulf since the 16th and 17th centuries. In 1784, the ruling family of Oman sought refuge in Gwadar, with approval from the Khan of Kalat. The port and surrounding area became part of Oman, but in 1958, Pakistan bought the land and port of Gwadar. Omani rule over parts of the Makran coast made it easier for Baloch people to move to Oman in search of work and to stay there. Because of this, many of them moved to Oman. Most of them live along the al-Batina coast, which runs along the Gulf of Oman from Muscat to the United Arab Emirates. There are also small groups of them in other places. Both Muscat and Muttrah have places where Baloch people live.

Baloch people have served in Gulf forces for a long time. The first modern army unit in Oman was made up of all Baloch people in 1921, and they were in high demand during the Dhofar uprising (1965–1975). Most Baloch are from Pakistan, but some Iranian Baloch came to the area when the Shah of Iran was in charge in the 1950s and 1960s. Some of these newcomers were asked to join the paramilitary group of the Sultan of Oman. Today, eastern Baloch people make up 40% of the army in Oman. They are also a large part of the Bahraini police force. Several Baloch have been officials in the government of Oman. Others have become well-known businesspeople or even led the air force. Major General Sharafuddin Sharaf, who was from western Balochistan, used to be in charge of the intelligence service in Dubai.

The Collier-Hoeffler Model says that diasporas are a second way that rebellions and insurgencies get money. The bigger the diaspora, the more likely it is that it will pay a rebellion. The study found that if the size of a country's diaspora changed from the smallest to the biggest in the study, the chance of a civil war went up by a factor of six. It's hard to find out what the Baloch diaspora thinks about their home country because political speech is illegal in the Gulf States and Pakistan is putting pressure on the Gulf States so that they don't become a safe haven for Baloch rebels. There is also pressure from within the

Baloch community not to do things that hurt the interests of the Baloch diaspora in the Gulf and cause diplomatic trouble. Baloch still have close family ties and active ties to their towns and villages on the Makran coast, but these ties are stronger for the first and second generation Baloch who still speak the language and follow the culture norms. About 5,000 people from Gwadar live in the Wadi Hattat neighborhood of Muscat City. There are flights every two weeks between Gwadar and Muscat. Some of the people who live there are well-known Baloch nationalist poets, like Abdul Majid Gwadari, who wrote the Baloch national song "Ma Chuken Balochaani!" and Gulam Hussain Shohaz, who has since died. More generally, a large number of Omani Baloch and other Baloch people who live in the Gulf Region agree with and support Baloch nationalism. This is because the Makran Division has been one of the most important places where a Baloch middle class and nationalist rising have been taking place. So, members of the Baloch diaspora, who are naturally worried about what's been going on, are angry at the Pakistan Army and its followers for being so cruel. For example, a Baloch major from Muscat who retired from the Oman army was quoted in the news as saying, "Pakistani army soldiers are like beasts and cannibals."

The Baloch have copied the transnational methods used by the Taliban, such as the triangular cycle of Federally Administered Tribal Areas (FATA)/Helmand, Karachi, and the Gulf (mostly Dubai). Khalid Sheikh Mohammed, who planned the 9/11 attacks, and Ramzi Yousef, who bombed the World Trade Center in 1993 and was involved in the Bojinka plot, are probably the most well-known cases. Both live in the Baloch Gulf and are linked to Osama bin Laden. Like the Taliban, secular nationalist Baloch get a lot of their money from the trade in drugs. Along with illegal goods, Baloch crime networks also move people. In the 1990s, heroin was being sold in Pakistan, and a document from the Central Intelligence Agency names some Baloch groups. Diplomatic sources generally agree that Baloch extremists are using this network of criminal activity to fund the uprising. The money is washed in Dubai and put together with money from the Baloch diaspora, where anger is high over the terrible things that are happening to the Baloch. Again, because there is no legal or obvious political action in the Gulf States, it is not possible to figure out where the money that is being collected and sent to the insurgents is coming from. But, like the Taliban, drug money and money from other sources is moved online through the informal Hawala network, through the secretive formal banking system based in Dubai, or by courier.

There are connections between the funding network and international arms-dealing groups. The Baloch buy guns from drug smugglers in Afghanistan. These drug smugglers then sell these weapons to the Taliban. There is no proof that the Baloch separatists are working with either the Taliban or Al Qaeda. Even though Darra Adam Khel and other parts of Khyber Pukthunkhwa have their own industries for making weapons, most terrorists prefer to use weapons made in other countries because they are more reliable. There are also some supplies left over from the operation in Afghanistan, which can be bought for a price, but these are added to by a number of other sources. Dubai's unrestricted free market is not only a major source of money, but also a major source of weapons. The weapons that the Pentagon gave to the Afghan army but that ended up on the black market are another important source. This pool of illegal weapons is easy for the Taliban and Baloch terrorists to get their hands on. Pakistan says that the United States and the United Kingdom back Baloch militants because NATO weapons are being sold on the black market. As can be seen, the Baloch rebels are also using the same networks that supply the Taliban uprising with weapons.

In the Gulf, diasporic support is often done in secret, but Baloch refugees in Europe and the United States do their work in the open. Transnational activists in the UK, USA, Norway, and Sweden are very noticeable. Exiles from Iran and Pakistan who live in Europe and the US work together to lobby the United Nations in Geneva and New York, the European Union, and individual countries. They are building a shared political identity for the Baloch and using the media to spread their ideas. Baloch websites with servers outside of Pakistan and Iran talk about people who have gone missing, say that they were killed without a trial, post statements from separatist leaders, and give news about Baluchistan in general. They do this to challenge the story that Islamabad and Tehran tell about Baluchistan and show an alternative history and cultural memory. Because of this, Internet service companies in Pakistan and Iran are told by the government to block these sites. Still, this diasporic action worried Pakistan so much that President Musharraf was able to get the British and American governments to label the Baloch Liberation Front a terrorist group. In 2007, his government also tried to send Mehran Baloch to another country and charged Hyrbyair Marri and Faiz Baloch of being terrorists.

Khan of Kalat, Hyrbyair Marri, and Brahamdagh Bugti, who are in exile, are working hard to create a single stage where the different Baloch groups from Pakistan and Iran can come together and speak with one voice. To this end, there are talks, which are held up by personal rivalries, about making a constitution, which would lead to the formation of a government in exile in the end. Republican Congressman Dana Rohrabacher, Chair of the US House of Representatives Committee on Foreign Affairs Subcommittee on Europe, Eurasia, and Emerging Threats, has pushed for Iranian and Pakistani groups, as well as different groups within Pakistan, to work together. Rohrabacher doesn't like Pakistan because he thinks it helps the Taliban. He thinks that a united Baloch resistance could get Congress to see the area in a different way. Baloch activists in exile were able to convince Rohrabacher to hold a congressional meeting on the situation in Balochistan in February 2012. This scared the Pakistani government. Baloch activists brought up the idea of a free Balochistan at this meeting. The plan was offered to the US as a package in which Iran and Pakistan would be split up and Gwadar would be given to the US as a base for the US fleet. This is a minority opinion in Congress, and it is more of an attempt to shame Pakistan. However, these events have caused a lot of worry in Pakistan's security establishment, which is already worried about what exiles are doing abroad.

Washington's worst-case situation for Pakistan is that Al Qaeda would get access to nuclear weapons because of the country's instability. These worries keep it from getting involved and make it very unlikely that the country would break up and Balochistan would become a separate country. But there is a small chance that a war with Iran could lead to a change in the government and the creation of a de facto independent western Balochistan like Iraq's Kurdistan. This would be a big setback for Islamabad because it would give Baloch terrorists a safe place to hide.

The separatists are getting help and money through the diaspora and international activities. They get money from selling drugs and get guns from people who sell drugs. They are using the well-established financial, drug, and money laundering networks in the area that the Taliban have set up to further their own goals. In the Gulf States, where they have settled as diasporic populations, they are giving money, but this can't be checked because the area isn't democracy. Exiles living in the West have done the most visible things. They have tried, but failed, to support their cause, bring the opposition together, and lobby governments. Some Congressmen who don't like Pakistan have helped them and given them a place to talk about how an independent Balochistan would be good for US interests in the area. Diasporic action gives the nationalists a breath of fresh air, and transnational circuits are used to raise money and get weapons. So, they are a part in figuring out what is going on with the insurgency, but not necessarily a cause.

Diversity Management

Most nation states have put a lot of thought into how to deal with differences. Some have tried to get rid of differences, while others have tried to recognize cultural differences. McGarry and O'Leary found eight different ways to deal with ethnic conflicts. These ways are not always used separately, but are generally used together, either one after the other or at the same time. Genocide, ethnic cleansing, secession and partition, and political homogenization (which can mean anything from integration to assimilation) are four grand strategies for getting rid of differences. The other four grand strategies for dealing with differences are hegemonic control, arbitration, federation, and autonomy and consociation.

Hegemonic control, on the other hand, has been the most usual way that historically divided societies have been brought back together. Authoritarian or imperial governments deal with cultural differences by co-opting elites and dominating them by force. Ethnic divides, both dormant and active, were put down, especially during times of fast modernization. Control was hegemonic when openly violent ethnic threats to state power costed too many lives. So, hegemonic control was a system in which it was unthinkable or impossible for subordinate communities to use their ethnicity to question the power of the state. In the name of the ruling nationality, which O'Leary calls the Staatsvolk, regulators try to erase some of the differences between ethnic groups. To do this, the most powerful group needs to be organized, which in a liberal democracy means taking over state institutions and making sure that minorities can't vote. Hegemonic control in authoritarian regimes didn't always depend on the support of the largest ethnic groups. Instead, it depended on which ethnic group was in charge of the coercive apparatus. There are many examples of ethnic minorities who were in charge of the police and security forces, which helped them keep hegemonic control.

Federations usually start out as multi-ethnic colonies, where the people in charge want to keep the federation going because it gives them access to bigger markets and makes them feel safer. Federalism can be a good way to deal with differences if the groups that make up the government are divided by ethnicity and disadvantaged groups are given special treatment, like in India. In Pakistan's constitution, the legal way to deal with differences in ethnic groups is through federalism, which has been changed a lot by the Eighth Amendment and is now moving towards consociationalism. As a way to deal with ethnic conflicts, it can work if the borders between ethnic groups meet the units of the federation. However, this is not the case in Pakistan, where most provinces are made up of people from different ethnic groups.

Even though Pakistan is a federation, hegemonic control became the most important way to deal with racial issues. Authoritarian governments ruled over more than one culture by dominating by force and getting elites to join them. Hegemonic control, on the other hand, can only happen if the Staatsvolk is in charge of the institutions of state power. The military and the bureaucracy were the most important institutions. The military was more important when Pakistan was under military rule, which was most of its past. People have called this change the Punjabization of Pakistan. Punjabization isn't just about how many Punjabis live in Pakistan; it's also about how ethnicity and institutional power are mixed together. This happens when there are too many Punjabis in key state institutions, especially in the military. The army is the biggest employer in the country. It also works as a development agency that promotes strategic industries, owns the most land in the country, and hires people with fairly high levels of education. Another important industry that has a lot of power in Pakistan is the military-industrial complex. But the Punjabi service class had to work together to take control of these important organizations. Before Bangladesh came into being, an alliance of Punjabis and Muhajirs ran the military-bureaucratic oligarchy. As a result of the Soviet Invasion of Afghanistan, the military-bureaucratic oligarchy changed in a way that gave the Pukhtuns more power at the cost of the Muhajirs. Today, Punjabis, Pukhtuns, and, to a smaller extent, Muhajirs work together to rule the Staatsvolk.

Even though the political situation has changed, Balochistan's past from the time it joined Pakistan until now is full of examples of coercion and manipulation. When Mir Ahmed Yar Khan wasn't sure if he wanted to join Pakistan with the Baloch-Brauhi confederacy in 1947, the center did things to force the state to join Pakistan. By recognizing the feudal states of Las Bela, Kharan, and the district of Mekran as separate states, which quickly merged with Pakistan, the State of Kalat became landlocked and shrunk to a small fraction of its size. So, on March 27, 1948, Ahmed Yar Khan was forced to sign the document of accession. This led to the Khan's brother, Prince Abdul Karim, raising the flag of revolt in July 1948, which started the first of many Baloch uprisings. In the 1970s, Zulfikar Bhutto also used coercion and co-option to deal with the National Awami Party coalition in Balochistan. He fired Ataullah Mengal's provincial government on false charges, which led Ataullah Mengal and Khair Bux Marri to flee to Afghanistan. Akbar Bugti was chosen to be the governor of the province, but he quit after a short time because of the harsh methods that were used to make the province calm down. The harsh method turned the Baloch into political activists and made them want to be independent even more.

Several local issues come together in the current dispute: the problem of development, the share of revenue from energy and mineral resources taken from the province, and the building of the Gwadar port. At first, it seemed like the problem in Balochistan was about resources. However, the building of Gwadar poses a much bigger risk that differences will be lost through integration. Assimilation is a way for states to get rid of racial differences. If a few million people moved to the port city, the Baloch would become a minority. Because of this, Baloch leaders pushed for a 12-year ban on voting rights for newcomers to the province. The security establishment, on the other hand, didn't have much patience with the Baloch nationalists and quickly moved from negotiations to coercion with military operations in the Marri-Bugti areas. This allowed the agencies to run a province-wide "kill and dump" policy and get pro-government sardars, some of whom had religious ties, to run a vigilante campaign against suspected nationalists that has turned into sectarian violence against Hazara Shias.

To explain why the security establishment is so impatient, groups that aren't allowed into key institutions have found that their problems aren't taken seriously and that the military uses force very quickly. Compare, for instance, how the center dealt with the Waziristan conflict and how it dealt with the Balochistan dispute. In contrast to Washington, which sees the tribal areas through the lens of the "War on Terror" and Islamic militancy, Islamabad has a more nuanced view. This is because a number of senior officers are from the area, which is why they suggested negotiations instead of military campaigns in FATA. As in Balochistan, the army has also fought against ideas to get rid of local levies, and the dozen or so attempts to kill Musharraf were not taken personally, as they were in Balochistan. Baloch complaints, on the other hand, were dealt with more harshly through assimilation strategies related to development or through coercive strategies, because Baloch people were a disenfranchised minority and couldn't get to the power centers in the armed forces. This group is not reflected in the top levels of the military-bureaucratic oligarchy, especially in the army, which is the most important institution. This is why the move to force was made so quickly. Baloch aren't part of the Staats-volk, so hegemonic control is the best way to deal with racial issues in Balochistan. The current conflict is part of a long-term trend of how the province has dealt with political unrest. Hegemonic control has been the most common way to deal with difference, which suggests that it is the cause that interacts with other factors to make this conflict worse. It sets the stage so that other things can make the war and Baloch nationalists' resistance worse.

But in the framework of federalism, there have been attempts to move away from hegemonic control and deal with the problem of differences. With the election of a PPP government in 2008 and the swearing in of Asif Ali Zardari as President on September 9, the government tried again to deal with the problem directly. It did this in two ways. First, it made changes to the constitution that affected provincial rights across all of Pakistan. Second, it took steps to deal directly with the problem in Balochistan. In 2010, the 18th Amendment to the Constitution was a step in the right direction. It made parliament the highest authority, limited the ability of the center to get involved in provincial matters, and changed the name of the North-West Frontier Province to Khyber Pukhtunkhwa. The combined list was taken away, and the Government made it easier for the provinces to have a say in some things on the Federal List by giving the Council of Common Interests more power. The provincial assemblies were given more power. For example, the power of the ruler of the provinces to declare emergencies and extend ordinances was limited, and the provincial assemblies had to agree to it.

Plans to give the provinces more freedom were made to handle the problems of the smaller provinces, especially Balochistan. Federating units were made equal partners with the center for mineral, oil, and gas reserves in the provinces, and parliament was given the power to pass laws that made up for the fact that the provinces were underrepresented in Pakistan's services. Also, if the federal government decided to build a hydroelectric power station, it had to talk to the local government about it. Under Musharraf, the Council of Common Interests, a quasi-executive body that was supposed to handle problems in the center province but wasn't doing a good job, was expanded, seems to have been strengthened, and is now required to report to Parliament regularly. The National Finance Commission Award stopped distributing money based on the number of people in a country. Instead, it uses a method that takes into account several factors, such as underdevelopment, how much money is collected and generated, and the inverse population density. The center's share of income was cut down by a lot, and the provinces could now borrow money on both the domestic and foreign markets. The 18th Amendment and the Balochistan Package, or Aghaaz-e-Huqook Balochistan, were both passed by Yousaf Gilani's government. Together, they were supposed to solve the province's problems. This political plan was also backed by the largest opposition party, the Muslim League (N), which was ready to put the weight of the Punjab behind a solution to the conflict.

The Baloch were skeptical, even though it was seen as a step in the right direction. Militants called for an end to all fighting on their own and asked that military operations stop, prisoners be freed, and a probe into extra-judicial killings be held. On the ground, though, it had no effect because the army was out of control and the cease-fire fell apart. Neither the federal government nor the local government has been able to negotiate with the army to solve the problem. The 2013 general elections were won by Nawaz Sharif's Muslim League, and he backed Abdul Malik Baloch's bid to become chief minister and lead a coalition regional government. The chief minister is not a sardar and is from the Makran coast. He is a member of the National Awami Party and continues the political discussion with Baloch nationalists that was started by his predecessor. He has admitted, though, that he hasn't made much progress on the problems of disappearances and extra-judicial killings. Abdul Malik Baloch is now bringing the problem of disappearances and executions to the

All Party Conference. He wants to find a way for the security forces and their vigilante allies to be held in check, which is a requirement for serious talks with Baloch nationalists. Only time will tell if the move away from hegemonic control will work and if consociationalism will be a good way to deal with differences in a changed federal system.

Conclusion

When you look at the different points of view on the Balochistan problem, it's clear that the main cause of the insurgency in Pakistan is bad management of differences, which then affects how resources are shared and who has power over them. Baloch history shows that coercion and bribery have been used to control the ethnic group, and the current crisis is the result of this approach still being used. Baloch objections and worries about how the Gwadar development plan could lead to assimilation and how mineral extraction and energy projects that wouldn't help the Baloch people much were overlooked. First, they didn't have legal ways to disagree because key parts of democracy had been taken away. Second, they didn't have a voice in the Staatsvolk, which is where important decisions were made. During this time, most decisions were made by the army, where Baloch impact was very small. It also shows how quickly the military went from negotiating to using force and a brutal effort to get rid of people who didn't agree with them. Even though there seems to be a strong emotional case for independence, many people think that the violence of the operations against the nationalists is just political posturing. The 18th Amendment and the Balochistan Package could help end the crisis by addressing all of the sensitive issues that Baloch rebels have brought up and allowing for a certain amount of consociationalism. But these plans have failed because no civilian government has been able to control the army, which is eager to crush the opposition. Dialog and compromise are still the only possible options, but they will only work if the detainees are freed and the extra-judicial killings are looked into.

As for the sardars, they are split between people who are pro-government and people who are against the government because of personal rivalries. Only three tribal leaders are involved in the revolt, and parts of Balochistan where there are no sardars are very busy in mobilizing against the center. There seems to be some proof that outside forces were involved, but Pakistan's claim about how much India was involved has not been proven. There does seem to be some proof that Delhi is giving resources, and given how bad things are between Pakistan and its neighbor to the east, it's not easy to say for sure that neither India nor Afghanistan are fishing in troubled waters. But outside interference, with or without the help of tribal leaders, is not a strong explanation for the current problem.

The resource argument has some merit, not because it is what funds the rebellion, but because it emphasizes how poor the province is and how it is being used. Clearly, if the many pipelines that are being planned are to be built, the conflict must be resolved and a certain level of security must be reached before big companies are willing to make the big investments that are needed to do business in Balochistan. So far, there is no proof that geopolitical competition between the US, China, India, Iran, or any other country is making the area less stable. In different ways, the Baloch diaspora and transnationals are active. Since political action is illegal in the Gulf States, support from the diaspora is secret and underground. In many ways, the international networks that connect Quetta, Karachi, and Dubai are similar to the networks that the Taliban use to fund and keep up their war against NATO in Afghanistan. In the case of the Baloch, drug trafficking is a major source of money that is used to buy arms on the same black market that the Taliban, Al Qaeda, and other criminals use. Baloch exiles in Europe and the United States, on the other hand, work together with their Iranian counterparts to come up with joint views on media coverage and lobbying. In 2012, a small US Congressional committee held a meeting on Balochistan, which shocked Islamabad and showed how well this strategy works.

Contributing Elements to Insurgency in Balochistan

The region of Balochistan, which has seen a period of relative tranquility lasting three decades, is currently undergoing a comprehensive insurgency. For a considerable duration, the area has witnessed instances of forceful demonstrations characterized by explosive detonations, indiscriminate homicides, and acts of deliberate disruption targeting critical infrastructure. The ongoing episode of violence in Balochistan, which commenced in late 2003, persists without abating and recurrently resurfaces with remarkable frequency. In December 2005, a comprehensive military campaign was initiated by government forces targeting the Baloch militants in the Kohlu District. This territory is primarily inhabited by the Marri tribesmen, who are known for their combative nature and represent one of the several Baloch tribes. In 2005, security forces engaged in a direct military confrontation with Baloch nationalists for the third instance. Nevertheless, in prior occurrences, the focal point of activity was the adjacent Dera Bugti District, which is predominantly controlled by the Bugti tribe, the largest ethnic group in the Baloch community. The Baloch community was further incensed and several clans were unified as a result of the subsequent assassination of Nawab Akbar Bugti, the leader of the Bugti tribe, during an armed operation in August 2006. The Baloch constitute a relatively small proportion of Pakistan's population, making it unlikely for them to directly overpower the state forces. However, despite the state forces' significant military advantage, they have been unable to assert their authority in the province. Despite the diminished media attention due to the killing of Benazir Bhutto, following political upheavals in Pakistan, and the increasing influence of fundamentalism, the ongoing violence in Balochistan has persisted without interruption. Despite the occurrence of the death of Nawabzada Ballach Marri in November 2007, who was widely believed to hold a leadership position within the Baloch Liberation Army, the ongoing violence has not been effectively suppressed. The government has employed helicopter gunships and artillery to engage with Baloch nationalists, who are contesting the authority

Figure 2.1. Map depicting Balochistan in Pakistan.

Source: Indian Army's Eastern Command Website, http://www.eastarmy.nic.in/ images/pakistan-map.gif (accessed 1 May 2008).

of the state by specifically attacking various symbols of government power, such as cantonments, police stations, railway lines, power transmission lines, and telephone exchanges. The presence of ethnic violence and the manner in which the Pakistani state is addressing the concerns expressed by the Baloch community highlight the inherent vulnerability and rigidity of the state apparatus.

The ruling elites in Pakistan have consistently sought to repress any manifestation of authentic federalism, viewing it as a potential catalyst for secession, as they strive to promote nationalism and national unity. The primary obstacle to Pakistan's pursuit of a unitary structure can be ascribed to the profound ethnic consciousness and robust socio-cultural identity exhibited by the majority of ethnic groups dwelling within the country. Despite the initial inclusion of the concepts of "constituent units" with autonomy and sovereignty in the Lahore Resolution, the Urdu-speaking ruling elites of Pakistan, who championed the 'Two Nation Theory' and spearheaded the movement for a separate homeland for Indian Muslims, expressed significant concerns regarding these ideas. This ultimately led to the partition of India. The individuals held the belief that the cohesion of the newly formed state could alone be achieved by prioritizing its religious identity over all other identities. Additionally, they expressed concerns regarding the potential collapse of the recently constituted state due to ethno-linguistic divisions. As a result, they strongly disapproved of endorsing sub-national identities, either via symbolic means by acknowledging their socio-cultural and linguistic identity, or through political means by incorporating them into the state structure based on ethnicity. From its very beginning, the central authority encountered challenges in effectively devolving functions to the provinces in alignment with the envisioned federal structure of the state. Furthermore, it took on powers to govern the provincial governments that were not legitimately within its jurisdiction.

The majority of the Baloch population exhibited a lack of enthusiasm in their decision to align with Pakistan, displaying a general reluctance towards joining the newly formed state. The State of Kalat held a prominent position among the Baloch princely states in the region of Balochistan. It was officially recognized as a princely state of British Balochistan and maintained treaty relations with Whitehall, distinguishing it from other princely states that were integrated into British India. The Khan of Kalat, as the ruler of the princely state, expressed a desire for a status comparable to that of Nepal. He asserted that his pursuit was endorsed by Mohammed Ali Jinnah, the inaugural Governor General of Pakistan, who at the time served as the legal counsel to the kingdom. The Baloch assert that the British transfer of sovereignty over the Baloch areas was afterwards delegated to the State of Kalat prior to achieving independence. Following the attainment of independence, both houses of parliament in Kalat unanimously declined the proposition of merging with Pakistan. However, the regions of Balochistan that were formerly under the direct governance of the British Empire were included into Pakistan. This proposition was officially approved by the city authorities of Quetta, an administrative body predominantly composed of non-Baloch settlers. Following a series of events, the Khan of Kalat was compelled to affix his signature to the merger contract, resulting in the annexation of Kalat. The aforementioned circumstances precipitated the inaugural armed insurgency in 1948, spearheaded by Prince Karim, who happened to be the sibling of the Khan.

Subsequently, the Baloch population has engaged in three instances of rebellion, confronting the security forces during the periods of 1958, 1963-69, and 1973-77. The Baloch chronicles depict a consistent narrative of betrayal and dishonesty on the part of the leadership in Islamabad. Despite the utilization of forceful measures to suppress previous insurgencies, the enduring consequences of these conflicts continue to manifest in unresolved wounds. The intensity of each insurgency has progressively escalated, accompanied by a corresponding growth in the organizational capacities and public backing for the insurgent groups. During the peak of the insurgency in 1973, a total of 55,000 insurgents were confronted by a force of 80,000 Pakistani forces, who received help from both the Pakistani Air Force and the Iranian Air Force. The insurgency that persisted until 1977 resulted in the deaths of more than 5,000 rebels and over 3,300 soldiers. The Pakistani Armed Forces employed a robust approach to suppress the insurgency, driven by their desire to restore their reputation following their significant loss in Bangladesh. The insurgent group expressed a desire for Soviet intervention, however, their hopes were not realized. Zia ul Haq pursued a policy of collaboration with Baloch leaders, offering broad amnesty and facilitating the reintegration of a majority of the insurgents. Subsequently, a faction of Baloch nationalists consistently held a presence within the provincial government located in Quetta.

The attribution of violence in Pakistan by the elites is often oversimplified, as it is primarily linked to the Baloch sardars' inclination to maintain their fiefdoms. Their opposition to development stems from the concern that it may lead to increased awareness and expose their tribes to democratic ideals, which could potentially challenge their leadership. Furthermore, it is believed by some that the resurgence of the insurgency in 2004 can be attributed to the absence of Baloch nationalists, who had previously maintained a certain level of influence within the province government but were subsequently excluded following the most recent elections. Nevertheless, it should be acknowledged that the Baloch insurgent movement is mostly spearheaded by urbanized and educated Baloch youth who have been affected by Marxist ideology, despite the backing they receive from the sardars. Furthermore, it is worth noting that this support extends beyond tribal boundaries. It is noteworthy to observe that among the approximately 250 Baloch sardars, only the sardars belonging to the Bugti, Marri, and Mengal tribes have been actively expressing opposition towards the government in recent years. The Baloch people, transcending tribal divisions, possess legitimate issues. The issue of Baloch grievances is around the intersection of ethnicity, political marginalization, and economic exploitation, which remains a significant catalyst for mobilization within the Baloch community. The sentiment described is particularly heightened within the Baloch community in Pakistan, relative to other ethnic groups, due to historical and economic factors.

Inadequate Participation in Government

Pakistan's national government has never had a lot of Baloch people in it. General Musharraf made Zafarullah Khan Jamali the prime minister. Before that, no Baloch had reached a key post in the federal government. During the first 30 years that Pakistan was around, only 4 of the 179 people who served in the cabinet at different times were Baloch. Even though they have been called a "military race," they haven't played much of a role in the Pakistani Army. This seems to be a result of British rule, as "77% of the people recruited by the British from what became the state of Pakistan came from Punjab, 19.5% from NWFP, 2.2% from Sindh, and 0.6% from Balochistan." But after Pakistan got its freedom, no one tried to fix this problem. In 1970, about 70% of Pakistan's military leaders were Punjabi, 15% were Pathan (Pakhtoon), 10% were Mohajir, and 5% were Baloch or Sindi. The situation was much worse at the top of the military. In June 1959, 11 of Pakistan's 24 generals were Punjabis and 11 were Pathans. So far, there haven't been many Baloch in the highest ranks of the military. Ataullah Mengal, who used to be the Baloch chief minister, said, "There are only a few hundred Balochs in the whole Pakistani Army." There are no Baloch in the well-known Baloch Regiment. During the rule of Ayub, a group called the Kalat Scouts was formed. Only two people from Kalat were in the group. The same goes for the Sibi Scouts, who were made to keep order in the Marri lands. It has no Baloch people in its ranks. The leaders are from Punjab, and the soldiers are from the Frontier. Pakistan hires troops based on quotas, and the percentage of soldiers from Balochistan and Sindh was raised to 15% in 1991. At the same time, height and schooling requirements were lowered for these groups, which had been underrepresented in the Army until then. This was done to make it easier for them to join. But in December 1998, there were still about 10,000 other ranks from Balochistan and the heart of Sindh that weren't there. Since the limit is based on the province, most of the people from Balochistan who join the Army are Pathans and other settlers, not Balochs.

One estimate says that there were 830 higher civil service jobs in Balochistan in 1979, but only 181 were filled by Balochs. Each position of secretary, director, and deputy commissioner was held by the same Baloch. As far as the police force was concerned, only 25% of its officers were Baloch, and the whole top level was made up of officers who were not Baloch. The same thing happened in the court system. After the insurgency ended in 1980, Zia tried to make peace with the Baloch by giving them a share of central jobs proportional to their number in Pakistan. As a result, 3.9% of central jobs were set aside for people from Balochistan. But Baloch people are still not well represented in the government. Even now, they don't make up 3.9% of the government, which is what the law says they should. Even among those who came from Balochistan, most of the recruits were from outside the country. Most of them were Pakhtoons, who live mostly in the northern areas. Few Baloch people work in the Pakistani Army, government, or foreign service. In 2002, only four of the fourteen provincial government secretaries in Quetta were Baloch, less than 500 of the 3,200 students at Balochistan University were Baloch, and only 30 of the 180 staff members were Baloch. Abdul Rauf Mengal, a Baloch member of parliament, said that as of March 2005, there were very few government workers from Balochistan in Islamabad and not a single Baloch working in foreign offices. Balochistan is still not well represented in any part of the Pakistani government, which makes it hard for people to feel like they belong to the government. So, the government and its agencies are seen as foreigners who rule over Baloch land.

Exploitative Financial Practices

Balochistan is the region in Pakistan with the lowest income. It has the lowest income per person out of all four provinces in Pakistan. Not that it doesn't have any natural resources, but its natural resources, which help the rest of Pakistan's economy grow, haven't been able to provide jobs or raise living standards in the province. Even though the state doesn't have a lot of plants, it has a lot of natural resources. It has a lot of natural gas and a lot of minerals like chromium, copper, iron, and coal. Sui and Pirkoh have enough gas to be useful for business. Pakistan gets most of its energy from the gas sources in the area, and nuclear tests can be done there because there aren't many people living there. Balochistan should have been rich because of its long shore and abundance of fish. But the Baloch people say that they don't get any benefits from the natural riches in the province, especially gas.

The state also has a lot of marble and limestone reserves, and about 95% of the world's asbestos is thought to be there. It also has a lot of barytes, chromites, silica, gypsum, magnesite, antimony, manganese, graphite, sulphur, fluorite, and iron ore. People also think that the ground has a lot of oil, but Baloch groups have made it impossible to look for it because they are so angry. In the Marri area, the government wanted to improve the economy by building roads that would make it easier to look for oil. But since the gains were going to the national government and foreign companies instead of the provincial government, Baloch nationalists saw it as a way for Islamabad to take advantage of the province. So, the Baloch Peoples Liberation Front (BPLF) stopped the building of a 57-kilometer road, which they thought was being built for oil drilling, for more than five years. The road couldn't be built until the Army had some success in putting down the insurgents. Things are still pretty much the same. Pakistan's search for oil in the area was one of the main reasons for the latest round of military operations in Kohlu district.

The Pakistani government often says that Balochistan is a "wasteland of deserts and mountains" and "an economic liability," but nothing could be further from the truth. "Balochistan is not only self-sufficient, but it also helps support the Federal Government with its own resources." There are a lot of natural riches on and under the land, in the sea, on the mountains, and even over and under the deserts. The Baloch have always thought that the state doesn't give them a fair share of the money it makes from their land. Baloch nationalists talk a lot about how their natural resources are being used, and Baloch political leaders have always been interested in how resources are shared between the center and the areas.

The Baloch see the difference between how much the gas created in Balochistan is worth and how poor the province is as proof that outsiders are taking advantage of them. Baloch nationalists have been upset for a long time about how the federal government stole Sui's gas supplies. Sui Gas field, which is made up of five gas wells, was found in 1952. It provides 38% of Pakistan's energy needs for homes and businesses, but only 6% of the people who live in Balochistan have a gas connection. Even this gas didn't get to Balochistan until after it was sent to the rest of Pakistan, and that was only because General Zia chose to set up a cantonment in Quetta. Even now, only 6% of Baloch homes are hooked up to a gas line. Since the federal government controls the extraction and distribution of gas and the federal government is "dominated by the Punjab," the gas went where the Punjab wanted it to go. This proves the Baloch nationalists' point that the Punjabis are taking advantage of their resources.

Balochistan gives Pakistan 80% of the gas it needs and most of the coal it needs. This saves Pakistan hundreds of millions of dollars in energy imports. Baloch separatists have always said that the Punjabi-dominated center takes all of their resources. The gas tax is one of the lowest in the world, at 12.5% of the well-head price. Because of the royalty problem, angry people in Balochistan have been able to fight for the people. The Baloch nationalists think that the federal government should pay them a huge sum as a fee for the gas they have given over the years. The late Nawab Bugti was always upset that Pakistan Petroleum Ltd. had broken promises to the Sui people. In response, the government tried to pay or threaten him into staying quiet. When that didn't work, they spread the idea that the tribal sardars were greedy and didn't want their areas to grow. This made the tribes more determined, but it also made the fight more personal. Almost none of the coalmines are owned or run by Baloch. "Balochistan's coal goes to the Punjab, so the Baloch have to burn wood trucked in from Sindh. Its onyx and marble are sent to Karachi to be finished, and its natural gas is piped to industrial belts in the Punjab and Sindh, where it is used in factories. The gas is then sent back to Balochistan in tanks. All of these have failed to make the people in the area feel like they own the place.

Ethnic Marginalisation and Exclusion

Before the 1970s, neither the Pakhtoons nor the Balochs saw it as a problem that the north of Balochistan was mostly Pakhtoon and the south was almost completely Baloch. After the "One Unit Formula" was thrown out and Balochistan became a province in 1970, the problems became clearer. During the war in Afghanistan, a large number of Pakhtoon refugees fled the country. This caused a sudden and disturbing mismatch in the number of people in each community. The Baloch are "no longer the dominant ethnolinguistic group in large parts of the province." This is because the large number of Afghan refugees has made Balochistan's population grow a lot. In 1991, when things got really bad between the two groups, there were violent ethnic battles. Balochistan's population has changed because many Afghan refugees didn't go back home. If the refugees decide to stay for good, the usual balance of ethnic groups between the Baloch and the Pakhtoons would change in favor of the Pakhtoons. This has made Balochs feel like they don't know who they are and "added to ethnic tensions between Balochs and Pakhtoons." The Pakhtoons of the province are with the nationalists in the current standoff with the government, and the party that represents the Pakhtoons of the province, the Pakhtoonkhwa Milli Awami Party (PMAP), has been working with other nationalist groups.

Fundamentalism has also grown because of the large number of refugees and people who support the Taliban who have come to the area. The group of Islamic parties called Muttahida Majlis-e-Amal (MMA) did very well in the last election. This also showed that most people in the area were pro-Taliban and anti-American, since the MMA had run for office on an anti-American platform. People have a lot of anger toward the government of Pakistan because they think it bows down to American orders. But the rise of fundamentalism and Islamic political parties in Balochistan briefly overshadowed the Baloch nationalist movement, which has always been linked to some kind of leftist ideology. Some people in the government think that the major reason for the violence in Balochistan is that the voters pushed the feudal lords who control the nationalist parties to the side in the last elections, and now they are using violence to try to get back in the spotlight.

Recently, a lot of people from Punjab and Sindh have moved to the Makran Coast. Land gang has bought and sold big chunks of land along the coastal highway to people from outside the country. This, along with the fact that big projects are being done in the area, has made the Baloch even more worried about being left out as an ethnic group in their own traditional home.

Deterioration of Self-Rule

The Baloch leaders think that the Constitution's definition of provincial authority has been slowly lost over time. When the Constitution of 1973 was passed with the help of the Balochistan regional government, it was agreed that the Concurrent List would be phased out over the next ten years. "However, even though it's been more than 30 years, the list is still there, and the federal government keeps getting involved in things that should be up to the provinces, like tourism, environmental pollution, worker's rights, property transfers, newspapers, school curriculums, etc." Under the present constitution, the federal government controls most of the country's economic resources and political power. The situation is the worst in Balochistan, where law and order are even in the hands of militia troops who are controlled by the government. "There, the relationship between master and servant is more clear than in any other region. The situation got even worse when the military took over again. Even the current military-friendly province government doesn't have much power. This has led to "Balochistan's economic backwardness and the Baloch's lack of job opportunities." Most Baloch nationalists think that the military government has either gone up against the political groups in the province or tried to push them to the sidelines.

In this situation, "Baloch leaders have been speaking out against the creation of new cantonments in the province loudly in parliament and outside of it." Today, local governments in Pakistan can't charge a tax on entertainment or a tax on property on any property inside a cantonment, even if it's a private property. The cantonments have become "a kind of parallel government" that is not controlled by the local government. The Baloch people think that these cantonments are just the army taking over their land. "Over 500 acres of land were taken by force in Sui" when people refused to sell their land, and the same thing is happening in Kohlu, which is "causing the same anger."

Suppression of Cultural and Political Rights

The Baloch live in an area that is part of three countries: Iran, Pakistan, and Afghanistan. As a result of the "great game," the British split Balochistan between these three countries in the 1800s. The Baloch don't have much political or cultural freedom, despite the size of their land and the number of people who live there. The Baloch have always been known for their music and poetry, and they have songs for almost any event. They have a lot of cultural history, and they are proud of it. Baloch separatists have mostly talked about "concerns about political and cultural autonomy." The Baloch live in countries where the governments haven't done anything to help their culture and language grow. Even though Balochistan covers a lot of land, it is the least developed region in Pakistan and has the lowest literacy rate. There aren't enough ways to read, teach, or spread the Balochi language, and the Pakistani class thinks Balochi is a primitive language that hasn't been developed. So, the Baloch feel like they haven't been given the chance to learn in their own language or participate in their own songs and culture.

Huge Infrastructure Endeavors as Means of Colonial Control

Mega projects that are being done in Balochistan, supposedly to help the province's economy, are the thing that has upset Baloch people the most in recent years. The Baloch and Balochistan's basic problems with underdevelopment are no longer important because of the way politics works and the attitudes that come with it. In order to gain power and money, political groups try to make each other look bad. This has often hurt the poor people of the area. Since most of the non-Baloch, mostly Punjabi bureaucracy was in charge of distributing funds, it was said that the Baloch's request to be in charge of choices about development projects had been ignored. On top of this, there is the question of colonization. "The Baloch said that Punjabi settlers were taking over good farmland, and Punjabi real estate investors were buying up property in Quetta,"

One of the main reasons for the return of conflict in Balochistan is that people there are very against development projects. Mega infrastructure projects like the Gwadar port and coastal highway, the Saindak copper project, and the Mirani dam are being built in the state. These projects have been long overdue. They could help the region in Pakistan with the worst economy get on its feet. "For example, the Mirani dam could turn 33,000 acres of desert land in the Turbat area into farmland. The seaside highway will make it easier to get around and bring in more tourists, and Gwadar will become a major port that Afghanistan, China, and Central Asia can use. Analysts in the West and other Pakistanis who think the rebels don't care about Balochistan often don't understand why they go after these projects. But the Baloch leaders are upset that most of the people working on the project, which is being run by the central government, are not from the province. They think the Saindak copper project and the seaside highway are both good ideas.

People keep telling the Baloch that the mega projects will give everyone a lot of business, trade, and investment opportunities, as well as job chances. Abdul Hakim Baloch, who used to be the top secretary of Balochistan, says that the main problem is not with building or running these projects, but with who owns them. The land mafia has taken over the state land around Gwadar and the coastal highway, which goes to the province. They have done this with the help of the Mekrani underworld and its members in government and the legislative bodies. Because of this fraud, the regional government has lost a lot of money. Also, Gwadar is being linked to Karachi but not to Quetta through the Baloch hinterland. This means that the rest of the province doesn't have a stake in the project. People are upset because they think they are becoming a landlocked region, even though they have the longest coastline in the country.

On the other hand, people from outside the country will not only make money, but they will also move into the coastal areas and live there. Baloch nationalists think that the benefits of these development projects won't go to the Baloch people. Instead, they think that these projects will bring a lot of people from outside Balochistan, making the Baloch a minority in their own province. 'There are also worries that too much foreign impact will come from unchecked foreign investment and development projects, threatening the social and cultural patterns of the native people. Ataullah Mengal said, "If there were jobs in Gwadar, people would go there in droves, both Pakistanis and people from other countries." They would get the right to vote in time. The trouble is that even just one Karachi in Gwadar is enough to make all of Balochistan a minority. Gwadar will end up sending more people to the Parliament than the rest of Balochistan. We would lose our culture, our language, and everything else. So, we don't want to go along with these huge projects. Baloch nationalists also think that the government isn't focusing on economic growth as much as it should. Instead, they think the government is more interested in getting a strategic advantage over the insurgents. In the past, the army decided where roads went instead of economic forces. Since the only goal was to get rid of rebels, roads were built to get to places where they were hiding.

Outside Influence

An uprising of this size can't last without a fair amount of help from other countries. "Intelligence agencies in Islamabad and government circles in Quetta say that the Baloch Liberation Army's (BLA) monthly operating costs are between 40 and 90 million rupees." Reports in the Pakistani Urdu press say, "There is a plot to get Balochistan to leave the federation." A lot of men are being trained to do terrorist acts against the Pakistani government. The immediate reason for this is that the province is expected to have a lot of oil. Outside forces want this resource to be under the control of an independent Balochistan instead of Pakistan. Many people think that the BLA is supported by outside forces that want to have an interest in the province. The BLA seems to have well-trained members, and their choice of targets shows that they know what their tactical and strategy goals are. They also seem to be everywhere and have a good way of talking to each other. All of these things tend to show that at least a core group of BLA members, if not a bigger number, have been trained by people who know a lot about the military. Since there probably aren't any BLA supporters in the Pakistani Army, it seems possible that foreigners are teaching the BLA how to use weapons. Also, the guns used by the BLA are Russian, which means that the Pakistani Army does not have them.

Director General of the Institute of Strategic Studies in Islamabad, Shireen Mazari, said, "A pattern can be seen that points to a deliberate targeting of communication systems and national assets, which affects the whole country across provincial boundaries." With more advanced explosives, which show that the BLA has better access to weapons and money from outside sources, they have switched from going after civilians to going after installations, military setups, and communication lines. The acts of mischief are clearly not random, but instead have been carefully planned and are also technically advanced. There is also the very important question of money. All of these signs show that what is going on in Balochistan is strongly connected to events outside of the country. Ayesha Siddiqa, a fellow at the Woodrow Wilson International Center in Washington, DC, said, "The Indians or the Iranians could add fuel to the fire." There are even rumors that the United States has spies in Balochistan.

If an outside force is at play, who could that force be? Iran and Afghanistan are the countries that are next to Balochistan. The BLA has always had plenty of high-tech weapons and ammo, and they have a lot of rockets and rocket launchers. In 2004, there were more than 626 rocket strikes and 122 bomb blasts. In January 2005, during four days of fighting in Sui, insurgents fired 14,000 small arms rounds, 436 mortar rounds, and 60 rockets. On March 17, 2005, insurgents and security forces shelled each other all day in Dera Bugti. The insurgents refused many offers to stop the fighting, which showed they had a lot of weapons and ammunition. The first question that comes to mind is where do they get all of these weapons and bullets? Afghanistan seems to be the most likely place where they came from. In the early 1970s, when Bhutto had to start a military operation in Balochistan, Afghanistan was the only place where the rebels could get weapons and ammo. However, President Hamid Karzai has neither a reason nor the means to make trouble in Balochistan. Second, having Americans in Afghanistan would make it impossible for the government to do things that go against its plans. Pakistan also thinks that Iran is against the Gwadar Deep Sea Port Project because it would compete with Iran's newly built Chahbahar Port on the coast of Balochistan, which is being built by India as a way to get to Central Asia. "Pakistani intelligence agencies think that Iran and India, which are unhappy with the building of the Gwadar Port, are giving money and weapons to the rebels." This seems very unlikely, since Iran has a large Baloch population and most of the people in their region of Seistan are Baloch. Any uprising in Iran that supports the idea of a Baloch homeland is sure to cause trouble in places where Baloch people live. This is exactly why the Shah of Iran went out of his way to help Pakistan with its troops during the last Balochistan uprising.

Some Pakistani lawmakers and journalists have said that India is behind this insurgency, just like they do for everything else that goes wrong in their country. The chief minister of Balochistan said that at least 40 camps were being run by the Research and Analysis Wing (RAW) in the province. They also think that "Indian presence on the Pak-Afghan border and in Zahidan has made it easier for India to sponsor Low Intensity Conflict." Even though many people in India might be tempted to fish in the troubled waters as a trade-off for Inter-Services Intelligence (ISI) activities in India and to keep ISI busy in Pakistan so it can't do its bad things in India, the timing of the insurgency makes it unlikely that this will happen. Even though Pakistani media has been very quick to say that Indian intelligence agencies are very powerful, the fact is that not a single Indian spy has been caught. Also, India does not share a border with Balochistan, so it cannot give the BLA the big weapons they are using. At the edge of Sindh or on the Makaran Coast, no arms shipment has ever been caught. Even if India wanted to, it couldn't get involved in the troubled seas by itself because it isn't connected to Balochistan. It could, though, help out if it worked with other countries in the area. But India shouldn't make trouble in Balochistan when ties between India and Pakistan are getting better.

Some Pakistani media people think that Russia has something to do with the Baloch conflict because the BLA uses weapons made in Russia. Their participation in the last insurgency made them familiar with Balochistan, and the idea that they are angry with Pakistan for making them look bad in Afghanistan and giving a lot of help to Chechen rebels may give this theory some weight. A Central Asian website says that Soviet spies who used to work in Balochistan are still there and are running camps in Afghanistan and Balochistan with the help of India and the USA. But Russia is too busy with its own problems and problems in its own neighborhood to spend time and money making trouble in faraway Balochistan. Since the fall of the USSR, Balochistan is no longer a key location for Russia. It's also hard to believe that the US would let Russia run camps like this in Afghanistan. The presence of some people who have been to Balochistan before can't be ruled out, though. But the people wouldn't have nearly enough money on their own to start an uprising of this size.

So, the only superpower, which is currently occupying Afghanistan and has clear access to Balochistan, could be involved. At first glance, it seems crazy that the US could cause trouble inside Pakistan. After all, Pakistan is their most important partner in the fight against the Taliban and Al Qaeda. But the top English-language Pakistani magazine, The Herald, says that the USA is the most likely place for the BLA to get money because it "may want to stop the growing Chinese presence in Balochistan." People say that a lot of cash is coming into these camps, and it is thought that a number of CIA spies are moving cash from Afghanistan to Balochistan.

The USA doesn't like that the Chinese are in Gwadar, which is close to their main base in the area, because it sees China as a possible foe. Gwadar, which could be a Chinese naval base and could make the Baloch a minority in their own region, is a problem for both the Baloch and the United States. "It brings together dangerously conflicting interests at a time when geopolitics are already tense." "As long as Balochistan is unstable and the law and order situation is uncertain, Gwadar can't reach its full potential, and the Chinese will have to rethink their growing economic involvement in Pakistan." In recent years, a few Chinese people have been attacked in Balochistan. This was likely done to discourage China from investing in the difficult province. "The recent conflict between the US and Iran has made US policymakers think that Balochistan is even more important because of its location." Even though it's not in the US's best interests to upset the way things are in Pakistan right now, "the Pentagon has reclassified China as a "strategic foe," and China's strategic presence in Gwadar is reason enough for a well-timed, low-intensity boil in Balochistan," according to a report. Also, the planned oil pipeline between Iran, Pakistan, and India can't happen as long as there are problems in Balochistan, and the USA hasn't tried to hide how uncomfortable it is with the idea.

There is also a need to look at what a free Balochistan would mean. It would be the best way to get to Afghanistan and the rest of Central Asia, so there would be no need to go through Pakistan or Iran. It would also make Iran smaller without having to go to war with it, which would be disliked around the world. These things are good for the US, and even if they weren't, the Baloch nationalists are not Islamists. Instead, they are secularists who move to the left.

Baloch people in general are not very religious, and the rise of Baloch nationalists has started to push out MMA, which is in power in Balochistan and has a lot of support from Pakhtoons in Balochistan. So, growing Baloch nationalism has started to roll back the impact of the Taliban and fundamentalists in Balochistan, which is something the USA has always wanted. This doesn't mean that the US wants Balochistan to be independent; it just wants to keep that option open in case a future government in Pakistan doesn't want to work with them or if Islamic hardliners kill their ally in Islamabad. On February 14, 2005, in Karachi, US Ambassador to Pakistan Ryan Crocker met with Baloch nationalists. This was a sign that this was going to happen.

Also, "instability in Balochistan is much better for the US than stability and economic growth in Balochistan, given its strategic location," especially since economic growth in Balochistan would be good for neighboring Iran. The US wants to put Iran on its own in the region and would like for relations between Iran and Pakistan to get worse by spreading rumors that Iran is involved in Balochistan. "As the US has become more hostile toward Iran, the number and severity of acts of sabotage in Balochistan have also gone up." The US knows that sanctions won't work against Iran. What's more, sanctions will cause oil prices to go through the roof, which could cause a world recession. At this point, when US forces are already spread too thin in Iraq and Afghanistan, the military choice is also out of the question. So, the best thing that could be done right now is to get Iran involved in an internal war with the ethnic minorities that live around Iran's edges. The Baloch, the Ahwazi Arabs, the Azheris, and the Kurds are these communities, and all of them are upset right now. Seymour Hersh has also written about secret operations that are run from Balochistan against Iranian nuclear assets. Mahmoud Ahmadinejad, the president of Iran, has already said that the US and its partners are trying to cause ethnic unrest in Iran to make it less stable.

Shireen Mazari says, "What is going on in Balochistan is part of a much bigger picture for the US." Part of the new strategic plan is to break up bigger Muslim states, change the borders between some of them, and make new political units. In the context of Pakistan, it's important to remember that the Afghan polls showed a clear split between ethnic groups, and that going after Iran also means looking for ways to promote old ideas of "Greater Balochistan." The new US plan might include making a Kurdish state. It wouldn't be surprising if this led to the creation of a new Baloch state. If Balochistan was its own country, the US would have a great base that could possible replace Afghanistan and Pakistan. It would be a straight path for pipelines and other things from the Indian Ocean to Central Asia, with no troublemakers like the Pakhtoon, the Taliban, or the Pakistani military junta, which has its own power problems.

Conclusion

If bloodshed in Balochistan gets worse, the Pakistani Army will have no choice but to get involved in a war that could make Pakistan sick and make it bleed. Already, the rising tide of fundamentalism has moved from the Federally Administered Tribal Areas (FATA) and threatens to cover the whole North-West Frontier Province (NWFP). Musharraf is the main person the fundamentalists want to kill, and the recent murder of Benazir Bhutto shows that they are ready to kill anyone who stands in their way to power. The political upheaval and constant bloodshed have not only worn down the Pakistan Army, but they have also made it less motivated and less united. The dry desert of Balochistan could put the Pakistan Army in a hostile environment where its mechanized troops are unlikely to be useful. The suicide bomber is the newest type of tool that can kill a lot of people, and Pakistan has a lot of them. Even though the Pakistani Army is made up of professionals, it hasn't done a good job in the past of dealing with problems inside the country. They have used suicide bombs against "infidels," but it would be hard to stop them if they started to target them, as they have been doing since Dargai in October 2006.

Most Baloch have developed a strong sense of being persecuted over the years, and there is a lot of proof that Balochistan has not gotten its fair share from the federal government for the natural resources it gives to keep Pakistan's economy going. Since Pakistan got its freedom, the country's leaders haven't been able to build a strong government. This was made clear by what happened in East Pakistan from 1958 to 1970. The problems that Pakistan is having now are mostly the same ones that caused Bangladesh to form. Even though the Baloch are poorer and less united than the Bengalis were in 1971, their complaint against the federation is the same: that the Punjabi army tries to run the state according to its whims. The Army's assumption that it could crush the Baloch "in the absence of a hostile neighbor to provide arms and shelter" has made them lazy, but this will only make the lack of trust worse and throw the economy off track. With 70,000 troops in Waziristan and six brigades in Balochistan, the Pakistani Army is already pushed too thin. Pakistan is playing a dangerous game by using its power in a colonial way and using force to force the Baloch to submit. Also, people from other minority groups are speaking up to help the Baloch. The death of Nawab Akbar Bugti has brought Baloch groups together like never before. After he was killed, the current Khan of Kalat called a grand jirga that was a lot like a declaration of Balochistan's freedom. Today, there are more guns in Pakistan than ever before, and everyone there, Baloch or not, is better armed than ever before. If the problem isn't handled wisely, the ethno-national fires coming from Balochistan could be the death knell for the state of Pakistan. Sardar Ataullah Mengal's words about the current conflict, "This could be our last battle," could be a good way to sum up the problem. Either their men will still be standing at the end, or we will.

Chapter 3
Balochis of Pakistan

Rise of Baloch Rebellions from 1948-1977

The current insurgency in Balochistan is a continuation of the rebel war against the Pakistani government that has been going on there off and on since 1948. The only difference between the uprising in 2004-2005 and the ones in 1948-1952, 1958-1960, 1962-1969, and 1973-1977 is the size of the violence and how far it has spread. The causes, the problems, the expectations, and the end goal haven't changed.

The Khan of Kalat claimed independence on August 15, 1947, one day after Pakistan was formed. The Muslim League and the Kalat National Assembly had both said many times that Kalat was a separate country. Even so, on April 1, 1948, the Pakistani Army marched into Kalat and arrested the Khan, who had already given up. His brother, Prince Abdul Karim, on the other hand, started a revolt with the Khan's tacit support. He said that Kalat was independent and that the Baloch National Liberation Committee was against the Khan's accession agreement. Karim wanted Afghan help because Afghanistan didn't want the Baloch and Pashtun areas to be part of Pakistan. Afghanistan also didn't want Pakistan to join the United Nations. Pakistan says that Afghanistan gave Karim a lot of help, but Baloch nationalists say that Afghanistan didn't help because it wanted Balochistan to be part of Afghanistan instead of being a separate country.

Initial Guerrilla Uprising

In late May 1950, Prince Abdul Karim started guerrilla operations against the Pakistan Army in the Jhalawan area. However, the Khan was afraid of retaliation from the Pakistani Army, so he convinced his brother to give up by promising him safety and amnesty from the Pakistan Army. Reports say that Pakistani officers signed a safe conduct deal with Abdul Karim's people and swore on the Koran to keep it. But Pakistani troops broke the deal by ambushing the Prince and 102 of his helpers on their way to Kalat in 1950 and arresting them.

In Baloch history, Karim's revolt is important for two reasons. First, it was clear that the Baloch did not want Kalat to join Pakistan. Second, it made a lot of Baloch people think that Pakistan had broken the deal to keep the peace. The Baloch see this as the first in a series of broken deals, which has made them doubt Islamabad. Karim and the people who followed him were all sentenced to long prison terms. They became symbols of the Baloch fight to free their people.

Subsequent Rebellion

The next time Baloch anger turned deadly was in 1958. This was a clear result of the way Pakistan's leaders tried to control everything. In the 1950s, the Punjabi leaders who ran the country were afraid that Bengalis would take over. To stop this from happening, they made the Western Wing of Pakistan into a single region. The Baloch fought against this One Unit plan. Abdul Karim, who had finished his jail sentence in 1955, and the Khan, who used tribal chiefs to organize large-scale protests, were both against it.

Balochi nationalists in the Khanate were very unhappy with the One Unit scheme. In October 1957, they met with Pakistani president Iskander Mirza and asked him to exempt Kalat from the One Unit scheme and spend more money on developing Kalat. But Ayub Khan's ambitions changed the way politics worked in Pakistan. When some Baloch sardars refused to work with the Pakistani commissioner, saying that Khan had raised a parallel army to attack Pakistani military, Ayub Khan ordered the Pakistani army to march into Kalat on October 6, 1958, one day before he put martial law in place in Pakistan. The army captured the Khan and his followers and said they were planning a full-scale Baloch rebellion in secret with Afghanistan.

The arrest set off a chain reaction of violence and retaliation, with the government bombing towns where guerrillas were thought to be hiding. The Jhalawan Sardars who were loyal to the Khan fought against the Pakistani troops in Danshera and Wad. Nauroz Khan, the 80-year-old leader of the Zehri tribe in Jhalawan, fought hard in the Mir Ghat mountains, but the Pakistani military swore on the Quran and told Nauroz to give up his weapons and get ready for talks. Nauroz gave up his arms in hopes of being let go and getting a clean slate, but as soon as he did, the army put him and his boys behind bars. Soon after, in July of 1600, Nauroz's sons were killed in Hyderabad and Sukur. Soon after, Nauroz was taken to Kohlu jail, where he died in 1962. The Balochis of Kalat, who were the first people to question the power of the Pakistani state, got a clear message from Ayub. He is said to have said that if Balochis didn't change, they would all die out.

After the revolt in 1958, the Pakistan Army put up new garrisons at key places inside Balochistan. This made the Baloch plan for more armed rebel groups that could protect Baloch interests. Sher Mohammed Marri was in charge of the movement. He had enough foresight to know that the random, unorganized fighting that had been going on so far would have to change into a classic form of guerrilla warfare. To do this, he set up a network of base camps from the Mengal tribe areas of Jhalawan in the south to the Marri and Bugti areas in the north. The rebels were called "Pararis," and they attacked convoys, bombed trains, and so on. In response, the army set up cruel retaliations. For instance, the Army used bulldozers to destroy 13,000 acres of almond trees that Sher Mohammed and his family owned in the Marri area. Fighting went on here and there until 1969, when Yahya Khan canceled the One Unit plan and got the Baloch to stop fighting. Even though there was a truce, the Pararis thought that fighting with Islamabad would start up again sooner or later. So, the machinery of the organization stayed the same and cadres kept getting trained.

Rebellion of the 1970s

During the time that "Basic Democracy" was used in Pakistan by Ayub, the patriot Balochis got involved in politics. When the One Unit plan broke up in 1970, they found a way to work together with the Pakhtuns in NWFP. Together, they made the National Awami Party (NAP). In the 1971 elections, Bhutto's PPP won everywhere in West Pakistan, but Balochistan and NWFP went to the NAP. Attacks on Punjabi settlers in Quetta and Mastung in early 1973, what was seen as defiance of the Ataullah Mengal-led government in Balochistan, and the discovery of a large shipment of weapons in the Iraqi embassy were all used as proof that the Balochis wanted to fight, and General Tikka Khan was sent to Balochistan to lead the second military attack on Baloch nationalists. Pakistan, still hurting from the shock of vivisection in 1971, did not handle the Balochi nationalists' claim well.

The first thing that made the Baloch rebel was when Bhutto fired the Baloch provincial government, which was led by Ghaus Bux Bizenjo as governor and Attaullah Mengal as chief minister, in February 1973. Bhutto said that the government had often gone beyond what it was allowed to do by the constitution. She also said that this was done with the help of Iraq and the Soviet Union as part of a plan to break up both Pakistan and Iran. The dismissal came at the same time as the news that 300 Soviet sub-machine guns and 48,000 rounds of ammo were found in the house of the Iraqi Defense Attache in Islamabad. The weapons and ammunition were said to have been sent to Baloch leaders. It was later found out, though, that the arms were actually found in Karachi. They were meant for Iranian Baloch as a way to get back at Iran for helping Iraqi Kurds, and the Iraqi Defense Attache worked with Iranian and Pakistani intelligence agents to set up the arms exposure to put pressure on Iran.

After their government was thrown out, Baloch rebels started to attack army convoys in April 1973. In response, Bhutto sent the army to Balochistan and put three experienced nationalist leaders from Balochistan behind bars: Ghous Bux Bizenjo, Ataullah Khan Mengal, and Khair Bux Marri. Over the next four years, there were different levels of violence in the violent conflict. During the worst part of the war, more than 80,000 Pakistani soldiers were in the area. Fighting was going on in more places than in the 1950s and 1960s. By July 1974, the rebels had cut off most of the main roads that connected Balochistan to the provinces around it. They also occasionally messed up the Sibi-Harnai rail link, which stopped coal shipments from the Baloch areas to the Punjab. Attacks on drilling and surveying operations also made it hard to look for oil.

The Shah of Iran at the time thought there might be trouble in Iranian Balochistan, so he helped Pakistani troops wipe out the Baloch resistance. The Shah sent 30 US Cobra helicopters with Iranian pilots to attack the areas of resistance in the Baloch region. In September 1974, the turning point was the 6-day fight at Chamalang in the Marri area. As part of its "scorched earth" policy, the Pakistani army launched a ground and air offensive in the winter of 1974 against the Baloch tribes, mostly Marris, and their families who had come to the Chamalang plains to graze their flocks. Many people and animals died in this attack. Both sides lost a lot of people, but the Baloch couldn't get the upper hand in the military in the years that followed. Most of the Balochi leaders left Pakistan and went into exile in Afghanistan, the UK, and other places outside of Pakistan. Several groups of Baloch people moved to Afghanistan, where Mohd Daud let them set up camps. Even though Bhutto said he had ended Baloch opposition, he was a big part of how the Pararis became the Balochistan People's Liberation Front (BPLF) in 1976. The BPLF was led by Mir Hazar Khan Marri, who had broken away from the BSO, which was led by Sher Muhammad Marri.

Zia ul Haq used the anti-Bhutto feelings of Baloch nationalists to his advantage after he took power in 1977. His show of mercy was well received by many Baloch leaders, including the Baloch trio of Ghaus Bux·Bizenzo, Ataullah Mengal, and Akbar Khan Bugti. But a group of rebel Marris kept fighting against the Pakistani government. And to show that Baloch nationalism and Pakistani state-nationalism are incompatible, the Baloch Students Union (BSO), the most aggressive and strongly independent Baloch group, reorganized and re-established itself in the early 1990s.

The Baloch Rebellion 2000-2006

Introduction

Some of the older Baloch rebels may have given up after the uprising in the early 1970s and the harsh way the Pakistani army put an end to it, but since the beginning of 2004, there have been signs of a new rebellion in Balochistan. Since July 2004, it has been bad enough to need army action, and when the army and rebels have fought, a lot of people have died. Since early 2000, people have seen the Baloch Liberation Army (BLA), an armed rebel group that operates secretly. It doesn't have a boss, but it's been getting stronger over time. It helps to look at the situation from a strategic point of view.

Balochi resistance has been growing for a long time, especially since Pakistan's federal government started building the Gwadar port and road and rail links to it as part of an ambitious plan to create a trade route similar to the Silk Road through Chaman, Kandahar, Afghanistan, and into central Asia. During the late 1990s, when Nawaz Sharif was in power, this was a popular idea. Sharif was crazy about highways, and there were good business reasons for this. This plan got a boost when China supported it, and it kept going even after Musharraf took over. From the Balochi side, only a small group of nationalists opposed these federal efforts. They said that even if it brought growth to Balochistan, it would still help the Punjabis in the long run. But the Balochi struggle was lost in the Islamist fervor that grew in the area after 9/11 as a result of the war on terror. This was clear from the way the nationalist parties were wiped out in the 2002 elections, even though they didn't give up the areas where the traditional Sardars had power, like Khuzdar, Kohlu, Dera Bugti, Kalat, Nushki, and Awaran.

But Baloch discontent grew after the attack on Afghanistan, when US bases were set up in Pasni, Gwadar, Dalbandin, and Jacobabd (in Sind). This wasn't so much because the US army was there, but because the Musharraf government decided to set up some army cantonments in Balochistan so that they could help fight terrorists. Part of a bigger plan to strengthen the army's position in the border provinces, this was done. Balochi nationalists argued through the Pakistan Oppressed Nations' Movement (PONM) platform that building cantonments would help Punjabis keep a tighter grip on Balochis and Balochistan. Neither the army nor the government led by the MMA could convince Balochi nationalists that this wasn't true. The fact that the federal government didn't care about the Balochis' reasonable requests that they be hired first for so-called "developmental activities" only made people's feelings even worse. In a way, Musharraf gave the Balochi nationalists a reason to fight again, which they had been looking for a long time. This helped bring the Balochi nationalist opposition back to life.

During all of this, it was interesting to see Balochi leaders from a younger generation take over the resistance effort. This new leadership is different from the old one in terms of where it gets its power, how well it can explain things, and how it can look at the Balochi problem without getting upset. Young leaders like Sanaullah Baloch, Hameed Baloch, and Amaullah Baloch, who are all part of the Baloch Students Organization (BSO, which has become BSO-United), were the sparks that started the resistance in the 1970s. They don't look to the old, traditional Sardari-based system of loyalty and privilege as a sure way to get support. Instead, they use appeals and persuasion to bring together a group that is modern in

This is not to say that the "famous four"—Ghaus Bux Bizenzo, Khair Bux Marri, Nawab Akbar Bugti, and Ataullah Mengal—have lost their attraction. They were all part of the resistance movement in the 1950s and 1970s. Hasil Bizanzo, Balach Marri, and Akhtar Mengal, who are part of the second generation of Sardari leaders, are less feudalistic and have said they are ready to work together in the ongoing movement.

It doesn't need to be said again that the current Balochi uprising began in the areas that are still controlled by some of these warrior families. In the areas of Dera Bugti and Kohlu, where the Marris and Bugtis were in charge, the city grew up around gas-rich land. Khair Bux Marri and his two sons, Balach Khan Mari and Hyrbyahr Marri, along with the Bijrani Marris, led by the unstoppable Sherbaz Marri, have kept the flag of resistance flying in Kohlu, while Nawab Akbar Bugti's successors have jealously guarded their power in the Bugti region. Since October 2003, the Frontier Constabulary and the Levies have been attacked from time to time in the Kohlu and Bugti areas. They also have strong feelings about the idea of building a cantonment in Kohlu. These attacks may have made Baloch nationalists in the south around Kech (HQ Turbat), Gwadar, and later Khuzdar less open to the idea of a bigger and stronger army presence in Gwadar. In fact, the nationalists have been against the Mirani dam project near Turbat since June 2004. They have fired several rockets at the project site, destroying some of it.

Since early July 2005, when Musharraf told the Gwadar Port Implementation Authority (GPIA) to move to Gwadar in response to the rising number of terrorist attacks in Karachi and told the army to give them tight security because of the attack on the Chinese engineers in April, the army and Balochi nationalists have been fighting more often and with more force. Since the normal army joined the fight against the Balochi nationalists, the fight has gotten worse, and the attacks on the MMA Chief Minister and army men who were just on leave in July and August 2004 made it look like the insurgency was getting stronger.

The Situation

Even though the Baloch resistance began in a low-key way at the end of 2000, it picked up speed in 2003 and 2004. Since 2003, a group called the Baloch Liberation Army has been claiming that it has planted mines, shot rockets, exploded bombs, and even attacked military convoys. But it wasn't until 2004 that the Pakistani government started to worry about the Baloch rebellion. As the work around Gwadar, the building of highways, and the building of cantonments picked up speed by 2003, the Baloch rebels made their position known just as quickly by attacking all the development work. The main point that the Baloch nationalists made was that all this growth would benefit outsiders, who would then move to their area, take all the jobs, and get involved in trade and business. Because many Balochis are illiterate and poor, they will never be able to use the chance that these growth projects offer.

People thought that the Balochi rebels were going after foreigners and important facilities to stop foreigners from helping with the projects and to stop people from working on the projects themselves by messing up important facilities like power and gas. Every day, there were also more attacks on security troops. The most well-known things the liberationists did were kill three Chinese engineers working on the Gwadar Port Project, attack the Chief Minister's car, and attack the Sui Airport Building. They also regularly attacked military and government buildings, power lines, and railways, among other things.

In 2004, there were 626 rocket strikes. 379 of the rockets were aimed at the Sui gas fields, and some were also aimed at the railroad tracks. The gas pipeline was hit by 122 bomb blasts. At first, the government ignored the problem. However, as the attacks became more frequent and violent, the government sent in troops from outside the province to take charge of important buildings and fight the nationalist rebels. Early in 2005, it was said that security forces raped a Sindhi female doctor. This gave the Baloch movement new strength. When the government showed that it didn't care about the problem, the BLA launched a huge attack. Hundreds of rockets and mortar shells were fired, and for 11 hours there was a fierce gun fight. Residents' and Pakistan Petroleum Limited's (PPL) property was severely damaged, and the town of Sui was cut off from the rest of the country. In January 2005, the rebels tried to take over the gas field at Sui, which showed how strong and determined they were. In four days of battle, the rebels used 14,000 small arms rounds, 436 mortars, and 60 rockets, according to the Pakistani government. By this time, Nawab Bugti had given his whole life to the Baloch nationalist fight, and his help gave the movement even more power.

According to news accounts, more than two dozen security forces were killed in the fighting in Sui, and the gas supply to large factories in Punjab and Sindh was cut off. After that, the Pakistani army sent thousands of regular army men to the area as quickly as they could. Even gunships on helicopters were used to stop the Bugtis and the Marris. The government blamed Nawab Bugti for the attack, and the Pakistani media was full of stories about how a seventy-year-old Bugti boss took charge because Pakistan Petroleum Limited (PPL) wouldn't pay for Nawab Bugti's lavish lifestyle. It was also said that the PPL paid Rs 122 million per year for the salaries and benefits of Nawab Bugti's personal staff. Even worse, in March 2005, security forces used a small fight between tribesmen and FC members as an excuse to attack the Hindu ghetto in Dera Bugti, which was right next to the ancestral home of the Nawab, where he was thought to be hidden. The shooting for an entire day killed 67 people, 33 Hindus and 8 FC soldiers. Homes and temples were badly damaged, and more than 100 people were hurt. All of this was happening at the same time that a senate committee on Balochistan was trying to settle the disagreements and meet the real needs of the people of the state/province. The leader of the ruling PML (Q), Chaudhary Shujat Hussain, was sent to Dera Bugti to try to stop the fighting.

The nine months after that were mostly quiet. Both sides dug into their own areas and planned to go on the attack again when the time was right. Ayaz Amir, a well-known commentator on Pakistani politics, wrote that the Pakistani army needs to be more careful about taking on the Bugtis: "The Bugtis, in particular, are a proud and warlike people with a strong sense of injustice against Pakistan's permanent ruling party, the military-bureaucratic oligarchy. Even though the army is nothing like the Bugtis, fighting the Bugtis would not be a walk in the park. You can be sure that the Bugtis will go to the hills, giving the army another South Waziristan.

In December 2005, the quiet ended. On December 14, 2005, at least eight rockets were fired at a paramilitary camp in Kohlu. Two hours later, the president was going to speak to the tribal leaders there. Three of the rockets fell near the camp of the Frontier Corps (FC). After that, the BLA said they were behind the attack. The President, on the other hand, went ahead and built the fortress. This was the much-needed cover story that the army had been waiting to use. The security troops attacked the Marri tribes in Kohlu district on December 17, 2005. The Marri camps were hit by more than 200 troops and helicopter gunships. Several attacks from the air were made on the areas held by Marri tribesmen. Baloch sources say that the security forces' bombs had a lot of unintended consequences and caused a lot of damage and loss of life and property. On the first day of the operation, it is said that more than 40 people were killed. Every day, the operations got bigger and bigger until they included not only the whole Kohlu district but also the nearby Dera Bugti district. The President of the National Party, Dr. Abdul Hayee Baloch, went so far as to say that the situation in Balochistan was the same as it was in East Pakistan in 1970.

Baloch nationalists quickly reacted by doing what they did best: blowing up gas pipelines, railway lines, communication towers, and electricity towers. Not only did they question the authority of the state all over the province, but they also went outside of the province and attacked pipelines in other states. The government said it had taken over some rebel training camps and started an attack with all of its power. In parliament, opposition parties have said that the government is killing "innocent citizens" in Balochistan by using poisonous phosphorus gas and airplanes to drop bombs on the "people." They have also complained about how the air force was used in the action. Even Asma Jehangir, who is in charge of Pakistan's Human Rights Commission (HRCP), couldn't go to Balochistan.

Violation of Human Rights

The HRCP asked the government to stop killing Balochs in Kohlu as part of its military operations, call for an instant stop to the fighting, and find a political solution to the problem. It said that the military operation broke both national and foreign laws. It also said that it was worried about people going missing in the area and blamed intelligence agencies for their part in this. It also said that President Pervez Musharraf's military-led government was responsible for "gross human rights violations" in Balochistan, where a "war-like situation" existed. The HRCP also doesn't believe what the government says about how it didn't use normal armed forces in the December 2005 crackdown in the province. It said that it had "received evidence that actions by armed forces had caused civilian deaths and injuries" and that "populations had also been bombed without reason." The HRCP report said that between 22,000 and 26,000 of the 22,000 people who lived in Dera Bugti had left their homes after militia forces shelled the town several times. The HRCP report also said that there have been many cases of torture, killings without due process of law, and disappearances. It also said that security forces have carried out summary executions and said it had proof to back up its claim. In February 2006, Amnesty International also said that Pakistani security forces had broken people's rights. In a January/February 2006 story, Nir Rosens also talked about how the Pakistani government was dealing with the Baloch insurgency. He did this by quoting many Baloch leaders, such as BSO activists Allah Nazar and Imdad Baloch.

Human rights abuses in Balochistan have caught the attention of people around the world and will continue to do so. Selig Harrison has called these violations "slow-motion genocide," but unlike the humanitarian crises in Darfur and Chechnya, they haven't yet worried the conscience of the world. But he would say, "As the number of deaths rises, it will be harder to ignore the human costs of the Baloch independence struggle and its political effects in other troubled minority areas of Pakistan's many different ethnic groups." It looks like this new wave of Baloch nationalism could be a much bigger problem for Pakistan than any of the other uprisings.

Assassination of Nawab Bugti

Human rights groups' reports didn't stop the army from going after rebels. On August 26, 2006, Nawab Akbar Khan Bugti, an experienced Balochi leader, was killed in the Kohlu District of Balochistan. The Pakistani government did a bad job of handling the killing. But it didn't have the result that was hoped for. The government in Islamabad, which was led by Musharraf, thought that this would teach the Balochi rebels a lesson and cause them to stop their movement. But what's happened since then says otherwise. The death of Nawab Bugti seems to have brought the Balochis closer together and made them stronger as a group. The situation on the ground hasn't changed, and the BLA continues to attack government icons at will in all of Balochistan and the areas around it.

In fact, the killing of Nawab Bugti led to more violence and protests, not just in Balochistan but all over Pakistan. The Pakistani government had been trying to kill Nawab Bugti for a long time, so his death was a hollow win for them. In fact, he had been on the security forces' radar since March 2005. But he lived through up to 17 shells hitting his apartment building. In July 2006, his hideout was attacked again, but he was able to stay safe. His death in August shows that Pakistan's military leaders think they can solve the problem with force. But many experts and opposition leaders have tried to make his death look like a big problem for the federation. They have compared how things are going in Balochi to what happened in East Pakistan in 1971. In a report from September 14, 2006, the International Crisis Group (ICG) asked the rest of the world to put pressure on the Pakistani government to stop all military action in Pakistan and all actions that violate international human rights, such as torture, arbitrary arrests, and killings that don't follow the law.

Factors behind Baloch discontent

Many Pakistani analysts have said that the sardars want to keep their fiefdoms and are against development because it could make their tribes more aware of modern ideas of democracy, which would be a challenge to their authority. But the truth is that this time around, the Baloch movement is led by young, educated Baloch people who live in cities and are inspired by Marxist ideas. These people are getting support from people of different tribes. It's important to note that only Bugti, Marri, and Mengal sardars have been against the government in recent years, out of about 250 Baloch sardars. Some people are quiet about their support for Balochistan. They are sure they know what makes Baloch people unhappy. The Baloch opposition movement is driven by a strong sense of ethnic identity, a sense of political isolation, and a lack of money. Even though people of some other Pakistani groups feel the same way, the Balochis feel it more strongly. Some of the most important reasons are listed below.

Status of Resources and Poverty

26 percent of people in Punjab, 38 percent of people in rural Sindh, 29 percent of people in NWFP, and 48 percent of people in Balochistan live below the poverty line. Balochistan also has the highest rate of people who don't know how to read or write—50%. Estimates for the years 1973 to 2000 showed that Balochistan and Sindh's GDP growth went down, while Punjab's GDP grew by 2% despite having a very large population. Even though the gas has brought in about US$ 1.4 billion for the national budget, the average amount given to the state from the center has only been about US$ 116 million per year. In almost all human development indices for the year 2003, Balochistan was at the bottom of the list. These indices were made by the UNDP.

Balochistan has a lot of natural gas and minerals, such as chromium, copper, iron, and coal. Sui and Pirkoh have enough gas to be useful for business. Seventy to eighty percent of the gas and most of the coal in the country come from this area. Some figures say that the total royalty from gas in Balochistan is about US$114 billion each year. The 600 miles of shoreline and abundance of fish haven't helped the Baloch either. But the Baloch's main complaint has been that they haven't gotten their fair share of the money they've put into the national budget. Baloch political leaders have always talked about how resources should be fairly shared between the center and the areas. They think that the difference between how much gas created in Balochistan is worth and how poor the province is because of how outsiders have taken advantage of them.

The way Islamabad took Sui's gas reserves for itself is one reason why the Baloch have been against oil and gas development in their area. Five gas wells at Sui were found in 1952. They provide 38% of Pakistan's energy needs for homes and businesses, but only 5% to 6% of the people in Balochistan have a gas link. In a strange twist, these links didn't happen until a decade after gas had been sent to every part of Pakistan. In fact, there would still not be gas in Quetta if the Zia regime hadn't chosen to put an army corps headquarters there.

Table 3.1 Ranking of Provinces by Overall Human Development Index

Name	HDI	HDI Rank
Punjab	0.557	1
Sindh	0.540	2
NWFP	0.510	3
Balochistan	0.499	4

Source: Pakistan National Human Development Report 2003, UNDP, Pakistan Estimation by Wasay Majid and Akmal Hussain. http://www.un.org.pk/ nhdr/htm_pages/cp_1.htm

Table 3.2 HDI Index of Provinces in Pakistan

Name	Literacy Ratio % 1998	Enrolment Ratio % 1998	Infant Survival Ratio %	Immunisation Ratio% 1998	Real GDP per capita (PPPS) 1998	Educational Attainment Index	Health Index	Adjusted real GDP per capita (PPPS) Index	HDI
All Pakistan	45	71	95.5	49	1715	0.537	0.82	0.272	0.541
Punjab	46	75	95.4	55	1770	0.557	0.83	0.281	0.557
Sindh	51	64	94.9	38	1804	0.553	0.78	0.287	0.540
NWFP	37	70	96.3	54	1364	0.480	0.84	0.213	0.510
Balochistan	36	64	96.4	34	1677	0.453	0.78	0.265	0.499
Islamabad	72	58	95.9	72	1743	0.673	0.89	0.277	0.612

Note:
GDP per capita and Infant Survival Rates for Islamabad are calculated as an average of Punjab and Pakistan.
Enrolment rate is for primary level only.
Immunisation refers to fully immunised children based on record and recall having received BCG, DPT1, DPT2 DPT3, Poliol, Polio2, Polio3 and Measles.

Source: Pakistan National Human Development Report 2003, UNDP, Pakistan

The Pakistani constitution says that the province where the natural gas well head is should get priority over other parts of Pakistan when it comes to meeting needs from that well head. However, 83 percent of the gas produced in

Balochistan is sent to the other provinces for use in factories and homes, while only four of Balochistan's 28 districts have piped gas. Compared to this, gas is delivered to almost every village in Punjab, but there is not a single CNG stop in the whole province of Balochistan.

These unfair practices prove that the Baloch nationalists are right. The project to find and spread gas was run by Islamabad, which is run by Punjabis. Since Punjabis ran the government in Islamabad, the gas went where the Punjabis wanted it to go. And there aren't many good arguments against what they say. In the Marri area, the government wanted to improve the economy by building roads that would make it easier to look for oil. But Baloch conservatives saw it as a way for Islamabad to take advantage of the province, since the money would go to the national government and foreign companies instead of the provincial government's coffers. So, the BPLF stopped the building of 57 km of oil-related roads for about five years. The road could only be built because the army was only partially successful in stopping the rebels' armed resistance.

The Baloch nationalists say that the province only gets 12.5% of the well-head price in gas payments. This price is set by the government at what the Baloch say is one of the lowest rates in the world. The Balochis say that the center owes them a lot of money in fees for the gas it has given them over many years. Nawab Akbar Bugti always said that Pakistan Petroleum Ltd. had broken its promises to pay the Bugti people who lived in Sui. Reports said that different federal governments tried to pay or threaten him. But Islamabad has started spreading the idea that the tribal sardars are against growth in their area and only care about their own wealth. Najam Sethi would say that this has made the war more personal and made the tribes more determined to win. Also, almost all of the coal mines are owned and run by people who are not Baloch. The coal from Balochistan goes to the Punjab, so the Baloch have to burn wood from Sindh that is brought in by truck. It sends its onyx and marble to Karachi to be finished, and its natural gas is piped to industrial belts in the Punjab and Sindh and then sent back to Balochistan in tanks.

Absence of Participation

The Baloch people aren't well represented in either state or national government. Pakistan's central and state governments, ministries, and military forces are mostly run by people who are not Baloch. One study shows that only 4 of the 179 people who were named to central cabinets from 1947 to 1977 were from the Baloch ethnic group. The number of Baloch in the military forces has been very low. An academic study shows that the British recruited 77 percent of their soldiers from Punjab, 19.5 percent from NWFP, 2.2% from Sindh, and 0.6 percent from Balochistan. After the British left Pakistan, the ratio didn't change much. In the 1970s, about 70% of Pakistan's military officers were Punjabi, 15% were Pathan, 10% were Mohajir, and 5% were Baloch and Sindi. As for higher military posts, it was said that until June 1959, 11 of Pakistan's 24 generals were Punjabis and 11 were Pathans. Even after that, there were almost no Baloch in the top ranks of the military. Ataullah Mengal, a past leader of the Baloch people, said, "There are only a few hundred Balochs in the whole Pakistani Army. There are no Baloch in the well-known Baloch Regiment. During the rule of Ayub, a group called the Kalat Scouts was formed. Only two people from Kalat were in the group. The same goes for the Sibi Scouts, who were made to keep order in the Marri lands. It has no Baloch people in its ranks. The leaders are from Punjab and the soldiers are from the Frontier."

Even though the number of soldiers from Balochistan and Sindh was increased to 15% in 1991 and their height and school requirements were lowered, there was still a shortage of about 10,000 other ranks from Balochistan and the interior of Sindh in December 1998. Since the limit is based on the province, most of the people from Balochistan who join the army are Pathans (Pakhtoons) and other settlers, not Balochs.

One estimate says that in 1979, only 18 of the 830 government jobs in Balochistan were filled by Balochs. Each position of secretary, director, and deputy commissioner was held by the same Baloch. As for the police, all of the top officers and three quarters of the police force were not Baloch. Status in the court system wasn't that different. In 1980, the Zia regime promised to give the Baloch the same amount of representation in the federal bureaucracy as their 3.9% share of Pakistan's total population. This was done to fix an old problem and give the Baloch a feeling of participation in government. But Baloch people are still not well represented in the government. Baloch people aren't very common in the Pakistani Army, government, or foreign service.

In 2002, only four of Quetta's 14 provincial government secretaries were Baloch. Less than 500 of the 3,200 students at Balochistan University were Baloch, and only 30 of the 180 staff members were Baloch. According to Baloch MP Abdul Rauf Mengal, there were not many government workers from Balochistan in Islamabad in March 2005, and there was not a single Baloch working in foreign offices. Even now, most of the top officials in Balochistan come from Punjab or other provinces. This includes the chief secretary, the inspector general of police, and most of the government secretaries who work in Balochistan.

When people came to see him, the late Nawab Bugti would often say, "If you go to the Balochistan cabinet, look at the name plates outside each office.

Almost no people will be in charge of running a province." Balochistan is still not well represented in any part of the Pakistani government. This makes it hard for people to feel like they belong to the government. So, the government and its parts are seen as foreigners ruling over Baloch land.

Provincial Autonomy

The Baloch leaders also think that there has been a slow loss of what the Constitution calls "provincial autonomy." When the Constitution of 1973 was signed into law, it was also said that the Concurrent List would be phased out over a period of 10 years. But 30 years later, the list is still the same, and the central government is still meddling in things that should be up to the provinces, like tourism, environmental pollution, worker welfare, property transfers, newspapers, school curriculums, etc. Under the present constitution, the federal government controls most of the country's economic resources and political power. Balochistan has the worst situation. Even keeping law and order is the job of militia troops that are controlled by the government. "The master-servant relationship is clearer there than in any other province," said an observer. The situation got even worse when the military took over again. Even the pro-military local government we have now doesn't really have any power.

The son of the late Nawab Bugti, Jamil Bugti, says that the chief minister of Balochistan is just a worker because everything is run from Islamabad. Every month, he has to run to Islamabad to get the pay for his secretariat workers. So, he gets a check for the month's pay and is sent home. The next month, he comes back with his hands out. So, under the current military system, Balochistan's regional government is almost like a branch of the central government that works for it and does what it says. The political and economic choices that are made in Islamabad do not affect any province. Because of this, Balochistan's economy is weak and the Baloch don't have many job prospects. Baloch separatists tend to think that the military government in Balochistan has either tried to ignore the political forces there or put itself in direct conflict with them.

In this situation, Baloch leaders have been speaking out loudly in parliament and outside against the creation of three new cantonments in the province at Sui, Kohlu, and Gwadar. Balochistan already has too many security systems. In addition to the four cantonments in Quetta, Sibi, Loralai, and Khuzdar, there are 3 naval stations, 4 missile testing sites, 2 nuclear development sites, and 59 other paramilitary facilities. Today, provincial governments in Pakistan don't have the right to charge an entertainment tax, a property tax, or a property tax on private land that is inside a cantonment. The cantonments have become a kind of parallel government that is not controlled by the local government.

Over time, these islands have become places where more than just the province and local governments have power. Baloch people see these cantonments as nothing more than the army taking over their land. When people in Sui refused to sell their land, it was taken over by force. The same thing is happening in Kohlu, which is making people there just as angry. The Baloch see the cantonments as tools of colonization and abuse because of this.

Resistance against Development

Mega-developmental projects that are being done in Balochistan, supposedly to help the province's economy, are the thing that has upset Baloch people the most in recent years. The Baloch people think that the benefits of these kinds of development projects in their area will spread to people who are not Baloch. These include the Gwadar port, the seaside highway that goes from Karachi to Gwadar and beyond, the Saindak copper project, and the Mirani dam. All of these projects were long overdue in Pakistan's most backward state. When finished, these projects could be very important for Balochistan's social and economic growth. The Mirani dam, for example, could turn 33,000 acres of uncultivated land in the Turbat area into farmland. The coastal highway will increase transportation and improve tourism, and Gwadar will become a major port that Afghanistan, China, and Central Asia can use. Analysts in the West and other Pakistanis who think the rebels don't care about Balochistan often don't understand why they go after these projects. But the Baloch leaders are upset that most of the people who work on the project for the federal government come from outside the province.

The Baloch people are told over and over that the mega projects will give everyone a lot of chances for business, trade, and investment, as well as jobs. Abdul Hakim Baloch, who used to be the top secretary of Balochistan, says that the main problem is not with building or running these projects, but with who owns them. The Gwadar Deep Sea Project, which is Pakistan's biggest infrastructure project, makes the Baloch the most angry of all the big projects. The land mafia has taken over the state land around Gwadar and the coastal highway, which goes to the province. They did this with the help of the Mekrani underworld and its members in government and the legislature. The government of Balochistan has lost a big source of income that could be worth trillions of rupees because of this huge amount of theft. Also, the state government has no say in how the project is developed. All decisions about the port have been made by Islamabad on its own, and the navy, coast guard, and paramilitary forces have taken over big areas of land. Also, Gwadar is being linked to Karachi, but Turbat, Panjgur, and Khuzdar have not been linked to Quetta. This means that these projects won't help the rest of the state in any way. People are upset because they feel like they are becoming a landlocked region, even though they have the longest coastline in the country.

On the other hand, Baloch nationalists think that these projects will bring a lot of new people to Balochistan, making them a minority in their own region. "There are also worries that unchecked foreign investment and development projects will bring too much foreign influence, threatening the native social and cultural patterns." Ataullah Mengal said, "If there were work in Gwadar, people would go there in droves, both Pakistanis and people from other countries. They would get the right to vote in time. The trouble is that even just one Karachi in Gwadar is enough to make all of Balochistan a minority. Gwadar will end up sending more people to the Parliament than the rest of Balochistan. We would lose our culture, our language, and everything else. So, we don't want to go along with these huge projects.

The Current Landscape of National Politics

To understand the current rise of nationalism in Balochistan, it's important to figure out what makes people feel the way they do as a group. The strength of nationalist politics depends first and foremost on how people see themselves and their history, how they rewrite their collective memory and build a sense of community based on shared values, goals, and attachment to a specific culture and territory.

Expressions of Balochi Nationalism

The fact that the Balochis have stuck out both as a group that is different from others and as a group that is different from itself is proof that they are a separate ethnonational group. A close look at the history of the land where the Baloch people settled, which has been called "the place where God dumped all the trash of the earth," shows that their cultural identity has thrived despite the politics of war and subordination. This is because their culture is a mix of the Dravidian culture from the Indus valley civilization, the Aryan, Hindu, and Buddhist cultures that came after that, and then the Islamic culture that came after that. In the 1600s, under the leadership of Nasir Khan the Great, the Baloch national identity became clear, and other people began to see them as a different cultural and ethnic group. This isn't to say that the people who lived here from the time of the Greek attack until the British came didn't have their own unique traits. They did, and it will be helpful to see how the following things shaped Baloch identity.

Linguistic Aspect

All of these cultures and societies have left their mark on the Balochi and Brahui languages, which are the two most common local languages in the area. Even though these languages have played a big role in the growth of a sense of ethno-national identity, the lack of work to standardize the Balochi language and the inability to promote it as the language of the people has made it harder for Balochis from different regions to feel like they belong to the same group. But it is true that the Baloch language has been around for a long time and has a lot of history. It is also true that the Balochi and Brahui languages have become more similar over time. Baloch patriots haven't been able to use it well in their fight for Baloch independence. In 2003, it was interesting to see that Balochistan's provincial assembly voted to make Urdu the only official language. The patriots in Balochistan didn't even say anything about it.

Religion

Balochi national identity, as it has been built up by nationalists, puts a focus on their unique tribal nature, their culture that has been around for hundreds of years, and their presence in a certain area. From my talk with the leaders of the Balochi movement today, it's clear that they don't see Islam as a key part of their national identity, especially when they look at how Islam is woven into the state-nationalist mindset of the Pakistani elite, which they support. Many people would say that, even though they see Islam as an important part of their lives, they don't see it as competing with India or Hinduism.

Slave System

Up until the 1990s, one of the most important things about the Balochi nationalist movement was its preference for a Sardari-based social and cultural system. Irrational nationalists often point to this as a sign of Balochi ethnic identity. Some people who know a lot about Balochi politics have said that "Baloch is a slave of his Sardar." Because they didn't want to make the Sardars angry, neither the British nor the Pakistani government have done anything to replace the Sardari system with a more open and equal one. They have followed the imperial strategy of ruling through collaborators, which has made the Sardari system stronger in a roundabout way over time. This has been a sign of the Baloch national situation, but it has also made it harder for a pan-Sardar national unity to grow. The Balochis haven't been able to build a strong base of resistance because of the rivalries between tribes and Sardaris, which are partly traditional and partly kept up by the Pakistani government.

It's interesting to note, though, that over the past few years, a new group of Baloch leaders has emerged, coming from different parts of the country and different social classes. They are going in a different direction and telling the Sardars to stop working together and instead support nationalist causes. The Balochi culture and government may have just begun to become more equal. The Balochi nationalists may have started a long trip.

Aversion towards Punjabi and Pathan Immigration

The most important thing about Balochi nationalism as it exists today is the widespread fear and suspicion that the Pakistani government wants to make Balochis a minority in their own region. Many young Balochi nationalists would even hint at the difficult situation they are in now when they see how Pakistani government projects like building highways and improving the port of Gwadar are bringing in a new wave of Punjabi and Pakhtun/Pushtun settlers to Balochistan. The Pakistani government has also made the Baloch feel less safe by ignoring their feelings and going ahead with plans to set up more military cantonments or a permanent presence in Gwadar, Kohlu, Sibi, Ormara, and Pasni to protect the passageways that are being built to make it easier for trade and commerce to move through Balochistan.

The way the Balochis are taken advantage of economically has also brought the Balochis together in recent years. The Pakistan National Human Development Report 2003 from the UNDP shows that 10 of the top 20 poorest areas in Pakistan are in Balochistan. Balochistan is the province with the least number of people working for national forces. Baloch people aren't well represented in the government of Pakistan. For example, there were only 3,753 ex-servicemen from Balochistan from 1995 to 2003, while there were 1,335,339 from Punjab and 229,856 from NWFP during the same time period. Their leaders have said that the province has not been paid enough for the money made from the Sui gas fields (which have a total stock of 25.9 trillion cubic meters) and the use of the province's mineral resources. In the same way, they say that the people of Balochistan will never benefit from the success of Gwadar port, and that the growing number of Punjabis and Pathans in the province will give these forces more ways to steal Balochistan's economic resources.

Period following 1980

Even though the Zia-ul-Haq government made a strategic show of support for the Balochis, their politics after Bhutto have been about making peace and putting their demands in a less aggressive way. Even though famous Baloch writers like Mir Gul Khan Naseer, Gul Rasool Mullah, and Sayad Zahoor Shah kept telling the Baloch people to fight against the wrongs done to them, the political leaders who stayed behind were careful about pushing their nationalist ideas. Balochi nationalists talked a lot about how they were ready to accept Balochi nationalism as a sub-national strain of Pakistani nationalism, no matter how it was thought of, whether it was Islamic or not. People who were in self-imposed or forced exile, like Ataullah Mengal in London and Khair Bux Marri in Afghanistan, kept making big claims.

But most of the other Baloch leaders were more calm, in part because Zia was able to work with them and calm them down. Former BSO president and guerrilla fighter Khair Jan Baloch gave up the fight, and former Governor Bizenjo started the Pakistan National Party (PNP) to put pressure on the regime from the inside and help the federal structure set out in the Constitution of 1973 work better. Many of the Sardars liked working with the center because it was the most willing to accept them.

From 1988 on, the process of democratization gave the Baloch notables even more room to move in politics. However, the more they ran for office in competitive elections, the more divided they became. Sardar Akhtar Mengal started the Balochistan National Movement in November 1988. This group was a key part of the new government alliance, the Balochistan National Alliance of Nawab Akbar Bugti, which came into power in January 1990. But as the 1990 temporary elections got closer, the fights between the different groups got worse. Bugti left the BNA and started the Jamhoori Watan Party (JWP), which joined forces with Nawaz Sharif's Pakistan Muslim League. That was a clear sign that the Baloch politicians had changed their approach. Rivalries between Baloch groups led them to make deals with national parties that could help them get into power. In 1996, Zulfikar Ali Khan Magsi also put together a government with help from the PPP, the PML-N, and the JUI.

The Balochistan National Party (BNP) was formed in December 1991 by the parts of Mengal and Bizenjo. In the February 1997 elections, none of the candidates won a majority of the seats in the provincial assembly. With 10 of the 43 seats, the BNP was the single biggest party, so Sardar Ataullah Mengal put together a coalition government with the help of the PPP. At the same time, the BNP backed the PML (N) in the National Assembly. This is another sign that the Baloch leaders and the national mainstream parties are becoming more pragmatic.

Mengal quit his job in 1998 because he didn't agree with the decision to do nuclear tests in Balochistan. He said that the decision was made without asking him and that the honor of the Balochis was at risk. After he quit, Mengal went back to speaking in the usual Baloch nationalist way. In an interview with

The Muslim, he said, "We have to look for who we are." But the main points of disagreement between his government and Nawaz Sharif were not just about who they were. Mengal didn't like how the center kept an unfair amount of the income from gas that was mined in Balochistan. He also had a lot of negative things to say about the choices made by the National Finance Commission, which he thought were very bad for Balochistan.

The Ongoing Socio-Political Setting in Balochistan

Marxists who study Baloch history would tell us that the Baloch people are in a terrible state of disorganization. As a slow but steady process, modernization seems to have helped change the way the economy worked in a society where the person in power, the Sardar, had access to all lands and had traditional rights of custody over these lands that he could pass on to his children. When the British first went to Balochi, they were confused by the fact that Baloch people rarely showed their Sardars respect. The Pathans in the tribal areas were called "slaves of the mullah," but he called the Baloch "a necessary part of the Sardar."

Throughout history, many onlookers have also pointed out the role of sardarship in building and keeping up small-scale local resistance. And many people have pointed out that the fact that these pockets of resistance are spread out and not linked to each other has made Balochi resistance easier for all the outside powers that have ruled over Balochi land to deal with.

If the Balochi Sardari system didn't work, it's important to talk quickly about the "whys" and "hows" of that. Arguments for this point of view focus on the following causes: the introduction of a modern education system, the introduction of a modern way to communicate, the increasing use of a relatively modern system of government, the appeal of democratic values during periods of democracy, the change in the traditional economic structure, and, most of all, the people's strong desire to give up traditional ways and a willingness to modernize their outlook.

There has been a counterargument that all of these changes haven't changed them at all, that they're still stuck in the past and proud of their traditional way of life, and that the only people who have been affected by the waves of change are the Sardars and their minions, who have been able to keep their power by absorbing the waves of change and using the knowledge they've gained. If you look at how little growth there is in Balochistan and how few people live in cities, you might agree with this point of view.

In this situation, it's important to think about how well the Pakistani government's forceful methods have worked since the 1970s. This may have caused the tribal sardars to change their minds about their dream of starting a rebel movement in Balochistan. Zia-ul-Haq used a strategy called "tactical accommodation," which needs to be talked about here. Zia-ul-Haq gave all Balochis who were taken as prisoners during the uprising a general amnesty. He also sent Rahimuddin Khan, who was a lieutenant general and the corps leader of Quetta, to be the Martial Law Administrator and Governor of Balochistan. For the first time in Pakistan's history, a military government was set up in the province of Balochistan, and it was given a lot of power. Gen. Rahimuddin Khan had a lot of power, and he cut off places that were home to Baloch rebels. He put down the random Baloch rebels with an iron hand and is credited with stabilizing Balochistan during his time as the longest-serving governor, which ended in 1984 when he was made a full General. Zia offered pardon as a carrot, but Rahimuddin was free to use the stick in any way he wanted. It was strange to see that no Balochi leader spoke out against Rahimuddin's arrogance and his authoritarian ways of running things. Marri and Megal decided to stay away, and Nawab Akbar Bugti, who had helped Bhutto attack Balochistan by working with him, was left on his own. Rahimuddin's strategy was to keep Balochi sardars from getting involved in politics, and he ruled as a dictator. It's hard to think that Baloch nationalists ignored his rule most of the time. But it's important to remember that during this time, the Baloch People's Liberation Front (BPLF) strengthened its position and got ready to act in the future.

Since 1947–48, when they broke the Balochis' trust by lying to them, the Pakistani government has used a carrot-and-stick approach that works very well. After he killed the Khan and put down the Balochi rebellion at Wad (where the famous octogenarian Nauroz Khan fought with great bravery), Ayub pushed for a policy of national reconstruction and paid for all efforts to improve regional and local culture.

The Balochi clan sardars were fooled in large part by the Pakistani government's policy of using force and acting like nothing is wrong. Pakistan's government, which is mostly run by Punjabis, has taken over this old policy from the British and used it without getting in trouble or feeling bad about it at all. Whether it was a democracy or an army, the people in charge of Pakistan didn't care much about individual calls for autonomy, even from within Pakistan. They are still haunted by the ghost of East Pakistan (now Bangladesh), so they have tried all kinds of things to stop regional claims. They have done a good job of dividing Balochis into different administrative units, and their strategy of redistributing areas of tribal influence, which is similar to gerrymandering, has made the traditional institution of Sardarship less important.

In recent years, the Pakistani government has been very busy in Balochistan. This is because Balochistan is a very important strategic area for the Pakistani government. Aside from being a nuclear wasteland, the province has a lot of rich materials and, most importantly, the Sui gas fields have a lot of gas. The coast between Gwadar and Pasni also has a lot of business and military possibilities. The Pakistani government, on the other hand, didn't pay much attention to the tribal areas along NWFP, also known as the infamous FATA, which recently caught the attention of the world when Taliban and Al Qaeda remnants moved in after the war in Afghanistan. Balochistan has been getting a lot more attention from the Pakistani government instead.

Significance of Jihad

It is important to point out yet another thing that has hurt the clan system and made Balochi identity less nationalist. It's also important to know that there are a lot of Pathans or Pushtuns in the north of the province called Balochistan, and that Chaman is one of the best ways to get from Pakistan to Afghanistan. During the years of jihad in Afghanistan, there was a huge influx of Afghan refugees into Balochistan. At one point, it was thought that the urban centers of Balochistan, especially in the north, were overrun by Afghan refugees. Over time, these refugees got Pakistani citizenship through illegal means, making Balochis a minority in the state.

During these years, the state has also been slowly turned into an Islamic state. Many people point to the rise of MMA in Balochistan in October 2002 as an example of how the Islamist forces in Balochistan were hurt. This, they say, broke up the traditional structure of Balochi society and led to the end of the elite Sardari system, which had ruled for most of history. But these things aren't important and come from thinking that the northern part of Balochistan where the Pathans live is the real Balochistan.

Let us analyse this argument here. The following facts have to be taken into account.

- The 2002 elections were held after the delimitation of constituencies, which, if looked at closely and analytically, decreased the importance of the Sardar-led nationalist movements. It was a very shrewd move and it has been adopted quite successfully by all governments in Pakistan starting from Ayub onward.
- The popular participation was at an all time low. According to highly liberal estimates provided by Musharraf's administration, only 28 % voted in the elections, i.e., a meagre 971,814 out of a total registered voter population of 3,413,393. The elections were preceded by the War on Terrorism in Afghanistan which significantly affected the voting pattern.

- If the results are analysed in terms of constituencies, MMA won in the north, Pathan majority areas, while Balochi Nationalist Parties, the National Alliance, PKMAP as well as PMLQ and PPP fared well in other areas.
- The Bugtis retained their hold on the Dera Bugti area while in the southern Brahui and Balochi dominated areas non-MMA parties fared well.
- Even in Quetta, supposedly the hub of MMA politics, the margin of difference was very thin and in case of a larger turnout the MMA would have been less successful. The success of Pakhtun Khwa Milli Awami Party (PPMAP) in one of the segments of Quetta signals the continuation of the Pathan nationalist sentiment, which at the moment due to the widely prevalent pro-Taliban and antiUS sentiments among the Pathans might have translated into MMA support-base but it is too early to predict a sustained MMA constituency in the area.
- Even if MMA manages to prolong its influence it will be limited to the north.
- The issues like additional cantonments in Balochistan had not come up during the elections which would have acted as a spur for the growth of nationalist sentiments.
- The anti-Shia violence in Quetta and some other places in northern Balochistan is rather sporadic and indicative of the sense of acute frustration among the Afghan-returned Jihadis, who are out to exhibit their violence more to demoralise the Musharraf administration than to Islamise politics in Balochistan.

The Road Ahead

The Balochis are one of the smaller groups of people. They make up 4.9% of Pakistan's population, and their number was estimated to be 7.101 million in 2001. 24% of the people who speak Balochi as their first language live outside of Balochistan, while 54.76% of the people who speak Balochi live in Balochistan. The literacy rate in Balochistan is a shockingly low 24.8%, which explains why people don't know much about politics and why old social and economic structures keep the Sardari/feudal system going, which hurts the national interests of the Balochi people.

The path of the Baloch nationalist movement shows that four important things about ethnic problems in Pakistan are still true. First, self-determination movements become clear when the overcentralized and authoritarian State overreacts to demands for autonomy from the provinces. The response of the Pakistani government to Pakhtunistan, or Pakhtunkhwa, is an interesting example of this. Second, the co-opting of ethnic leaders or the making of alliances between their parties and national parties tends to stop the centrifugal trends. This shows how the Pakistani government has become better at bringing people together as democracy has grown. Third, the strength of nationalist feelings also relies on how power is shared and how well the economy is doing. Fourth, Pakistan's assertive nationalist policies have been very easy for the government to use force against.

The most recent part of Balochi nationalist politics shows this feeling of being left out of the economy. Some of the biggest groups that have been fighting for a long time, like the Bajrani-Marri tribal group in the Kohlu region and the Bugti rebel group led by Nawab Akbar Bugti and now his son, feel alone. For example, the Bugtis of Balochistan are sure that they are the rightful owners of the gas resources in Pakistan's Sui area. This is because the gas field is in an area (almost 37.5 acres) that the British gave to them as a thank you for their help against the Hurs in the 1880s. They think that the Pakistani government has taken many of the resources that should have been theirs. The Marris of the Kohlu valley have always shown that they don't like it when other people try to rule over them. Even though the British had a regiment stationed in the valley by the 1890s, they were still annoyed by their resistance.

The nationalist parties' loss at the polls hasn't hurt the morale of the Balochi resistance in these places over the past few months and years. In fact, you can't look at it as a whole nationalist resistance. You have to look at it only from the point of view of the individual tribal mentality. It is hard to say that the growing resistance movement in Balochistan will turn into a long-lasting pan-Balochi resistance movement in Pakistan because there is no leader who can bring them together into a bigger nationalist resistance. The military government in Pakistan, which is getting moral and material backing from the US to fight these kinds of uprisings, won't let these kinds of resistance grow past a certain point either.

But the fact that an army-led government is determined to spread its authority to the most remote parts of Pakistan has made the extreme Balochis more stubborn. In the past few years, the military government has set up cantons in Gwadar, Kohlu, Sibi, and even Ormara and Pasni to move the army deeper into Pakistan's difficult areas. This has led to strong criticism from Balochi nationalists. When you add the claim that Balochistan has gotten the short end of the stick when it comes to sharing state resources and the idea that Balochistan has made a huge addition to the national budget, you have an explosive mix.

The next generation of Mengals, Bugtis, and Marris will also be led by people who don't know how to read or write. Aside from them, people like Sanaullah Baloch, Amanullah Baloch of the BSO (Muttahid), Hameed Baloch, Bizen Bizenjo, and many others are working hard and passionately for Balochi liberty. If this new leadership is able to create an appeal that goes beyond the old Sardari sentiments that have shaped Baloch national struggle so far, and if they can find the money to spread their beliefs more freely and widely and explain their grievances well, they will be able to build a larger and more stable group of nationalist-minded Balochis who can carry the flame of Baloch resistance forward.

The Weak Points

The Balochis' new leaders will also have to deal with many problems along the way. The recent vote in the assembly to teach in Urdu instead of Balochi shows that the nationalists have not been able to take advantage of linguistic feelings that have been there for a long time. Also, the nationalists are worried that the Baloch are being encouraged more and more to think of their language as less important than Urdu and other languages spoken nearby.

The nationalists have lost some of their original power because of the temptation to link Baloch nationalism with Pakhtun nationalism. Also, the Pakistan Oppressed Nations' Movement, which is a political front for fighting for the rights of oppressed nationalities, makes the Pakistani government more aware of the situation and makes it more likely to use its power.

Many experts close to the Pakistani government have said over and over again that India is to blame for all of Pakistan's problems, even the sectarian killings that happened in Quetta on the day of Muharram. These ideas haven't done much to cool down the weather in Balochistan. If Balochis are able to keep their movement going, it could lead Searikis, Balwaris, and even Pakhtuns to start their own resistance activities.

The movement has a lot less power because tribes that are related to each other are fighting with violence. For example, the Bugtis led by Nawab Akbar Bugti are fighting with the Kalpar Bugtis. In the same way, the fact that the different groups of Marris aren't working together and that Marris and Bugtis are fighting each other opens the door for outside help and puts an end to the idea of a united Balochi resistance.

There are clear differences between the Brahuis and the Balochis, and it may not always be easy to bring these two groups together for a national cause. Baloch attractiveness at the national level in Pakistan is also affected by the fact that there are more Balochis outside of Balochistan and that they have "de-Balochized" themselves.

Last but not least, the Sardars' uncertainty in how they deal with the Pakistani central government may take the shine off of the movement. With the death of Nawab Akbar Khan Bugti, the sub-feudal leaders or second-tier Sardars may want nothing to do with the nationalist fight. They have been open to favoritism from Islamabad and would be the first to join the Pakistani nationalism movement in exchange for a political or economic gain.

What Lies Ahead

It is hard to think that a well-connected resistance movement will form in Balochistan in the near future without active help and direction from the outside. The current rise in Balochi militancy is a result of the Musharraf administration's indifference to Balochis' requests to remove cantonments from Gwadar, Kohlu, and Sibi and stop non-Balochi industrialists from taking over Balochi business. The current resistance movement along the Makran coast started when the Musharraf government moved the Gwadar Port Implementation Authority (GPIA) office from Karachi to Gwadar and beefed up security around GPIA. Since June 2004, Balochi nationalist groups have been fighting in Kohlu, Khuzdar, and Turbat. These fights now threaten to spread to the rest of the province. But the above-mentioned differences among Balochis and the fact that the Musharraf government is determined to crush any such movement with a hard fist will likely weaken the movement in the coming days. But, unlike in the 1970s, one hopes that the younger generation of Balochi nationalist leaders will be able to keep the Balochi resistance movement going with their drive and hard work in the years to come.

The Balochistan uprising doesn't get the attention it should from the Pakistani media. But people in Pakistan still think, based on what they hear from Pakistani sources, that the army is provoking the Balochis on purpose to get ready for a full-scale attack to stop the rebellion there, even though Baloch resistance is a fact of life in Pakistan right now. With advanced defense weapons for fighting the insurgency in FATA and the knowledge that the United States is on its side, the army will never let the insurgency get too big. But it would be foolish for the Pakistani government to compare Wana to Balochistan, as Balach Khan Marri suggests in one of his Urdu pieces. He would say that the Balochi rebellion of today is more explosive and more organized.

The resistance movement might have problems in the coming days, but they might come from within the movement. Because it will be very hard to keep the fragile pan-Balochi unity, which goes across groups, clans, and even ethnicity (Baloch-Brahui) lines. The Islamist enthusiasm of the majority Pushtuns/Pakhtuns of northern Balochistan, which seems to have spread to many Balochis in the Baloch-dominated corners of the western, central, and southern Balochistan, is also weakening the nationalist position, making the army's intrusion in the name of an anti-terrorist operation look more legitimate, and making more enemies than friends for the movement. Kissinger said in 1962 that he wouldn't know about the Balochi problem if it hit him in the face, and it's likely that his replacement at the US State Department won't be any different. To keep the cause going, there will need to be great leaders, a long-term plan, and money.

Chapter 4
Security Situation in Pakistani Balochistan

Introduction

Balochistan is ruled by two different ethnic and religious groups that are at odds with each other. These groups control large parts of the country's rough and hilly terrain. Balochistan is being formed by both local nationalism and jihadist groups, from Quetta in the north to the coast of Makran in the south. Domestically, the issue of Balochistan has always been a weak point for Pakistan's leaders, leading to five different uprisings since the end of British rule. All of these uprisings were caused by the need of a centralizing elite and the stubbornness of a local elite who didn't want to be assimilated. On the religion front, Balochistan has been under more scrutiny since 2009. The Americans say that Quetta and the area around it are safe havens for Mullah Omar and other leaders of the Taliban. Also, there are more ethnic fights in Quetta, and the difference between Shia and Sunni in the city continues to be important in the War on Terror. In light of the rise of Baloch nationalism and jihadist activism, which includes sectarian killings, this chapter offers a critical analysis of the dynamics of religious activism and ethnic conflict in Balochistan, as well as the effects on security at home, in the region, and around the world.

Officials in Pakistan say that Balochistan should become part of Pakistan because it could not survive on its own economically. We have a lot of materials, oil, and ports. Where would Pakistan be if we weren't there? —Ghous Bakhsh Bizenjo Balochistan has a 760 km long coastline and is strategically important because it is next to Afghanistan and Iran. Balochistan was important to the Portuguese, the Russians, and the British in the past, both from a strategic and a business point of view, because it was at the center of trade routes between Central Asia, the Middle East, and South Asia. Big empire builders like the Achaemenians, Alexander the Great, the Scythians, the Kushans, the Arabs, the Seljuqs, the Timurids, and the Mughals all pushed their way south into Balochistan and opened the way to the sea or Indus land, which is now Pakistan. After the Mughals, Balochistan was just as important to the British imperialists as a major line of defense against the Russian empire, which was expanding into Central Asia, Iran, and Afghanistan. It was very important for the British to keep Balochistan as a friend so they could strengthen their control over Afghanistan. In 1854, the British made a deal with Nasir Khan II, the Khan of Kalat, that required him to fight against Britain's enemies and protect British trade with Central Asia and Southwest Asia through Balochistan. After the Treaty, the British got more and more involved in Balochistan. This led to the creation of the Sandeman System in the 1870s, which made it easier for the Sardars and the British to work together.

As happened in the past when big empires and colonial powers messed with Balochistan, the War on Terror has brought a lot of state and non-state players into Balochistan, which has made an already volatile province even more unstable. Balochistan is in the middle of a complicated security situation that involves not only Great Powers like the United States and China, but also regional powers like Iran and India, non-state actors like the Taliban, Lashkar-e-Jhangvi, and Jundullah, Baloch nationalist parties like the Baloch Liberation Army, Baloch Republican Army, and Baloch Liberation Front, and global multinational corporations like Tethyan Copper Company.

Balochistan is important to the US for many different reasons. First, the United States uses Pasni, Shamsi, and Dalbadin air bases in Balochistan for security activities in the War on Terror. Second, Balochistan is one of the main ways that NATO troops in Afghanistan get fuel and other important things. Third, the Americans are most worried about the rise of the Taliban and the possibility that they will be able to stay in power, especially in Quetta under the cover of what they think is the Quetta Shura. In the same way they did in the Federally Administered Tribal Areas (FATA), the Americans have thought about using drones to attack the Quetta Shura, which is said to be led by Mullah Omar. On the other hand, China, a rising superpower that has had close ties to Pakistan since the 1960s, looks at resource-rich Balochistan through the lens of replenishing its own dwindling energy resources. It played a key part in setting up the Gwadar Port for this reason. In a similar way, India, which doesn't have enough energy, has a hidden interest in Balochistan because of two possible gas pipelines that go through its territory: Iran-Pakistan-India (IPI) and Turkmenistan-Afghanistan-Pakistan-India (TAPI). Also, the Pakistani government has said more than once that the Baloch nationalism movement was started by the Indian government.

Iran is also worried about Pakistani Balochistan, especially because of the Jundullah, a Baloch Sunni religious party that is mostly based in Iranian Balochistan but has safe houses in Pakistani Balochistan from which it targets Iranian land. Jundullah supports a militant Sunni ideology that is opposed to the Iranian Shiite state and accuses it of trampling on the rights of the Baloch Sunni population inside Iran. Also, the Shia Hazara population in Quetta has been the target of more sectarian killings in Balochistan over the past few years. Lashkar-e-Jhangvi, which has its roots and most of its backing in the Punjab, is the religious group that has been killing people because of their faith in Balochistan.

Balochistan is home to both jihadist politics and sectarian killings, as well as a violent nationalist movement that openly challenges the power and authority of the Pakistani government. Since 2001, when a Baloch nationalist movement that was just getting started turned violent in the Marri-dominated Kohlu region, the conflict has spread to all of Balochistan, killing Baloch leaders like Nawab Akbar Khan Bugti and Balach Marri. In the last two years, Baloch nationalism militancy has become truly "ethnic," with targeted killings of non-Baloch people in the province, especially Punjabi speakers, who are not Baloch. Lastly, big companies from all over the world want to invest in Balochistan because it has one of the three largest copper and gold stocks in the world.

In order to explain how Balochistan fits into the War on Terror, this article will take a critical look at the rise of religious activism and sectarian conflict in Balochistan. This will include a look at the Quetta Shura (as well as the Tehrik-i-Taliban Pakistan), Lashkar-e-Jhangvi, and Jundullah, as well as the militant activities of these groups. Transnational religious currents from Afghanistan and Iran that affect Balochistan today have been given the same amount of weight when judging religious activity. In the second part of the article, the focus is on how ethnic conflicts happen and what role the Pakistani government plays. In this section, we'll look at the history and current state of the Baloch nationalist movement, the politics of energy and how it affects Baloch nationalism, the ethnic divide between the Baloch and the Pashtuns in Balochistan, Balochistan's uneasy place in Pakistan's political system, and the key policy steps the Pakistani government has taken to control and lessen the Baloch sense of deprivation.

Religious Advocacy and Sectarian Rivalry in Balochistan

The Soviet invasion of Afghanistan in 1979 was a direct cause of the rise of religious activity in Balochistan, which was mostly limited to the northern belt of the province, which was mostly populated by Pashtuns. The Baloch were not aware of this growing trend. To protect Afghanistan and Pakistan from the danger posed by the Communist Soviet Union, most of the help went to the religious seminaries. This aid, which came mostly from the United States and Saudi Arabia and was given out by Pakistan's Inter-Services Intelligence (ISI), was used to help the Mujahideen resistance in neighboring Afghanistan and to keep Shiite Iran from having too much power. One witness said, "If you look at where most Sunni madrasas were built, you'll see that they make a wall that keeps Iran from getting to Pakistan."

After the Soviets left Afghanistan, the madrasas in Balochistan kept getting better and better. In the 1990s, Taliban fighters were trained in these madrasas. One of the first things the new Taliban did had less to do with religion and more to do with breaking up the power of local leaders in Afghanistan, who were hurting trade between Quetta and Kandahar. In the early 1990s, Afghanistan turned into a brutal civil war, which hurt the Quetta-Kandahar trade nexus a lot. This was because there were greedy warlords in Kandahar, which put the transport mafia in danger. For the strong truck transport mafia in Quetta and Kandahar, this was a bad business situation that they could not stand.

The transport gang in Quetta wanted to open up safe routes to Iran and Turkmenistan, just like the government of Benazir Bhutto wanted to open up trade routes to Central Asia. On October 20, 1994, Naseerullah Babar, who was Pakistan's Interior Minister at the time, took six Western ambassadors to Kandahar and Herat. He told them that he wanted to get $300 million from foreign organizations to rebuild the road from Quetta to Herat. The Quetta-based transport gang had the same goals as the Pakistani government, which was now looking toward Afghanistan and even further into Central Asia. Three weeks after Naseerullah Babar's road trip, the Taliban rose to power and besieged Kandahar, the second biggest city in Afghanistan. The transportation mafia was thrilled, and in December 1994, 50 trucks from Pakistan bringing raw cotton from Turkmenistan arrived in Quetta after paying 200,000 rupees in tolls to the Taliban.

During the 1990s, when the Taliban were in charge of Afghanistan, the network of madrasas grew and did well. It continues to do well in the War on Terror in more ways than one because the connection between Quetta and Kandahar brings a lot of Afghan refugees to Quetta and the area around it. Americans think that the Taliban are regrouping in Balochistan and that Taliban activities in Kandahar and Helmand are being run from the city of Quetta because of this growing connection. The United States now says that the Quetta Shura, which is led by Mullah Omar, is a big security threat to its interests in Afghanistan and Pakistan.

The Quetta Shura Group

In September 2009, Anne Patterson, who was the US Ambassador to Pakistan at the time, told the world that the Taliban were in Quetta. She said, "Al-Qaeda was a threat to us in the past, so we focused on them. We didn't care as much about the Quetta Shura when we didn't have any troops in the area. Now that we do have troops on the other side of the line, the Quetta Shura is high on Washington's list. Most of the military operations in southern Afghanistan, where most of the British and American troops are, have been blamed on the Quetta Shura. What does Quetta Shura mean? What are its goals and purposes?

People say that the Quetta Shura is the most active enemy group in Afghanistan and that all enemy groups have sworn loyalty to Mullah Omar and the Quetta Shura to different degrees. Mullah Baradar runs the day-to-day business of the Quetta Shura. He has been in charge since Mullah Obaidullah was arrested in March 2007 and Mullah Dadullah Lang died in May 2007. The Quetta Shura and its recruits are mostly based in religious schools and Afghan refugee camps in the northern Pashtun belt of Balochistan. When the author went to Quetta, locals told him that the refugee camps in and around Quetta are a great place for Taliban fighters to hide. In fact, one study found that the refugee camps are a key place where foreign fighters are recruited and trained to fight against ISAF troops in Afghanistan. Most foreign soldiers come from Pakistan's madrasas, refugee camps in Balochistan, and possibly even as far east as Miram Shah in Pakistan's Federally Administered Tribal Area (FATA). Because militant activism and sectarianism are on the rise in Balochistan (which will be covered in the next section), the Balochistan provincial assembly passed a law in October 2010 that stopped madrasas from preaching militancy and terrorism and from publishing books that promote hatred and sectarianism. The bill also says that all schools have to register with the right government agencies.

In the Federally Administered Tribal Areas, the Tehrik-i-Taliban Pakistan (TTP), which also has a network in Balochistan, grew out of the Taliban. This group is different from the Quetta Shura. The TTP came together in December 2007, the same month that Benazir Bhutto was killed. This happened when many small terrorist groups that had been working on their own in the area began to work together. Baitullah Mehsud, a leader of the militant group, was named amir. Maulana Hafiz Gul Bahadur of North Waziristan was named senior naib amir, and Maulana Faqir Muhammad of Bajaur Agency was named third in charge. The main goal of the TTP is to get foreigners, especially non-Muslim secular Westerners, out of Pakistan. To do this, they want to bring back Khilafat and set up a Sharia-based country. In October 2010, NATO oil tankers bringing fuel to American troops in Afghanistan were attacked and set on fire in Balochistan, Khyber Pakhtunkhwa, and Islamabad. The Tehrik-i-Taliban was a big part of these attacks, and they took credit for them right away.

The Resurgence of Lashkar-e-Jhangvi

There are 300,000 Shia Hazara people who live in Balochistan. In 2004, they formed the Hazara Democratic Party (HDP), which is their political party. Since 2001, attacks on the Hazaras in Balochistan, most of whom live in Quetta, have been getting worse. In July 2003, more than 50 people were killed in an attack on a Shia mosque in Quetta. It was one of the worst acts of communal violence in Balochistan in a long time. In the same way, during the tenth Muharram parade in Quetta in the first week of March 2004, about four dozen Shias were killed. In September 2010, Shias in Quetta held a gathering called Al Quds to show their support for the Palestinian people. A suicide bomber attacked the rally, killing 55 people. This was another major attack. In September 2011, exactly one year later, gunmen stopped a bus and shot and killed 26 Shia travelers who were going through Mastung on their way to Iran. Lashkar-e-Jhangvi (LeJ), a banned group of militants, said they were behind all of these killings.

Riaz Basra, Akram Lahori, and Malik Ishaque started the LeJ in 1996 as an extreme branch of Sipah-e-Sahaba. The LeJ wants to make Pakistan a Sunni state, mostly through violence, and is part of a larger movement called the Deoband movement. It has ties to the Taliban, Al-Qaeda, the Harkat-ul-Mujahideen (HuM), and the Jaish-e-Mohammad (JeM). It is said that the LeJ worked with Al-Qaeda to carry out two bomb attacks on Western targets in Karachi in 2002. In one, 12 French citizens were killed, and in the other, a bomb went off near the US Consulate. Also, the LeJ has ties to the Taliban from its time in Afghanistan, and it has given shelter and resources to people accused of being terrorists after the US invasion.

It's possible that the killing of Shias in Quetta has gotten worse since 2001 because the Taliban and LeJ have been working together. Both the Taliban and LeJ are strong believers in a radical Sunni version of Islam that rejects and denies the Shia heterodoxy. The attacks against the Shias also have a political goal, which has to do with the fact that the Shia community worked with Pakistani and American intelligence agencies to give important Taliban and Al-Qaeda leaders in Pakistan information. Someone from the Hazara community is said to have told Pakistani intelligence agencies that Khalid Shaikh Mohammad was in Quetta. After that, Khalid Shaikh Mohammad ran to Rawalpindi and was caught there. One Hazara Web site says that since 2001, terrorist strikes have killed 600 Hazara people and left over 1000 permanently disabled.

The Sectarian Discord in Balochistan

Balochistan is troubled by more than just the Quetta Shura, the Tehrik-i-Taliban Pakistan, and the Lashkar-e-Jhangvi. The Quetta Shura and the Tehrik-i-Taliban

Pakistan want to fight against the United States in the global War on Terror. The Lashkar-e-Jhangvi is fighting a tribal war in Balochistan. This part of terrorism is also international, like the Quetta Shura and Tehrik-i-Taliban Pakistan, but it has to do with Iran instead of Afghanistan. In 2008, Seymour Hersh, an American journalist, wrote a story for The New Yorker that explained the Bush Administration's plan to make Iran unstable from the inside by funding covert operations against the country's religious leaders. In line with this strategy, Hersh talked about the militant Baloch Sunni group Jundullah, which is also known as the Iranian People's Resistance Movement. He said that the US was helping Jundullah, which is also known as the Iranian People's Resistance Movement.

Jundullah wants to bring attention to the repressed Baloch community in Iran by promoting a religious ideology that is in many ways different from the Baloch's secular nationalist politics on the Pakistani side of the border. Since 2007, the Jundullah has been behind some of the most violent and cruel acts against the Iranian Revolutionary Guards. In 2009, the Jundullah killed 42 people in Iran's Sistan-Balochistan province in a suicide attack. Among those killed were 15 members of the special Iranian Revolutionary Guard. General Noor Ali Shooshtari, who was the deputy leader of the Guards' ground force, and Rajab Ali Mohammadzadeh, who was the Guards' chief provincial commander, both died in the attack. Iran had a strong response to the killing of the top Guards, and it criticized the US, UK, and Pakistan for helping Jundullah fight against Iran. Mahmoud Ahmadinejad said that Pakistani spies were behind the suicide attack and asked Pakistan to arrest the attackers, who he said had come to Iran from Pakistan.

Because of pressure from the Iranian government, Pakistan worked harder to help Iran find Abdel Malik Rigi, who is the leader of the Jundullah. In February 2010, Abdel Malik Rigi was caught. This was about five months after the suicide attacks on the Revolutionary Guards in Sistan-Balochistan. He was taken into custody while on a flight from Dubai. The Iranian Air Force told his plane to stop while it was over the Persian Gulf. The Iranian government said that the Pakistani government had nothing to do with Rigi's arrest, but there are reasons to think that Pakistani intelligence told Iran what was going on. In a statement shown on Iranian TV, Rigi admitted that the US helped him and that he was on his way to meet a "high-ranking person" at the Manas US military base in Kyrgyzstan when he was caught. Rigi was put to death by hanging in Iran in June 2010.

Ethnic Disagreement in Balochistan and Pakistan

As the Pakistani government backed the American government in the War on

Terror, the Baloch nationalism movement became more radical at the same time. In one way, the radicalization of the Baloch nationalist movement wasn't something new. Instead, it was an example of something that has happened many times since Pakistan became independent. In 1947, when Pakistan became independent, the Baloch fought against being absorbed into the country. They said that the Khanate of Kalat was an independent princely state and should be treated the same way in the postcolonial age. The Baloch couldn't stand up to the power of the Pakistani government, so the Khan of Kalat had to sign an Instrument of Accession. This led to the first Baloch uprising in 1948. Then, in 1958, there was another nationalist uprising. This went on for most of the 1960s, and then from 1973 to 1977, the Baloch nationalist movement died down.

The current conflict in Balochistan started in a small, isolated area. However, in the last ten years, it has spread to most of Balochistan, especially among its young people. A small group of rebels called the Baloch Liberation Army (BLA) started attacking the province's infrastructure in February 2002, almost six months after the September 11 attacks. The BLA was known to take its ideas from Nawab Khair Bakhsh Marri, a fiery Baloch nationalist leader who wants Balochistan to be independent. The BLA was mostly based in Kohlu, which is where the Marri family comes from. At first, the BLA attacked the tools used by the local government, such as trucks and rollers. This led to attacks on the gas pipelines in the province. The fact that Balochistan's mining wealth was taken from them was one of the BLA's main complaints. In this way, Baloch nationalists were most upset about Gwadar and its growth as a port. They thought that the federal government in Islamabad would have a big stake in making exploration deals with foreign multinationals, which would leave the Baloch out in the cold. This fear kept the BLA's nationalist movement going from 2002 to 2005, when new events made Baloch nationalism even more extreme.

When Nawab Akbar Bugti joined the Baloch nationalism movement in 2005, the movement got a big boost. The fact that the Nawab joined the nationalist movement did not mean that the Nawab and the BLA had the same political goals. In reality, they were very different from one another. Even though the BLA wanted to fight the Pakistani government and give Balochistan full independence on a national level, the Nawab's fight with the Pakistani government was more local in nature. Captain Hammad of the Pakistan Army was accused of being involved in the rape of a female doctor in Sui, but the then Interior Minister, Aftab Ahmad Khan Sherpao, defended the thirteen people involved, including eight defense security guards and five employees of Pakistan Petroleum Ltd. (PPL), by saying in the National Assembly that DNA tests had been done and all had come back negative. After the Bugti tribe and the Pakistani government started fighting words over the problem, President Musharraf went on TV and told the Baloch, "Don't push us. We are not in the 1970s. They [the Baloch] won't even realize what's going on." Musharraf's explicit threat showed what most people in power thought, which is why the Nawab had to run to the mountains in March 2005 after rockets were fired at his home.

In the woods, Nawab Akbar Bugti was with his grandson Brahmdagh Bugti and the son of Khair Bakhsh Marri, Balach Marri. From the mountains, the Nawab continued to lead local operations against targets that were meant to weaken the infrastructure of the Pakistani state. The gas pipes around Sui were the most important of these targets. After hiding out in the mountains for a little over a year, Nawab Akbar Bugti was killed by Pakistani security forces in August 2006 when the cave he and his followers were hiding in fell in Kohlu. Balach Marri was also killed in a military raid near the Afghan border a year later. Since these two well-known people have died, Balochistan has become even more chaotic and unstable. In April 2009, the bodies of Lala Munir, Sher Mohammad, and Ghulam Mohammad, three well-known Baloch nationalists from the middle class instead of the Nawabs and Sardars, were found. The three were taken from their lawyer's office in the middle of the day, and their abused bodies were found in Turbat. Also, since July 2010, the security forces are thought to have dumped the bodies of Baloch patriots who had been cut up in different parts of the province. The Human Rights Commission of Pakistan (HRCP) says that between July 2010 and May 2011, 140 of these bodies have been found. This is still going on, and it, along with the problem of missing people (Baloch who are said to have been taken by security agencies and are waiting in jails and torture cells), is radicalizing young Baloch nationalists.

In reaction, Baloch nationalists are now going after people who are not Baloch, especially those who speak Punjabi in Balochistan. Balochistan has seen a rise in "ethnic" killings in recent years. These killings have happened to everyone from building workers and barbers to teachers in schools, colleges, and universities. Because there aren't enough skilled Baloch working in businesses, schools, and government offices, non-Baloch are in charge of many important jobs in the area. Unfortunately, the BLA and other groups like it, like Dr. Allah Nazar Baloch and his Baloch Liberation Front (BLF) in the south and southwest of Balochistan, are now going after these people who are not Baloch. On August 14, 2010, 16 Punjabis were killed in two different places, one near Quetta and the other in the city of Quetta. In the first episode, 30–35 people with guns stopped a bus going from Lahore to Quetta. The people were then taken off the bus, and 10 of them, all of whom spoke Punjabi, were killed. In the second attack, six Punjabis who were painting a house were shot and killed by shooters who broke into the house. Also, well-known non-Baloch teachers and professors at universities, schools, and colleges have been killed, and as a result, many schools have stopped working. This has happened in every district of Balochistan, including Bolan, Mastung, Kalat, Khuzdar, Kech, Awaran, Noshki, Chagai, and Panjgur. The Interior Minister says that almost 100,000 settlers have left Balochistan and moved back to their home province, while more than 250 settlers were killed in the first seven months of 2010.

Rift Between Baloch and Pashtuns

Baloch and Pashtun are two of the main groups of people who live in Balochistan today. In the 1970s, the Baloch and Pashtuns joined together formally under the National Awami Party (NAP) platform. During this time, however, important political differences between the Baloch and the Pashtuns also came to light. Baloch nationalist researchers say that Abdul Wali Khan, who was President of the NAP at the time, did not do anything about the Baloch uprising in the 1970s. Wali Khan probably promised not only the full support of the Pashtuns in the Baloch armed fight against the Pakistani government, but also moral and material support from the Afghan government. However, none of these things happened.

It is important to note that the NAP was mostly made up of Pashtuns from Khyber Pakhtunkhwa, while Pashtuns from Balochistan felt underrepresented and left out by the NAP. In 1970, the Pashtuns of Balochistan formed a group called the Pakhtunkhwa NAP, which was led by Abdus Samad Achakzai. Achakzai was upset that the NAP did not fight for a separate Pashtun region after One Unit broke up in 1970. Achakzai said that the Baloch and Pashtuns should have the same number of jobs in the provincial government of Balochistan. He also said that a Pashtun should be Governor or Chief Minister of the province, one of the two top jobs in the province. After he was killed in 1973, his son Mahmood Khan Achakzai took up the Pashtun nationalism of his father and changed the name of the party to the Pakhtunkhwa Milli Awami Party (PKMAP). Mahmood Khan Achakzai says that even though Pashtuns are a minority in Balochistan, they should be treated like any other resident. Mahmood Achakzai wants to change the way Pakistan is run politically so that each ethnic group has its own territory. Achakzai says, "Pakistan is made up of Pushtoon, Baloch, Sindhi, Seraiki, and Punjabi nationalities. Each should have its own motherland: Pushtoonkhwa/ Afghanistan, Balochistan, Sindh, Seraikistan, and the Punjab." Pushtoonkhwa/ Afghanistan should be made up of the NWFP (Pushtoonkhwa) and the chief commissioner's province (southern Pushtoonkhwa), minus the Baloch areas, and the Pushtoon region of Attock and Mianwali. For now, the Pushtoon and the Baloch should share the political, economic, financial, and administrative power in Balochistan.

What does Achakzai's plan mean for ties between Baloch and Pashtun in Balochistan, given that he wants to break up the Pashtun areas of Balochistan and make them part of a bigger Pushtoonkhwa province? It's interesting to see that these Pashtun nationalist comments don't bother the Baloch. Instead, they say that the Pashtun areas in Balochistan should be combined with Khyber Pakhtunkhwa and should not be a part of a future Balochistan. For the sake of Pashtun nationalism, the Baloch are ready to give up the northern part of their province that is mostly populated by Pashtuns. In this way, Baloch-Pashtun ties can be managed in a friendly way and do not involve a Gordian knot of intractable disagreements about territory. On the other hand, Achakzai believes and cares about what the Baloch say about how building the Gwadar Port will bring workers from Punjab and Khyber Pakhtunkhwa that will make the Baloch a minority in Balochistan.

Balochistan and Geopolitics of Energy

Since 2002, one of the most important parts of the Baloch nationalist movement has been its connection to the "energy" factor and the possibility that China and multinational companies will use the province's natural resources and raw materials. The 760 km long Balochistan sea coast and its ability to be a shipping route for global oceanic trade led the Chinese to develop the Gwadar coast, which made the Baloch national movement stronger. Gwadar is the end of a planned interstate transportation corridor that will connect Pakistan by road, train, air, and, to some extent, pipeline to China's Xinjiang province and, via Afghanistan, to the energy-rich Central Asian Republics (CARs). In 1992, when Nawaz Sharif was in charge of the government, the decision was made to build a deep sea port in Gwadar. The people who lived there were happy about the decision. But the Gwadar problem has changed in a big way, and it is now an important part of the Baloch nationalist agenda. When it comes to Gwadar, the Baloch are upset because they don't have a say in how the port is run or who runs it. The federal government is in charge of the Gwadar port. The provinces have no say in how it is run. Second, Baloch nationalists say that the growth of the Gwadar Port is making the Baloch a minority by bringing in blue collar and white collar workers from the Punjab, Sindh, and Khyber Pakhtunkhwa.

Balochistan's geostrategic position, in addition to Gwadar, makes it an important hub for the international supply of gas to and from Pakistan. In recent years, one of the two pipeline projects is the Iran-Pakistan-India (IPI) pipeline, which is 2700 kilometers long and can move 2.8 billion cubic feet (bcf) of gas per day from Iran's huge offshore South Pars field to ports in Pakistan and India. The other project is the planned Turkmenistan-Afghanistan-Pakistan-India

(TAPI) pipeline, which would be 1680 kilometers long and be able to move up to 3.2 billion cubic feet of natural gas per day from Turkmenistan's Dauletabad field to markets in Afghanistan, Pakistan, and India.

Balochistan also has a lot of gold and copper in the Reko Diq area of the Chagai district. The Tethyan Copper Company (TCC), which is a joint venture between Chilean copper producer Antofagasta and Canada's Barrick Gold, wants to mine the gold and copper at Reko Diq, but they have been at odds with the local government of Balochistan over licensing for the mines. In November 2011, the Balochistan Mining Committee of the provincial government of Balochistan said that the company's feasibility study wasn't complete, so they wouldn't give the TCC a mining license. On the TCC website, it says that the mines at Reko Diq can make 200,000 tons of copper and 250,000 ounces of gold every year for 56 years. In the mining project, the end product, copper concentrate, will be moved through an underground slurry pipeline that is 682 km long. This will be the longest copper concentrate pipeline in the world.

In more ways than one, Balochistan's natural resource wealth fuels the nationalist movement. It gives nationalists, especially separatist nationalists, the idea that they don't need the Pakistani government. Balochistan is important to Pakistan, but Pakistan is not important to Balochistan. Also, as long as the nationalist conflict keeps going, it will be harder for both government and nongovernment groups to explore and use Balochistan's natural resources. The fact that nationalists continue to say they will damage gas pipelines and other facilities in Balochistan is not a good sign for the long-term success or feasibility of such projects. In order for Balochistan to be safe and stable, the Pakistani government must take the political steps needed to stop the nationalist uprising. Balochistan is a political problem that needs a political answer.

Balochistan and Political Interventions

The main way to solve the Balochistan problem is through politics, not through the military. Baloch nationalists and the Pakistani government are currently fighting in the military. However, nothing will get better in Balochistan until all of the political players are brought to the table to talk. Before tensions in the area can be eased, the art of politics and negotiating says that both sides need to be calm, careful, and, most of all, patient. In this way, the Pakistani government was not blind to the fact that there was a way to handle the issue "politically." After three Chinese engineers were killed in the south of Balochistan in 2004, the government set up a parliamentary sub-committee on Balochistan to look into the Baloch's problems and make suggestions for how to fix them. The parliamentary subcommittee suggested solutions in the following broad areas:

a) royalty and gas development surcharge; b) representation of Balochistan in federal government employment; c) Gwadar; d) construction and maintenance of national highways in Balochistan; e) drought strategy; f) distribution of funds between the federation and federating units (NFC Award); and g) policy and administrative measures that can help build CBMs in Balochistan. But the subcommittee's suggestions were never put into action because the Balochistan National Party (Mengal) didn't agree with them and because fighting broke out in Dera Bugti in January 2005.

The current Pakistan People's Party government has done more to control ethnic unrest in Balochistan through two important policy packages: The NFC Award and the Aghaz-e-Huqooq-e-Balochistan Package. In November 2009, the Balochistan package was brought up at a joint meeting of parliament. The Package is meant to stop ethnic strife in Balochistan by focusing on four important areas: the constitution, politics, administration, and the economy. Political issues include starting talks with unhappy Baloch nationalist leaders, the controversial problem of releasing political workers, and the return of Baloch people who have been living abroad. Administrative issues include getting rid of the Army's position in Sui and replacing it with the Frontier Corps (FC), as well as stopping the building of new cantonments in Sui and Kohlu. Also, the Package calls for the creation of a commission to look into missing people, a judicial inquiry into the deaths of Ghulam Mohammad, Lala Munir, and Sher Mohammad, and a fact-finding mission to find out what happened when Nawab Akbar Bugti Shaheed died. In terms of the economy, the Package says that the federal government will pay Balochistan the Gas Development Surcharge it owed from 1954 to 1991. This will cost Rs. 120 billion, which will be paid over a period of 12 years. Also, the Package talks about making 5,000 more jobs available in the province right away. It also says that all new large projects in Balochistan would have to be approved by the provincial government. An important part of the constitutional reform plan is the reworking of the National Finance Commission Award (NFC). The old criterion (population) for how money was split between the provinces has been replaced by three new criteria.

The NFC Award was signed on December 31, 2009, in the port city of Gwadar. It "can be considered a landmark in Pakistan's financial history." The most important thing that the Seventh NFC Award did was to address one of the main complaints of Pakistan's smaller provinces, which was that the formula for distributing money based on population should be changed to take into account their financial needs and that the biggest province, Punjab, gets too much money because of this. Along with population, the new standards for distribution now include three more factors: backwardness (poverty) 10.3%, revenue collection/generation 5% (in the same proportion as population), and inverse population density 2.7%. So, the new model says that Punjab has the most weight for population, Khyber Pakhtunkhwa has the most weight for poverty and backwardness, and Balochistan is close behind. Sindh has the most weight for bringing in money and Balochistan has the most weight for inverse population density. Balochistan has gained the most. This is because: a) its share in the divisible pool among provinces has gone up from 7.17% to 9.09%; b) the Federal government has promised to pay the projected amount of Rs. 83 billion from the provinces' divisible pool each year; c) the formula for figuring royalties and development surcharges on natural gas to Balochistan has been changed; and d) the federal government has promised to keep giving money to the depressed areas

Unfortunately, all of these efforts have failed because both sides are stuck in a horrible stalemate. The Pakistani government is still killing Baloch people, and the Baloch are still killing people who aren't Baloch, and neither side shows any signs of stopping. Both groups need to be calm and willing to give in if they want to move toward a solution. The Baloch want the security forces to stop using violence, find the people who have gone missing, stop the "kill and dump" strategy against the Baloch, and stop building new military cantonments in Dera Bugti, Kohlu, and Gwadar. The military cantonment in Dera Bugti has been turned into a military college, and the Army Chief said in April 2011 that "no new cantonments would be set up in Balochistan and the idea of building four other cantonments had also been dropped."

But at the same time, Baloch fighters are still being taken away against their will and their bodies are still being found in bad shape all over Balochistan. Rehabilitating these missing people would be a good way to build trust and help end ethnic strife in Balochistan. On the Baloch side, the same steps need to be taken. For example, the Baloch need to stop using violence, stop killing people who aren't Baloch, and stop attacking the gas infrastructure of the area. Politically, the only way to move forward with the above government initiatives is for all fighting to stop. After that, both Baloch nationalists and the Pakistani government can work toward a negotiated solution to problems in Balochistan, such as making the Gwadar Port, Reko Diq, and provincial autonomy work.

Conclusion

On February 9, 2012, the Oversight and Investigations Subcommittee of the United States House of Representatives Committee on Foreign Affairs held a hearing on Balochistan. It was led by Congressman Dana Rohrabacher, who a week later introduced a resolution "Expressing the sense of Congress that the people of Balochistan, who are currently divided between Pakistan, Iran, and

Afghanistan, have the right to self-determination and to their own sovereign country." The State Department quickly distanced itself from the hearing and opposed the idea of an independent Balochistan. They did this because they knew the topic was very sensitive right now in terms of US-Pakistani relations. The fact that the Balochistan problem is being discussed in the legislature of the most powerful country in the world is a big deal. But the idea itself is complicated because it includes not only the Baloch people who live in Pakistan, but also those who live in Iran and Afghanistan. In this case, if Balochistan became independent, it would lead to the breakup of not just one country (Pakistan), but three (Iran and Afghanistan as well).

Balochistan is at the center of a new political, military, economic, and business strategy that includes global and regional powers, as well as non-state players. Not enough energy Both China and India have a lot at stake in Balochistan, because it is a place with a lot of natural resources that are easy to get to. The US looks at Balochistan mostly from a military-strategic point of view, focusing on how religious extremism is growing in the region and how the Taliban are coming back. Now that the U.S. is talking to the Taliban through diplomatic channels, a post-U.S. Afghanistan and Balochistan with safe havens for the Taliban would be a big threat to the security of Pakistan and other regional and global powers. A nationalist fight is still going on in Balochistan, which adds to the problems of energy and religious extremism. The demand for an Azad (independent) Balochistan will continue to haunt Pakistani politics until the Baloch nationalists are brought to the talking table. Force might work in the short term, but only a political answer can bring long-term stability to the way the state and society of Pakistan work together. In this way, the 7th National Finance Commission Award and the Balochistan Package are both good things, but they won't be useful until the Baloch agree that they can solve their problems. The feeling of isolation, neglect, and lack of resources that the Baloch have may not go away until the efforts of the Pakistani government start to help the Baloch in social, political, and economic ways. This is true not only for the Baloch who live in Pakistan, but also for the Baloch who live in Iran, where a strong Baloch nationalist movement is also taking shape, though it has different goals.

Chapter 5
Champions of Human Rights in Balochistan

Introduction

Standing up for the rights of others has since 9 December 1998 been under the special protection of the international community. On that date, on the occasion of the 50th anniversary of the Universal Declaration of Human Rights, the General Assembly adopted the UN Declaration on Human Rights Defenders, the first UN instrument that explicitly recognizes the importance and legitimacy of the work of human rights defenders and lays down their right to effective protection.

Human rights protectors are people or groups who find out about violations of human rights, bring them to the public's attention, and work for victims' rights in a peaceful way. Civil and political rights, like the right not to be tortured or the right to a fair trial, economic and social rights, like the right to clean water, and cultural rights, like the right to media in one's own language, may be among the rights they fight for. The Declaration on Human Rights Defenders is not a legally binding document, but it has many of the same human rights standards as the International Covenant on Civil and Political Rights (ICCPR) and the Convention Against Torture (CAT), which Pakistan signed in June 2010. Since it was passed by consensus in the General Assembly, it shows that everyone in the international world wants to protect people who fight for human rights. It's a big deal to put down the work and value of people who fight for human rights: Former UN Secretary General Kofi Anan said, "The Declaration rests on a basic premise: that when the rights of human rights defenders are violated, all of our rights are put at risk and all of us are made less safe."

Everyone has a duty to protect human rights, but the state has the most responsibility. Also, the state has to protect people who fight for human rights. The Declaration makes it clear that states have to protect human rights activists from violence, retaliation, and intimidation that might happen because of their work. Article 12(2) 2 of the Declaration says, "The State shall take all necessary measures to protect everyone, individually and in groups, from any violence, threats, retaliation, de facto or de jure discrimination, pressure, or any other arbitrary action as a result of his or her legitimate exercise of the rights referred to in the present Declaration, namely the monitoring and publicizing of his or her rights."

In the broadest sense, human rights defenders are all those in Balochistan who peacefully report human rights abuses. In a more specific sense, Balochistan's human rights defenders are journalists who report abuses, family members of victims of human rights violations who expose and fight abuses, lawyers who stand up in court to defend them, and professional human rights workers whose job it is to protect people's rights. All of these people have the right for the government to protect them fully under the law.

In Balochistan, the truth is very different.

Agents of the state have not only broken a lot of human rights, but they have also gone after people who point out their wrongdoing, despite the fact that this work is important and legal, and that the international community has promised to protect it. This study is meant to show how bad and widespread the attacks on people who stand up for human rights in Balochistan are.

In the past, people who worked to protect human rights in Balochistan were able to do their jobs, such as monitoring, documenting, publicizing, campaigning against, and fighting in court, without too much meddling. In the last ten years, this has changed: Human rights activists have not only had a lot on their plates because of a rise in human rights abuses, but they are also growing in danger from the people whose wrongdoings they expose. This not only goes against the letter and spirit of the UN Declaration on Human Rights Defenders, to which Pakistan has agreed, but it also cuts the very lifeline that victims of grave abuse depend on most in their time of need: a human rights community to support and sustain victims and make sure that the people who hurt them are brought to justice. Because of this, a lot of bad things that happen to people's rights in Balochistan go unpunished.

A lot of human rights violations are happening in the province of Balochistan, but the Pakistani media and foreign media don't talk much about it. This makes it harder for people who fight for human rights to get help. When there isn't a lot of national and foreign pressure on the federal and provincial governments and their agencies, people who do wrong get away with it.

The first part of this report looks at how journalists, who are often the first people to tell the public about human rights violations, have been mistreated. The second part looks at what happens to lawyers who take on human rights cases, and the last part looks at how human rights activists in the narrower sense have been mistreated. Here are some ideas for the government of Pakistan.

Suppression of Free Media

In the course of doing their jobs, journalists who report on human rights abuses and give victims and activists a voice have been harassed and threatened, had their freedoms of movement, expression, association, and assembly restricted or taken away, and have faced false criminal charges, arbitrary arrest and detention, torture, extra judicial killings, and forced disappearances. Human rights defenders' rights to life and security of the person, to due process, to freedom from torture and forced disappearance, and to freedom of expression, association, and assembly have all been violated. All of these rights are protected by both domestic law and international human rights law.

Baloch writers have gotten a lot of hate from the government, which does everything it can to hide its tracks when it tries to hide the truth. The International Federation of writers (IFJ) and the Committee to Protect Journalists (CPJ) say that Pakistan is "the most dangerous country in the world for journalists right now." Balochistan is likely the most dangerous place in all of Pakistan for journalists to work.

There are many dangers for journalists and people who work in the media in the area. Separatist groups, nationalist forces, political parties, clan leaders, and, most of all, the paramilitary Frontier Corps (FC) put a lot of pressure on them. So, when doing their jobs, journalists are always putting themselves in danger. A Baloch journalist called the situation of the Baloch press "Between Nationalist-anvil and Khaki-hammer," and senior journalist Mohammad Khan Sasoli, who was president of the Khuzdar Press Club at the time, explained: "If we report on the nationalists, the government will threaten us, and if we report on the government, the nationalists will kick our asses by calling us spies of intelligence agencies."

Baloch writers' work and safety are also affected by the rules that the government sets for the media. On October 29, 2009, the Pakistan Electronic Media Regulatory Authority (PEMRA) law was changed to include parts that make it illegal to publish statements from militants, live footage of a suicide bomber or terrorist attack, and any news that goes against Pakistan's ideology and state sovereignty. Materials that insult or make fun of the head of state, the military, or the executive, legislative, or judicial parts of the government were also not allowed to be printed. Even though regulating journalism is necessary for Pakistan's security, it doesn't take into account the fact that many Baloch journalists, especially those in far-flung districts, are often put under a lot of pressure by political groups to carry their comments.

Print and Electronic Media in Balochistan

In the past, it was easy for newspapers in Pakistan to get ads from the local Government's Director of Public Relations, which was the only place where ads could be bought in the province. There are no large businesses or industries that provide advertising for local news sources. But in recent years, it has been hard for newspapers and TV stations in Balochistan to keep going because the government took away the advertising contracts they needed to stay in business. Some have also been shut down by the government.

Asaap, the English-language daily Baluchistan Express, and the Urdu-language daily Azadi were among the newspapers that were very critical of the government and were punished for it. So were some electronic media and websites, and their staff members were also treated badly.

The Daily Asaap Case

The Urdu-language daily newspaper Asaap stopped coming out on August 18, 2009, after the paramilitary FC checked its office in Quetta for about two weeks. Its editor said that the Quetta office was "under the control of paramilitary security forces and intelligence personnel," and that there were dozens of FC soldiers inside and outside the office to check on visitors and staff. "When our staff comes in and out of the office, they are checked, and the safety of our workers is very important to us. Editor Abid Mir said, "The security forces are watching both what we publish and what we talk about. We see this as a complete intrusion into our job duties." Some accounts say that the Asaap management said the FC threatened to hurt its journalists physically and put them in false sedition cases if the paper didn't shut down.

In a front-page article on August 18, the day before Asaap shut down, an editorial stated why it was closing: "It breaks our hearts to tell the valued readers of Asaap and the Baloch people that our office in Quetta has been under siege by the Frontier Corps and security forces for the past two weeks. Every tourist and staff member who came to our office was put down by these forces. Asaap is the only paper where protection has been put in place. Staff members and guests are often searched by these forces and bothered by them. Since the government put a tank in front of the Asaap buildings, things have gotten much worse. Because of this, everyone on our team is freaking out and can't do their jobs. In this case, the Daily Asaap has two choices: it can either temporarily or completely stop publishing, or it can get ready for a fight between security forces and the newspaper's staff. Asaap is very concerned about the safety of all of its employees, most of whom are young people. So, the people in charge of Asaap have agreed that the newspaper won't come out of Quetta and Turbat."

Abid Mir said that the local government had been "helpless" and that it wouldn't help to go to court against the security forces. Later, he talked about the attack on Asaap's office: "We worked with guns pointed at us outside the window. We could see the tank parked in front of our office. They were the worst days of 13 of Balochistan's crackdowns on the media.

Baloch observers have said this about Asaap: "Asaap newspaper has always taken a balanced view of social, political, cultural, economic, and human rights issues of Baloch people and Balochistan." We know that Mr. Dashti was recently warned of bad things that would happen if the Asaap Group of publications kept exposing the wrongdoings of the agencies, which we think are behind this dastardly act against Mr. Dashti's life.

Balochistan Express and Azadi Case

A few days after Asaap was shut down, on August 21, 2009, members of the FC began a "siege" of the English-language daily Baluchistan Express and the Urdu-language daily Azadi. Staff members and people who worked at the printing presses were often searched by security and kept out of the office when they didn't want to or couldn't answer the FC's questions about the newspaper's policies, sources of funding, and political leanings. The FC also blocked the main exits to the office buildings, so no one could get in or out. It didn't say why the building was cordoned off for about four days. On August 25, 2009, the FC took down the cordon after the Human Rights Commission of Pakistan (HRCP) protested and the BBC and other media outlets around the world reported negatively on the situation.

Daily Tawar Case

Even people outside of the government have harassed and threatened journalists when they didn't like what they were covering. At the middle of May 2011, members of the Baloch Students Organization (BSO-Mohiuddin group), which is the student branch of the Balochistan National Party (BNP-Mengal), burned copies of the daily Tawar in Khuzdar district and then attacked the office of the newspaper in Lasbela district. Even though the paper is known to support the nationalist cause, this happened, even though the BNP and BSO might not have agreed with the paper's editorial policy. Because Tawar often reports on bad things that the government does, it has lost all public advertising. Several journalists who worked for Tawar as correspondents in different areas have also been taken away against their will, and some of them have been killed without a trial. Tawar has also been attacked by the government. On July 25, 2010, the newspaper was apparently threatened by intelligence agencies, and its reporters were allegedly told they would be killed if they didn't stop writing about Balochistan's violations of human rights.

Electronic Mediums

On October 4, 2010, members of the FC broke into the Hub office of VSHNews TV, a private Baloch-language TV station, insulted the employees, ransacked the office, and broke some equipment. Reporter Jabbar Baloch said that while he, photographer Ghulam Mustafa, editor Muhammad Salah, and intern Farooq Ahmed were working in the office, eight FC employees came in, told them to raise their hands, frisked them, and then told them to leave. The men from the FC then looked through everything, including computer files. Baloch said that when he told the FC spokesman about the event, the spokesman at first denied it because he said that the people involved were not FC employees. Later, the FC's spokesman admitted that the check had been done by FC employees, but that there had been a mistake. Baloch said that he had shown footage and critical comments by Baloch journalists about the activities of FC troops a week before. He thought that this was what led to the punitive operation.1

On April 25, 2006, the Pakistan Telecommunication Authority (PTA) blocked four Baloch nationalist websites. These were balochvoice.com, baloch2000.org, balochfront.com, and sanabaloch.com, the site of a Baloch politician. balochvoice.com has news about the fighting in Baluchistan and reports from international media. The PTA order says that the sites have "false information," but a PTA official said that the sites had "ties" with the 18 Baloch nationalist leaders and that the decision to ban them was made by the government and the PTA. In March 2011, PTA blocked access to the internet version of the Urdu-language daily Tawar. Again, they didn't say why, but observers think it might be because Tawar is very pro-nationalist. The Baloch Human Rights Council (BHRC), which is based in Canada, was against blocking access to the website of a newspaper "known for its critical coverage of the military operation and gross human rights violations committed by the Pakistan Army against secular forces..."

The Baloch Hal Case

On November 8, 2010, PTA stopped access to the website of The Baloch Hal, which was the first online English-language newspaper about domestic events in the province. It had been launched on November 20, 2009. The Baloch Hal had also written a lot about forced disappearances and other violations of human rights. According to its mission statement, it is "the first online English newspaper of Balochistan that strongly follows an independent editorial policy that aims to practice objective journalism." The online newspaper has honest opinions, in-depth analyses, revealing interviews, investigative reports, and new photos that can be shared immediately with people all over the world through social networks like Twitter and Facebook. We have a liberal and nonreligious strategy that says we will treat everyone in Balochistan the same. The newspaper believes in democracy and all kinds of freedom. It also teaches peace and understanding. The Baloch Hal is "one of the few Baloch voices still calling for reconciliation, a parliamentary solution, and dialogue," according to The News. Other Baloch websites, like blogs and sites that use the dateline "Occupied Balochistan," are also banned. Baloch Hal, however, does not use this dateline, despite pressure from nationalists. Moderate voices like Akbar and his Baloch Hal have to walk a tightrope between the military and the militants, where one person's hero is another person's traitor and vice versa. ... Baloch Hal tries to stay balanced, even though he is under a lot of stress. Baloch Hal gives people a place where they can say what they want to say with a pen instead of a gun. If reasonable, moderate views aren't allowed in Balochistan, it only shuts more doors. This is the last thing a civilian government that was chosen by the people and focuses on peace and dialogue should be doing.

The only reason PTA gave for blocking access to the Baloch Hal was that it had published "anti-Pakistan" content. The editors of Baloch Hal rejected the accusations, saying that the move was "just a way for the Pakistani government to silence independent media." In March 2011, the Baloch Hal said that its website was still not available in some parts of Pakistan because the government wouldn't say why it was blocked.

Baloch Voice TV

The idea of an independent Baloch-language TV station seems to have caused a lot of worry among state agencies that want to stop news from getting out in the province, which is why they responded with harsh repression. In April 2006, a businessman named Munir Mengal who wanted to start the first station like this, Baloch Voice TV, based in Dubai, was forced to disappear as soon as he landed in Karachi airport after going to Bahrain to hire staff. His arrest was random, and it happened just three months before Baloch Voice TV was set to go on the air via satellite. No one ever set up the channel.

Assault on Individual Journalists

Journalists have been mistreated, which means they have been harassed, given false charges, arbitrarily arrested and detained, made to "disappear," tortured, and killed outside of a courtroom in order to stop them from investigating and reporting abuses (such as the abuses or corruption of security forces) or to punish them for doing so. State agents like police, security, and intelligence workers, as well as non-state players like political groups, tribal leaders, or people with official support, have been responsible. All of the wrongdoings on this list have been done without consequences because law enforcement and the courts have been unable or unwilling to bring the people responsible to justice.

Detention of Media Persons

A number of journalists have been arbitrarily arrested, which means they have been held in jail for no reason.

On April 23, 2010, Mustafa Tarin, the bureau chief for ARY News TV, was arrested and beaten by police in Quetta for "negatively" reporting on a police gathering. The media, especially the electronic media, didn't like the vandalism and random violence that police did in January 2010 when they were trying to get pay raises. As a result, the Chief Minister took action against police rowdiness. From then on, cops thought that people in the media were not helpful and were on a "witch hunt."

Tarin later said at a press meeting at the Quetta Press Club that police officers had stopped him on April 23 in the suburbs of Quetta and asked to see the registration papers for his car. He showed them his press card and the papers for his car, but they still took him to the nearby police station. There, his cell phone was taken away, and his "negative" reporting was blamed for the police force not being able to get better pay.

Tarin said that the cops beat him, tore his clothes, and talked badly to him before putting him in a cell. Tarin was able to tell his brothers that he had been arrested, and they told Abdullah Magsi, a reporter for ARY News, where Tarin was. Magsi, on the other hand, was not allowed in the police office, and the police denied that they had Tarin. Later, he was able to tell the Chief of Police what had happened. On his order, Mustafa Tarin was let go after being held for four hours. The Balochistan Union of Journalists and the Quetta Press Club both said that Tarin's arrest and bad treatment were wrong and that the people guilty should be punished.

On April 25, 2010, when local journalists tried to get to the Chief Minister's Secretariat to hold a demonstration, in part to protest the earlier mistreatment of Tarin, police mistreated the journalists and arrested 20 of them. Provincial Minister Mir Sadiq Umrani and Senator Ismail Buledi helped get the journalists released. Later, the Chief Minister set up a group to look into what happened to Tarin. No one knows how the investigation turned out.

Abdul Latif Gola, a reporter for the Urdu-language daily Jang in Jaffarabad, was arrested without a reason on June 17, 2007. Police apparently said they did this on the orders of an army major. He was held against his will for four days, first in a cell for two days and then in a place he couldn't figure out.

Gola said after he was let go that he was held because of a "suspicious phone call," but he didn't say if it was one he made or one he got. He said that no one had been mean to him. Reporters Without Borders was told by a writer who didn't want to be named that Gola's arrest was likely related to his coverage of fights between security forces and Baloch nationalists that had happened not long before.

On June 15, 2007, a BBC reporter named Nisar Khokhar and a local writer who was with him were taken into custody by the border police near Dera Bugti. At the time, the army was in charge of Dera Bugti. They wanted to find out what was going on after hearing that seven women had been held in an army camp for three weeks. After two hours, the two journalists were let go.

Oppression and Abuse of Journalists

Recently, there has also been more harassment and bad treatment of writers who are doing their jobs.

Reports say that a leading news channel's Baloch Bureau Chief in Quetta (who wasn't named) was fired in 2009 on the orders of security forces after he interviewed the leader of Jundullah, an Iranian Sunni militant group whose members are wanted by Iran and who are thought to be hiding in Pakistan. According to the Pakistan Federal Union of Journalists (PFUJ), the authorities said that his links hurt the relationship between Pakistan and Iran.

On December 28, 2008, members of the mostly Punjabi and Mohajir Anti Terror Force beat up Behram Baloch, who was the station chief for the Urdu-language Daily Intekhab. He was doing his job at the main roundabout in Gwardar. In May 2009, the top reporter for Express, Kazim Mengal, and his cameraman, Mahmud, were harassed by security forces while reporting on the Sandak Gold Project in Chaghi district. Their equipment was also taken away from them. Shah Hussain, a top reporter for Express, said that they had been given permission to go into the area.

When photographer Irshad Akhtar of the daily Asaap tried to cover a fight between FC members and women protesters in Turbat district on September 4, 2009, he was beaten by FC members and had his video camera taken away. "I was doing my job as a reporter and cameraman when the FC staff started beating me. They pulled me by my hair and tried to take me into their camp, but some protesting women stopped them and helped save me. "I got hurt in a lot of ways," said Akhtar. He was upset that the FC officials wouldn't give him back his camera, which had pictures and videos of the protest gathering on it. Earlier, on August 26, 2008, he was attacked by FC members at a public gathering held to mark the second anniversary of the death of Nawab Akbar Khan Bugti, the former governor and chief minister of Balochistan. He was shot, and one other person was killed.

On June 13, 2010, while riding his motorcycle in the Khuzdar area, Samaa TV and The Daily Messenger reporter Munir Noor was stopped. Members of the FC mocked and hit him, and Abdul Latif's camera was taken from him. The two guys were going to cover the funeral of two Baloch students who had been killed. Noor was taken to the FC cars, and when he tried to use his phone, it was taken away from him. After the FC men who were holding him called their senior officer, he was let go. His camera and phone were also given back. An FC official later said they were sorry about what happened.

In June 2010, members of the FC beat four journalists, held them for more than an hour without a warrant, and took their cameras so they couldn't cover a strike called by a political party in Noushki District. The reporters had seen members of the FC beat up political activists. They were locked in a room until the protest ended an hour later. They were then given their cameras back, but the footage they had taken had been erased. Bashir Mohammad from ARY One, Dawood Mengal from Daily Zamana, Ghulam Rasool from Daily Intekhab, and Mohammad Ibrahim Baloch from Daily Mashriq were among those who were beaten and put in jail.

Some journalists were very close to being detained without reason and probably treated badly.

Security forces tried to take Qazi Dad Mohammad Rehan, the Secretary General of the Gwadar Press Club. Rehan is 27 years old, and he is also the bureau chief of Daily Tawar, the editor of Murwarid, a Baloch literary magazine, and the publisher of a blog. He has spoken out against the forced disappearances of Baloch youth and journalists, and he has also spoken out about how there is almost no news about human rights violations in Balochistan in Pakistan. In the middle of the night on December 13, 2010, about 30 FC soldiers and probably Military Intelligence agents broke into Rehan's house in Gwardar. They seemed to want to take him away. When the forces didn't find Rehan at home, they beat up his brothers and asked them where he was. While he was hiding, he sent urgent calls for help: He sent messages saying that he feared for his life because Gwardar was ringed by security forces who controlled all entrances and exits. He said, "There is nowhere to hide or escape, the circle of death is closing in on me, and the Pakistani security hounds are after my blood."

Jamal Tarkai, a photojournalist, and Dr. Baqir Shah, a police surgeon, were the most recent journalists to be threatened, held without a reason, and beaten because they exposed a serious violation of human rights by security forces. Under public pressure, a judicial investigation was set up to find out what happened. However, witnesses like Tarkai and Shah, who fought for human rights, were not protected when state agents tried to silence them. Even though this kind of abuse was reported by a lot of people, nothing was done to hold the abusers accountable.

On May 17, 2011, police and FC members shot and killed five people, including three women who were at first thought to be Chechen. They were near an FC picket on the National Highway near Kharotabad, which is a suburb of Quetta. Police and FC officials said right after the attack that the people who died were suicide bombers who were wearing suicide vests and had explosives on them.

After people complained, the Balochistan government set up a judicial investigation on May 20, 2011. It was led by a high court judge and heard from 28 people between May 24 and late June. Jamal Tarkai, a photojournalist who was there and took pictures of the event, was one of the most important eyewitnesses. He showed video of the killing, which included a shot of a wounded woman lying on the ground and waving her hand three times, which was probably a sign of surrender or a call for help. On Tarkai's video, it is said that the police head of Quetta stopped a police officer from shooting while the FC Colonel kept shooting at the victims. Tarkai also told the inquiry panel that he saw a Chechen woman sitting at the scene and being shot at by cops and an armored vehicle. Dr. Baqir Shah, a police surgeon, was another important witness at the trial. He had done autopsies on five foreigners and said that they had died from bullet wounds.

Both of the most important witnesses were bullied and mistreated within hours of giving their testimony to the court. On June 14, 2011, Jamal Tarkai was riding a motorcycle near Kharotabad when he was randomly arrested for two hours and beaten by police at the Kharotabad police station in Quetta, where he was taken. Two of the police officers who were responsible for his experience were suspended after he got out of jail. Later, Tarkai allegedly told a private TV station that he had been "threatened" for getting to the bottom of what happened and that his life was hard because of it. He told the inquiry tribunal that the police arrested him because of the statement he made against them. He also said that he had been threatened by an unknown man who called the Quetta Press Club and told the Vice President that Tarakai had made a "huge mistake" by giving the footage and photos to the tribunal.

In a similar way, Dr. Baqir Shah told a private TV station, "I was punished by police for telling the truth about the killing of five foreigners." He also said that he could name the police officers who had abused him. He said that on the night of June 13, 2011, a lot of police officers came to the Prince Road Hotel, where he was having dinner, in about 10 cars. He said that they asked him for his name and threatened him because of what he had said that day in court. He said that they told him, "This is the guy who gave a statement against us, beat him." They beat him up and hurt his head and arms so much that he had to go to a hospital for care. But Station House officers from the Ghawalmandi and Sadar police stations, who were fired soon after Dr. Shah was attacked, denied that they were the ones who did it in front of the inquiry panel. "Dr. Shah was drinking booze while sitting in his car. The SHO of the Sadar police station said, "All I did was tell him not to drink alcohol in public." The SHO Ghawalmandi said that this was true because they had "barely touched him."

Police coercion, such as forcing witnesses to lie in front of the judicial inquiry tribunal, was also overlooked by the public, even though this is clearly a crime. On June 12, 2011, the driver of the van in which the victims were riding, Atta Mohammed, told a fact-finding mission led by the Prime Minister's Advisor on Human Rights, Mustafa Nawaz Khokhar, and set up by the National Assembly Standing Committee on Human Rights, that police had forced him to say that arms and explosives were found in the luggage of the foreigners. He said he had been told that telling the truth would put him in danger. He told the team that was looking into what happened that the victims were not guilty and that the cops had asked them to pay bribes.

The report from the judicial investigation was given to the Balochistan government on June 28, 2011. On June 30, 2011, parts of the report were made public by the Balochistan Home Department. The part of the report that was made public said that police and FC members killed the five strangers, three of whom were women and one of whom was seven months pregnant. The outsiders got into Pakistan without permission, and evidence found on them suggested they might have been part of some banned groups. But at the time of the event, they did not have any weapons or explosives with them. They also did not plan to attack security forces, so they could have been safely arrested. In fact, the firing for no reason destroyed important information about these banned groups. The review panel said that the people who killed the people should be taken to court. At the moment, we don't know what steps have been taken in this area. From the excerpts in Pakistani media, it seems like no one cared that journalist Jamal Tarkai and Dr. Shah were wrongfully detained and mistreated, even though the head of the judicial tribunal had been very angry about the attacks on the key witnesses during the hearings.

Several other groups noticed that Dr. Shah and Jamal Tarkai were being harassed and mistreated. Late in May, the Supreme Court heard about the event and asked for more information. In June 2011, the Senate talked about how to protect journalists who report on serious violations of human rights. The Senate urged that those responsible be held accountable. Farooq H. Naek, the head of the Senate, said, "The country can't move forward if journalists can't do their jobs without interference." On June 8, 2011, the National Assembly Standing Committee on Human Rights put together a five-person fact-finding committee led by Mustafa Nawaz Khokar, Advisor to the Prime Minister on Human Rights. Khokar told the IG Police Balochistan to make sure that Dr. Baqir Shah, Jamal Tarkai, and the taxi driver were safe. The fact-finding team later said that at first they had to deal with lies and cover-ups, but they came to the same conclusion as the judicial probe and said that what happened to Dr. Shah and Tarkai was "inhuman and shameful."

Jamal Tarkai had been threatened and bothered by different people and groups in the past. He said, "Once, at a protest rally, members of the Balochistan Student Organizations were beating a photographer named Din Mohammad Watanpal. I was able to save him." Later that night, two guys came to my house and told me I had to leave Balochistan or they would kill me. Last year, I was on my way home in the evening when some guys in masks stopped me and beat me up. I have no idea who they were." He was also said to have gotten threats from the Balochistan Liberation Army (BLA) over drawings of the late Nawab Akbar Bugti of the Pakhtunkhwa Milli Awami Party and Mahmud Khan Achakzai, the leader of that party, as well as from Jamiat Ulema-i-Islam over a cartoon of Maulana Fazlur Rahman.

In the recent past, security forces arbitrarily held a few journalists for a long time in unknown places. The officials who held them denied that they were being held or that they knew they were being held. Forced removal is what happened to these people. Some of these people have already died. The people in charge of holding them must have killed them without going to court.

On January 5, 2011, the mutilated bodies of Mohammad Ilyas Nazar, 26, a student and journalist for the Baloch language magazine Dhorant, and Qambar Chakar Baloch, a student at Balochistan University of Information Technology, Engineering and Management Sciences (BUITEMS) and a member of the Baloch Students' Organization (BSO), were found in the Pidarak area of Kechh district, near Turbat.

On December 22, 2010, Ilyas Nazar was taking a bus from Quetta to his hometown of Turbat when he was taken by armed forces near Pasni. Eyewitnesses on the bus say that paramilitary troops stopped the bus in the

Badok neighborhood near Pasni and asked the journalist to show proof of who he was. He was taken away after he showed his ID card. No one knew what happened to him or where he was. No one was charged with stealing him, and the local officials said they didn't know anything about it. It was said that Qambar Chakar had been taken on November 26, 2010.

The bodies of the two men were taken to a hospital in Turbat, where tests showed that both of them had been shot in the head and had signs of torture all over their bodies. Ilyas Nazar was shot in the head and chest four times, while Qambar Chakar was shot eight times in the head, chest, and hands.

Zareef Faraz, a poet and director of the quarterly literary magazine Shabjoo, was shot and killed on April 25, 2011. His body was found in Turbat on April 25, 2011. Reports say that Zareef was taken from a bus a week earlier by a group of people, some of whom were wearing uniforms. Sami Ahmed, also from Tump, had also been taken. His body was next to his.

Rehmatullah Shaheen, a journalist who worked for the Daily Tawar and lived in Bolan, was forced to leave twice. The second time, he was killed without a trial.

Shaheen was first taken from his car on December 8, 2009, as he was driving from his office to Mach grid station. After a lot of people protested, the police said they had him on December 15, 2009, and that a case had been filed against him the day before, on December 14. They said that Shaheen was wanted under the Explosives Act and that a hand bomb had been found at his house after he told them that while he was in jail. Journalist groups pointed out that Shaheen was "known for his bold and factual reporting from the sensitive region of Bolan" and that "terrorism charges against Rehmatullah Shaheen would send warning signals to the rest of the rural correspondents across Balochistan to think twice before reporting objectively from their respective areas, regardless of the poor governance in the area."

In March 2011, Shaheen and four of his friends were taken again, this time by security officials in Dahdar. On April 1, 2011, his body was found in Ispelangi, butchered and with bullet wounds.

On November 18, 2010, the body of writer Abdul Hameed Hayatan, also known as Lala Hameed Baloch, was found by the River Sami in Turbat. This was the day before the Muslim holiday of Eid. He had written for the Urdu-language Daily Tawar, worked as a stringer for several other news outlets, and helped start the Gwadar Press Club. He was also the head of the Baloch National Movement, which is a political group that wants Balochistan to be independent. His friend Hamid Ismael Baloch, a student from Turbat, was dead next to him. Hayatan's body had torture marks and bullet holes in the head and chest. "Eid gift for the Baloch Nation" was written on a letter that was found in his bag. Reporters Without Borders, which is based in Paris, said that Hayatan had been shot in the head and chest. In a statement, the group said, "Marks on his body showed that he had been tortured before he was killed."

The two men were taken on October 25, 2010, while they were riding a motorbike to Gwadar from Dasht, where they had been to a wedding. They were supposedly taken into custody at a security checkpoint in the Karwaat area near Gwadar. Some of Hameed Hayatan's fellow journalists say that he was taken by people from intelligence agencies and then killed a few days later. His news stories were critical of the government, and he backed the Baloch national movement. Both of these things seem to have played a role in his forced disappearance and killing without a trial.

A small number of writers who were taken away by force were later found and were able to talk about what happened to them, which usually involved torture and other bad treatment.

Ameenullah Fitrat, a journalist for the Jang newspaper, said that he had been picked up by security agents, held for a while, and tortured more than once. In 2009, he said, "I used to report on conflicts from both Afghanistan and Pakistan. I talked to Al-Qaida's No. 2 leader, Ayman Al-Zawahiri, about three or four years ago near Kandahar, Afghanistan. I was taken away by security people months after that interview. I had to stay in jail for four days. A US officer would also come to me while I was being held and ask me where Zawahiri was, which I didn't know. They made me suffer. They made it very cold for me. During the cold days of winter, they poured cold water on my head. After four days, though, they let me go. .". Fitrat also said that he got a threatening phone call from a Taliban member after he told about the kidnapping of UNHCR employee John Solecki in February 2009 and said that the Taliban might have been involved.

Even though they didn't live in Balochistan, Baloch journalists have been abused in other parts of Pakistan when officials thought they were working with Baloch nationalists or writing about Baloch issues.

Mehruddin Marri, a reporter for the Sindhi-language newspaper Kawish, was taken from Sindh and made to disappear for four months. During that time, he was tortured. Marri was taken into custody without a reason on July 27, 2006, after being called to a police station in Thatta, Sindh province. Other media were there and saw it happen. Even though the police said they had nothing to do with his forced absence, it is now thought that after they arrested him, they gave him to the military, who took him to an unknown place. The Pakistan Federal Union of Journalists (PFUJ) says that Marri's work was about politics and human rights. On October 24, 2006, he was let go. He told the BBC Urdu Service in an interview that he was questioned by the military, especially about his family's connections to Baloch leaders. "I was hit and shocked with electricity, and I passed out," he said. "Then they made it so that I couldn't sleep for three nights. I had to stand in the middle of a room, and if I went down, someone would come in and wake me up. He said that the military tried to get him to say that he had ties to the Baloch nationalist movement. Before he was let go, a military officer told him, "Never go against the government or its secret services."

Non-state actors who get help from powerful officials or have ties to them have also apparently gone after journalists who report on abuses of power.

In 2007, security forces took journalist Riaz Mengal, who covered the Khuzdar area for Intekhab, and held him for about six weeks without a court order. Just before he was taken, he looked into the illegal trade in stolen cars in the area and reported it. He also said that the son of a former minister was involved in this illegal trade. "After Riaz did his research, he got death threats. Reporters Without Borders said that a Baloch writer said that the man's life was in danger.

On October 4, 2007, security forces in Khuzdar area grabbed him and took him away. His family made a complaint at a Khuzdar police station, naming the minister in question. Journalist groups held protests to call for his release, but it didn't help. On November 25, he escaped from his captors. The next day, he held a press conference at the Quetta Press Club and said that his kidnapping was related to stories about gangsters selling cars. He told the BBC that Atta-ur-Rehman Mengal, the son of former minister Sardar Naseer Mengal, was involved in his kidnapping "because he was part of this illegal trade," which he had written about. He said, "After my article came out, the police seized a number of the same kind of cars, but they must have given them back because the minister's son told them to." He said that he had been beaten and moved from place to place so that no one would find him. He said that he got away from Nushki while he was being held there. In 2008, security officials are said to have picked him up again and held him for five days. After being severely tortured, he was set free.

In some cases, it's still not clear if state or non-state players were behind a forced disappearance because the people who were taken away didn't want to talk or were too scared.

Khalil Khoso, a reporter for the newspaper Azadi, was taken by unknown men on February 29, 2008, after he went to a news gathering in Nasirabad. No one knew what happened to him or where he was. His family thought he was taken away because he wrote stories that were critical of Baloch nationalist parties that took part in parliamentary elections when other Baloch nationalist parties didn't. Asif Baloch, the editor of Azadi, said that local reporters told him that Khalil Khoso's disappearance might have something to do with photos he took on his cell phone that showed possible problems with the parliamentary election. Arif Baloch said that he had never seen the photos and that they had never been shown to the public. Khoso was freed on March 8, 2008. He didn't name his kidnappers or talk about what happened, but he did say that they told him "not to do this kind of journalism again." He also told a media friend in Quetta that they were looking for a picture he had taken during the recent campaign for parliamentary elections.

In Pakistan, it is common for people who are in jail to be tortured, and anyone who goes missing must have been tortured and treated badly. The psychological effects on their family members are almost painful because they know that these people will be tortured. Under international law, this means that they were also made to disappear.

Javed Lehri and Munir Mengal are two writers who were taken away against their will for several months and said they were tortured severely before they were let go.

On November 29, 2007, Javed Lehri, a 24-year-old journalist for the Urdu-language newspaper Azadi and secretary of the local press club in Wadh, and his friend Ibrahim Baloch were taken by about twelve trucks full of intelligence agents who came to raid the boys' hostel in Khuzdar district, according to eyewitnesses. He was beaten up, a rag was put over his face, and he was taken to Quetta that same night. Later, Lehri was seen in a Quetta jail run by the anti-terrorist force, according to the Daily Times. Lehri later said, "In the past, whenever I got frightening phone calls, I ignored them because I thought my friends were just playing a joke on me. This time, though, it wasn't a joke. I was, in fact, in the care of rude people who beat and hurt me. It took me three months to figure out that the new place I was living was called Quetta. I was kept in a 5x3 room that was totally dark. I found out later that I was at the Quli Camp inside the Quetta cantonment area.

Lehri is also a member of a political party, but his family and coworkers thought that he had been taken by intelligence agents because he wrote articles that were very critical of the government. He had been chosen by his paper to report on rallies protesting the death of Nawab Bugti and other events that caused political division. Lehri's captors allegedly told members of his family that they should keep quiet or be ready to get Lehri's dead body. After Lehri went missing, journalists held protests to show their support for him. A newspaper based in Quetta called Azadi had been critical of the military's work in Balochistan. Lehri was freed from jail on August 22, 2008, and he talked about how he was tortured during the nine months he was missing. He told the Daily Times in an interview that he was beaten and hung by his feet for the first three days of his arrest. He was then put in chains. "The pain was so terrible that I prayed to die. ... I hoped there would be something in my cell that I could use to kill myself. He was asked where the name of his newspaper, which means "liberation" or "freedom" in Urdu, came from. He said that the intelligence agents wanted to know "what kind of liberation" his newspaper was fighting for and asked that the name be changed. "I told them that I was only a reporter for the newspaper and that I couldn't change its name or its editorial line. They didn't believe me, so they kept beating me.

After his release, Lehri said he had trouble sleeping, felt sad, and had stomach problems, just like other people who had been through similar things. He has had to go to Karachi many times for treatment, but he said, "I can't pay for the care I need." I still get threatening phone calls on my cell phone, telling me not to talk about what happened to me in jail, which gives me nightmares. He said, "I've been interested in journalism since I was a kid. Now that I'm back at work, I regret that no one helped me during the hard time, not even my own media house or the media watchdogs. At this point in my life, all I really need right now is safety and help with my 78 medical care."

Munir Mengal, who tried to start a private Baloch language TV station, gave one of the most detailed accounts of torture and other bad treatment during a long time when he was taken away against his will. It shows that the intelligence agencies are determined to stop any knowledge about their work from getting out to the public. The idea of a private news station in the Baloch language seems to have made them go after the people trying to set it up in a harsh way. But the case also shows that in the middle of the 2000s, those who arbitrarily detained and disappeared human rights defenders still tried to make it look like they were following the law. By the end of the 2000s, this was no longer the case: the law was no longer followed at all, and journalists were increasingly kidnapped and killed without due process.

Munir Mengal was held without a charge at first by the military and its agents in an unacknowledged detention. He was then held under a series of preventive detention orders, some of which were thrown out by the provincial high court. Finally, he was charged with a crime. After being held without a reason for 22 months, Mengal was finally freed in February 2008. He is one of the few people who have come forward after being freed to talk about how he was tortured and treated badly.

In 2005, a Baloch businessman named Munir Mengal came up with the idea of starting a private Baloch language satellite TV station. He wanted to "give the Baloch their own voice" at a time when human rights violations in the province were on the rise and major Pakistani media was mostly silent. The Baloch were and still are the only ethnic and cultural group in Pakistan without a private TV station in their own language. At an event in Quetta in February 2006, where about 3,000 people were present, Mengal told the public about the launch of the TV station. After getting established in the United Arab Emirates, Baloch Voice was going to start sending out satellite broadcasts to about six million Baloch people in South Asia and the Middle East in June 2006. The Pakistan Electronic Media Regulatory Authority (PEMRA) called Mengal on March 28, 2006, and asked him to come to Karachi to talk about his desire for a license for Baloch Voice. Early in April 2006, Pakistani media stated that the company's board of directors would meet for the first time on April 5 in Dubai and that cultural programs had been set up in Pakistan, Dubai, Muscat, Saudi Arabia, the USA, the UK, and other places to encourage people to buy shares. People were getting jobs.

Instead, Munir Mengal was taken into custody by people from an intelligence service on April 4, 2006, when he arrived at Karachi International Airport from Dubai. Immigration officials told Mengal's family that he had been taken away by people from the Inter Services Intelligence. The police refused to take a report. The family filed a habeas corpus case. When the Sindh High Court heard the petition in July 2006, the Secretary of the Ministry of Defense said that neither the ISI nor Military Intelligence were holding Munir Mengal.

For 16 months, no one knew what happened to him or where he was. On August 4, 2007, he was freed from arbitrary and secret army prison in Sindh, near Kalat in Balochistan, on the RCD Highway. This happened after Baloch political parties, journalist groups like the Pakistan Federal Union of Journalists and the South Asia Free Media Association, and human rights groups like the Human Rights Commission of Pakistan (HRCP), Amnesty International, and Human Rights Watch fought hard for his release. Some observers say that their efforts led to Mengal being moved from Sindh to Balochistan. In February 2007, the HRCP filed a case with the Supreme Court of Pakistan about people who were taken away against their will. The list of "disappeared" people included Munir Mengal's name. In August 2007, the government told the Supreme Court that Mengal had been sent from Central Jail Khuzdar to an ATF jail in Quetta. At that time, he had been briefly freed in Kalat. But the local police took him into custody right away because he had a 30-day preventive detention order under the Maintenance of Public Order Ordinance (MPO). He was then taken to Khuzdar Jail. "It's likely that the cops already knew that Munir Mengal was going to be dumped in Kalat. "They arrested him officially and put him in the Khuzdar District Prison under the MPO," a local writer was quoted as saying. Another MPO detention order put him in jail for another 30 days on September 3, 2007. After his mother told the Balochistan High Court about his medical needs on September 6, 2007, the Court ruled that he get the right medical care.

In answer to Mengal's constitutional petition, the High Court ruled on September 10, 2007, that the order for his detention was illegal because he hadn't done anything wrong. However, he was detained right away under a new detention order. The Balochistan High Court threw out a new constitutional petition that was filed on September 12, 2007. In the meantime, on September 11, 2007, a criminal complaint was filed against him under the Anti-Terrorism Act with the Crime Investigation Department (CID), where he was held for further questioning on September 14. The charge filed with the police, called the "First Information Report," says that Mengal did things that were against the state and wanted to start Baloch Voice TV to get Baloch nationalists to rebel against the state. Also, he was said to have spoken at a public meeting of "separatists" in Quetta in February 2006, kept in touch with the Baloch Students Organisation, and suggested that he might help the Baloch fight to get the province's resources back for its people. The Balochistan High Court threw out an appeal against the FIR on October 10, 2007. The day before, on October 8, 2007, he was given bail, but the provincial home secretary quickly had him arrested again because of another report under the Anti-terrorism Act. After being locked up for 22 months, he was finally freed on February 23, 2008, but not before someone in the security forces threatened to kill him. "As I was still refusing their (the security forces') blackmail, an officer came to the prison to threaten to kill me," said Mengal, who was finally able to go back to his family. He went into hiding for a few weeks and then left the country through the Turbat airport. Reporters without Borders, a non-government group based in Europe that works to protect press freedom, helped him find a safe place to live in Europe.

Mengal talked about his time in prison from a safe place in another country. He said that on April 4, 2006, when he arrived at the Karachi airport, an army officer dressed in civilian clothes took his visa and took him to a military detention center. "Col. Muhamad Raza and majors Nadim and Atta tortured me physically and mentally in the Malir barracks." After not letting me sleep for 72 hours, they asked me more questions, like "Why do you want to start this TV station?" and "Who gave you the idea and who is helping you?" Then they put me in a small basement cell. I was blinded and handcuffed for several months. The first three days of torture were the worst. I'm still having back pain because I was kicked. At the same time, the long interrogation sessions during the first five months were mentally exhausting. "I still fear for my life," he said in an interview with the BBC World station's Urdu-language station. I'm still being watched by intelligence agents. "I sold all of my homes and stocks to get the 13 million rupees I needed to get the station up and running. While I was being held, the army took all of this money. They drained all 14 of my bank accounts."

Targeted Killings

Journalists are also being killed more and more by people who don't know who they are. These people could be government agents, groups close to or supported by parts of the government or insurgent groups, or people with a grudge because journalists exposed their wrongdoings. Most of the time, it's hard to figure out who did it and you can only guess based on the situation. In all cases, there should be quick and independent investigations to make sure the people responsible are held accountable.

Khadim Hussain Sheikh, who worked for Channel Five and Khabrain, was shot and killed in Hub on February 10, 2008, reportedly because he had written about theft in border areas. On February 17, 2010, Hameed Marwa, a freelance writer, was shot and killed on the Sariab Road in Quetta by people who have not been found. Police said that his killers shot at him as he left his home. On December 4, 2010, journalists in Chathar held a protest in support of Muhammad Luqman, the head of the district's Chathar Press Club, whose house had been shot at, reportedly by security staff. On February 19, 2011, two people on a motorcycle shot and killed Abdost Rind, a part-time writer for the Urdu-language Daily Eagle. He was on his way home from work in the Turbat area when he was killed. Rind's family said that they thought he was killed because of what he did as a writer.

Abdus Samad Chishti Mujahid, the bureau head of the Urdu-language weekly magazine Akhbar-e-Jehan in Quetta, was shot and killed by an unknown gunman as he left his home in Quetta on February 9, 2008. Reports say that the gunman and his partner ran away, and it took the cops 90 minutes to get there. Mujahid was a doctor by trade and worked as an eye specialist at a nearby hospital. For about 38 years, he had also been part of the Jang Group and regularly contributed to Akhbar-e- Jehan.

Later, a spokesman for the banned Baloch Liberation Army (BLA) called the Quetta Press Club and said that the murder was their fault. He told Jang's Ameenullah Fitrat that Mujahid was "against the Baloch cause" and that "Dr. Sahib's part was wrong. He did things that were against Baloch. He was a government worker. We tried many times to get him to understand, but he didn't." According to the Pakistan Federal Union of Journalists, Mujahid, who is of Punjabi descent, had gotten several threatening phone calls after writing a "strongly worded" report about the killing of a BLA leader in November 2007. "Baloch nationalists often tell us how to publish their reports," said a Baloch journalist.

So far, nobody has been caught for killing Chishti Mujahid. After he was killed, a First Information Report (FIR) was filed at the Satellite Town police station in Quetta. However, police are said to not have done a full investigation and have since closed the FIR.

Journalists who work in Khuzdar say that they are often pressured by different political groups. Muhammad Khan Sasoli, the head of the Khuzdar Press Club, said, "There are threats from all sides." Everyone wants us to write something good for them. All I want is to keep doing my job with honor and the public's trust." Malik Siraj Akbar, a journalist, said that Sasoli also told him that the Baloch Musallah Difah Tanzeem (BMDT), a secret anti-nationalist group, had regularly threatened him and other journalists in Khuzdar. Some people in the area think that the mysterious BMDT has ties to Pakistan's spy agency or is funded by it, and that it works with paramilitary forces. In April 2010, the BMDT frequently threatened the Khuzdar Press Club. BMDT spokesman Mir Jang Baloch told local reporters not to cover events held by Baloch nationalists, national parties, or parts of the Baloch Students Organizations. "The threats are serious," said writer Muhammad Khan Sasoli. "The government-backed groups will kill me if I cover the Baloch nationalist parties, which I am required to do as a journalist." No one listened when Sasoli and others asked the government to protect them.

Recently, several Khuzdar writers were killed because they were journalists.

Haji Wasi Ahmed, who worked for the Azadi and Balochistan Express in Khuzdar, was shot and hurt in a planned attack on April 11, 2009. He died two days later in a hospital in Karachi. The person who sold newspapers was also hurt in the shooting. It is thought that an armed Baloch separatist group did the attack, and that the target was Ahmed, who was from Punjab state.

On June 27, 2010, Faiz Mohammad Khan Sasoli, the past president of the Khuzdar Press Club and a reporter for Aaj Kal and Independent News of Pakistan, was shot and killed as he drove near the Faisal Hotel in Khuzdar. No one knows who did it. Faiz used to be the head of the Khuzdar Press Club. The BMDT had threatened him before, and he had narrowly avoided two attempts on his life.

Muhammad Khan Sasoli, a reporter for Royal TV, Balochistan Times, and INP in Khuzdar and head of the Khuzdar Press Club, was shot and killed on December 14, 2010, as he was walking home in Khuzdar in the evening. The unknown gunmen got away. No one took the blame for the planned killing.

A few photographers were shot on purpose, but they didn't die. Instead, they were "only" hurt.

Jan Muhammad Dashti, the editor and owner of the Urdu language newspaper Asaap and a senior bureaucrat, was shot and badly hurt in Quetta on February 23, 2009, by people who did not know who they were. His driver also hurt himself. Dashti was taken to the hospital and then treated in another country.

At the time, the government put pressure on Asaap because of what it said. In a phone call, someone who said they were a spokesperson for the sectarian group Lashkar-e-Jhangvi, which is said to have ties to Pakistan's security services, took credit for the attack. They said that one of Dashti's books, which came out 20 years ago and was part of Asaap, insulted the prophets. He asked the government to outlaw the book. Reports say that Dashti was warned that bad things would happen if the Asaap Group of publications kept writing about the bad things that the security services did.

Reporters Without Borders said at the time, "This shooting attack on a newspaper owner known for fighting for Baloch rights shows that the government can't or won't protect journalists." Dashti used to work for the government, but President Musharraf fired him in 2000, supposedly because he supported Baloch pride and didn't want the province to become more Islamic. He was later rehired by the court, though. In 2088, the government of the province put him in charge of running the mines in the province. He started Asaap in 2001 to fight for Baloch rights. It was very popular in the province, but the central government stopped advertising in it for the last five years it was in print.

Many people think that the attack on Dashti was connected to the fact that Asaap released a long list of missing people after the kidnapping of UN employee John Solecki in February.

When examining and reporting on events in Balochistan, which is a place with a lot of violence, media workers haven't always had enough protection. As a result, they have been killed or hurt while doing their jobs.

The following are some of the more popular ones:

In 2006, a bomb went off in Quetta and Mohammad Ejaz Khan lost an eye. He was the station chief for The News and Geo News. On February 12, 2008, a bomb went off near the office of an election candidate in Khuzdar, just before the candidate gave a press conference. Five journalists were hurt in the blast. On April 10, 2009, a roadside bomb in Quetta hurt Muhammad Khan Adil, a reporter for Dunya TV. At the time, tensions were high because three Baloch leaders had been killed.

On April 16, 2010, a suicide bomber blew himself up in Quetta's Civil Hospital, killing Malik Mohammad Arif, a reporter for Samaa TV, and about eight other people. In the attack, five other photographers were hurt. The journalists were covering a Shi'a protest outside the hospital. Arif was filming a well-known Shiite bank manager who had just escaped violence outside and was being treated at the hospital.

In September 2010, at least 73 people died and 8 media workers were hurt when a suicide bomber attacked the Al-Quds Day rally in Quetta. This was a worldwide protest in support of Palestine's sovereignty. Mohammad Sarwar, a driver for Pakistan's Aaj TV, died on September 3, 2010, from gunshot wounds he got after the suicide bombing. On September 6, 2010, Ejaz Ahmed Raisani, a writer for Samaa TV, also died from his wounds.

Human Rights Abuse towards Lawyers

In the last few years, lawyers who help people whose rights have been violated have been targeted by the government and have had their own rights violated more and more. There have been kidnappings, arbitrary detentions in places that aren't supposed to be detention centers, forced disappearances, torture, and killings that didn't follow the law.

At the time this was written, nobody knew what happened to or where Farzand Ali Mengal and Munir Ahmed Mirwani were. After being made to leave by force, some other lawyers were let go. Some of the people who are protesting the abuse of lawyers' rights have also been abused by state officials.

A lawyer who had been made to hide recently came back after more than three months. On February 22, 2011, Agha Zahir Shah, a senior member of the Balochistan High Court Bar Association, was taken by unknown armed people near Metri in the Sibi area. No one knew what happened to him or where he was. Agha Zahir Shah was still being held, according to a constitutional case filed with the Balochistan High Court. His lawyer friends thought that the state was to blame for his forced departure. In April 2011, at a press reception in the Bar Room of the Balochistan High Court, the President of the Balochistan Bar Association, Baz Mohammad Kakar, said that the two "missing" lawyers, Mir Munir Ahmed Mirwani and Agha Zahir Shah, had been taken by state officials and were still in the custody of "state functionaries." He also said that the government had not answered the lawyers' questions, strikes, or calls to stop going to court. Nasrullah Baloch, who is in charge of the Voice for Baloch Missing Persons (VBMP), a group that works to find Baloch people who have been taken away against their will, said that security forces and security agencies had taken Shah. "The lawyer has a full list of people who have gone missing and was often in Balochistan Court. He was taken by security personnel." A representative of the Bar Association said that Shah had helped the Balochistan High Court with cases of Baloch people who had been taken away against their will. His family also didn't believe that Shah had been taken for ransom and said that he was being held illegally by security forces.

After Baloch lawyers pushed for him for months, Agha Zahir Shah came home early on July 2, 2011, after being taken away against his will for over five months. Family members said that Agha Zahir looked weak and like he didn't know where he was. Dawood Kasi, who is the president of the Balochistan Bar Association, told the media that Agha Zahir Shah looked dirty, weak, and like he had lost his balance. It was said that he couldn't talk and didn't answer questions. No one knows if he told anyone who took him, where they kept him, or why they did it.

Farzand Ali Mengal, a lawyer from Usta Muhammad, Jaffarabad, was taken by armed men near Sourab on March 29, 2011. He has not been found. Malik Aminullah Kakar, who used to be the head of the Balochistan High Court Bar Association, said that Farzand Ali was taken while he was on his way to Hub to take part in a case.

Munir Ahmed Mirwani, the secretary general of the Jhalawan Bar Association, was taken by force by armed men in Khuzdar district on June 17, 2010, while he was eating at a roadside restaurant. Even though lawyers have protested and skipped court hearings in public and more than once, no one knows where he is. Several lawyers have said that the kidnapping was done by a government body.

So far, no luck has been had in trying to find Mirwani. A habeas corpus case was sent to the Balochistan High Court, but it hasn't given any information about where Mirwani is. After lawyers' groups met with important government officials and influential tribal leaders to try to find Munir Ahmed Mirwani and get him released, and after "mounting pressure from the lawyers," the chief justice of the Balochistan High Court eventually took notice on his own that he had been taken. He said, "The performance of the police and other law enforcement agencies is not good enough to fight this threat [of kidnappings] effectively." Even though there were reports from people who saw the kidnapping, it was hard to find Mirwani. Mir Abdul Salam Baloch, a lawyer, was there when the two men took the girl, and he later found out who they were. Even though the kidnappers' faces were supposedly covered, the masks of the van driver and another kidnapper had slipped, allowing Salam to recognize them. The court told the cops to make sketches of the people who took the kids. The Supreme Court was worried about Mirwani's "disappearance" when it talked about how dangerous it is for lawyers in Pakistan. Activists said that during protests against the kidnapping of Munir Ahmed Mirwani, security officers beat and insulted a lawyer named Mir Abdul Salam Baloch for taking part.

Several Baloch lawyers may have been killed without a trial, usually after being taken away for a time. This was probably because of the work they did.

Advocate Ali Sher Kurd, a lawyer, writer, poet, and regular contributor to Daily Ostoman, was taken from the home of his relatives in Quetta on September 20, 2010, by unidentified men who other lawyers thought were from the intelligence or security forces. His whereabouts were unknown until his bullet-riddled body was found on September 23, 2010, in a deserted area of Ibrahim Road in the Khuzdar district. His neck was broken, and different parts of his body showed signs of torture.

Ali Sher Kurd's cousin, speaking about the Baloch columnist and lawyer's early life, said, "He was against injustice and exploitation even when he was a student." He started his fight on the stage of BSO, and he even spoke out against bad behavior in his group of friends. He wanted to be a great leader of the Baloch Nation and didn't like the Sardari or old clan system. Kurd's sister, Banok Sakeena Baloch, spoke to protesters in front of the Press Club. She said that Ali Sher Baloch was sick when security forces broke into his home, arrested him, and made him "disappear." In September 2010, the President of the Balochistan Bar Association, Baz Kakar, said that the families of Ali Sher Kurd and Mir Ahmed Mirwani, two lawyers who had been taken hostage and killed, had blamed the security forces and intelligence agencies for the deaths and kidnappings. "If the institutions aren't taking hostages, then they need to explain where they stand, because it's their main job to make sure people's lives and property are safe," he said.

Zaman Khan Marri was a lawyer at the Balochistan High Court. His body was found at Pashkaram Farm in the District of Mastung early on September 6, 2010. Reports say that the body was so badly damaged that it could not be identified right away. People who saw his body said that there were signs of chains on his hands and feet and bullet holes on his head. He was kidnapped on August 18, 2010, as he was walking home from his office in the Kabir Building in Quetta. The Kabir Building is a private room for Baloch lawyers that is part of the Balochistan High Court. His lawyer friends think that he was taken away by people from the security forces.

Before he was taken, Zaman Khan Marri looked into the cases of several detained or "disappeared" Baloch activists. This included the case of his nephew, Ali Ahmed Marri, who was arrested on April 7, 2010, along with three friends, Kamal Khan Marri, Lala Marri, and Lal Mohammad Marri, by people in plain clothes. Ali Ahmed Marri's disfigured body was found in the same place as Zaman Marri's body on September 11, 2010.

After Zaman Khan Marri "disappeared," people tried to find him and then the people who killed him, but they were not successful. For his safe and quick recovery, a habeas corpus petition was made with the high court. However, his body was found just one day before the petition was to be heard. In late August 2010, the Chief Justice of the Balochistan High Court, Qazi Faez Isa, was very worried and took action on his own. He said that "abductions cause alarm and fear in the general public." The law enforcement system, on the other hand, was not able to find out who did it. In November 2010, the Supreme Court of Pakistan said that on August 27, 2010, the Balochistan High Court told PPO Quetta to choose a top officer to look into the murder. The SP City was chosen to do this. On September 6, 2010, Hazar Khan told police station Mastung (FIR No. 71/2010) that his brother Zaman Khan Marri had been killed by people he didn't know. Under the direction of the Regional Police Officer in Khuzdar, an investigation team made up of the SP, DSP, IP/IR, and SI/SHO found that the death was caused by a gunshot but couldn't figure out who fired the gun. So far, there has been no progress in figuring out who did it and putting them in jail.

Another lawyer had to go into hiding and then leave the country to feel safe. Lawyer Kachkol Ali Baloch fought hard against the forced disappearance and extrajudicial execution of the three nationalist leaders Mir Ghulam Muhammad Baloch, Lala Munir Baloch, and Sher Muhammad Baloch, who were taken from his office. (See section on human rights defenders.) He had also spoken out about human rights violations in the past, both in Pakistan and around the world. Kachkol Ali Baloch said in public that the three politicians were taken by people from Military Intelligence. He also said that he saw two Frontier Corps (FC) vehicles without license plates following the cars that took the three men away. Because of this, he was told over and over again by state agencies to stop what he was doing. In May 2009, he said that intelligence services had called him and said they were going to kill him. He reportedly went into hiding a few days later. Local journalists said that intelligence agency workers were trying to find Kachkol Ali, that his homes in Quetta and Panjgore were being watched, and that his office in Turbat city was surrounded by people in plain clothes. Kachkol Baloch went to Norway in October 2010 and was finally given political asylum there.

Infringements on Human Rights Campaigners in Balochistan

Human rights campaigners who try to stop people from breaking their rights have often been broken against themselves. They include people who are part of organized human rights groups as well as people from the families of people whose rights were violated and who worked to stop the abuses.

In the past few years, security services have gone after several members of the non-government Human Rights Commission of Pakistan (HRCP).

On March 1, 2011, two people on a motorcycle shot Naeem Sabir Baloch, a well-known social worker and human rights campaigner. They did this near a bookshop on Chakar Khan Road in Khuzdar. He was shot, but he died in the Civil Hospital. Since 1997, he had been a part of the HRCP and was in charge of it in the Khuzdar area. More recently, he helped the HRCP record cases of forced disappearances in the province. This information was going to be sent to the Supreme Court of Pakistan and the High Court of Balochistan.

The BMDA (see above) said that they were the ones who killed Naeem Sabir. Many people think that the Pakistani military funds this mysterious group and uses it to go after political opponents of the government, such as media and other professionals. There were also rumors that the student younger brother of Naeem Sabir was on their list of people to kill. The Asian Human Rights Commission said that Naeem Sabir "had been getting constant death threats from people thought to be in the intelligence agencies for several months." He once said that... that his life was in danger and that one day he would either be taken by police and killed or taken by police and killed. Local people are also sure that the killing was related to his political work, especially his work on forced disappearances. The HRCP was outraged by attempts to "eliminate human rights advocates who speak out against persecution for any reason" and said, "Naeem Sabir... had been working hard and with bravery to promote human rights in Khuzdar. State stooges had sometimes gone after him because of what he did. But in recent years, he didn't seem to have upset anyone except for the local satraps, who couldn't stand his honest reporting on human rights crimes.

The official police reaction to the shooting of Naeem Sabir is very out of touch with what's going on in Balochistan. A police officer was quoted as saying, "Naeem Sabir worked as a sub-engineer for the Irrigation Department." The officer also said that it wasn't clear why Sabir was killed. "The police are looking into it," he said. Since there had been no movement in finding and charging his killers, the HRCP said a month later, "These killings show how dangerous it is to work for human rights in Balochistan."

Another HRCP worker, Siddique Eidho, was killed while he was being made to disappear. He was a writer who, with the help of other reporters, set up a network of human rights reporters in the Makran area. He was also a senior member of the Pasni Press Club and worked as the HRCP Core Group Coordinator for Pasni. On December 21, 2010, he and his tailor friend Yousaf Baloch were taken. The two men were going from Gwardar, where they had been to a court hearing unrelated to this case, to their home town of Pasni in a police van with four police constables and an ASI. At the FC checkpoint in the Karwat area on the Coastal Highway, armed people in security outfits stopped the van and put the two men in their own cars. Even though the police officers who were with them protested, they were taken away. Some of the police officers were beaten during the event and were held in FC custody for several hours.

The HRCP held personnel working for the country's intelligence agencies responsible for the abduction and enforced disappearance and expressed "serious concern" for the safety of Eidho and Baloch and demanded their immediate release and that "the rights of people working as human rights defenders [be] respected without exception." Efforts to trace Siddique Eido and Yousaf Baloch did not yield any result, their fate and whereabouts remained unknown. Other journalists thought that "the government was annoyed with his coverage of the disappearances and extra-judicial killings of political workers from the Baloch ethnic minority at the hands of the secret services" Later, his friends told him that Eido had gotten threatening phone calls from "private numbers," which are often used by secret services, telling him to stop reporting on "sensitive issues."

On April 28, 2011, the bodies of Siddique Eido and Yousuf Baloch, which had been cut up, were found dumped near Ormara next to the Makran coastal highway. The HRCP said they were "deeply shocked and outraged" by the killings. They blamed the government for not making sure their safe recovery, and they called for justice for their deaths. It said, "The uniforms his captors wore and the cars they drove made it more likely that they were state agents." Siddique was taken from his home in front of several police officers, but despite this clear proof, nothing was done to identify or prosecute his kidnappers or get Siddique back. Siddique had worked to bring attention to cases of forced abduction and other violations of human rights in the area, and his own disappearance was recently questioned in the Supreme Court. HRCP warned the government and security officials many times that Siddique's life was in danger. HRCP is saddened that not enough was done to save Siddique's life. HRCP can't say enough about how disappointed they are by the government's lack of action and lack of care, which comes to collusion in Siddique's murder.

People have also hurt members of the Voice for Baloch Missing Persons. In April 2010, the group's leader, Nasrullah Baloch, said that KD Baloch, the group's finance officer, and his two friends, Mushtaq and Mohiudeen, had been taken by FC members near the Bolan Medical College in Quetta. At the moment, there are no more information.

Shams Baloch, the Khuzdar Coordinator for Voice for Baloch Missing Persons, was taken by FC members from the Luckpass area on July 1, 2010. He was taking his 80-year-old mother from Khuzdar to a hospital in Quetta in a government van. Other family members were in the ambulance with them and saw what happened. They said that when they got to the Mia Ghundi Border Check Post (near Hazar Gunji Park), FC staff stopped the ambulance and told the government driver and Shams Baloch to get out. At gunpoint, they beat Shams Baloch, and then four other armed men took him away. His family thinks that they were working for the Frontier Corps Intelligence Unit (FCIU) or another spy outfit. When Shams Baloch's family went to the police station to file a FIR, officials reportedly told them on behalf of the FC that Shams Baloch would be freed soon. After first refusing to file a FIR about Shams Baloch's arrest and detention without a reason, police finally did so on July 6, 2010, because the court told them to. A plea for habeas corpus is still being considered. The family said that they got anonymous phone calls that were meant to scare them away from continuing the case. A team of people from the police and intelligence agencies was put together to look into what happened. They came to the conclusion that Shams Baloch had been stopped by FC employees and taken away from them by people they didn't know. Relatives of Shams Baloch say they have been getting threatening phone calls telling them not to talk to the police or judges about what happened. Since then, Shams Baloch has not been seen.

Yasin Muhammad Shahi Baloch, who was an active member of Voice of Baloch Missing Persons, was killed because of his work with the group. He was the brother of Mujeeb Baloch, who was a top member of BSO-Azad. On September 1, 2009, Mujeeb and four of his friends were taken from the University of Balochistan by people who seemed to be from the FC. Yasin Muhammad Shahi Baloch started helping the Voice of Baloch Mission Persons after his brother was taken away against his will.

On October 10, 2010, Yasin Muhammad Shahi Baloch was riding a motorbike on his way home to Malghozar Kalat when he was shot by people who didn't know who they were. This happened near Roshare, Kalat. The attackers, who were wearing masks, killed him right away and then ran away. Family members and other activists have said that the extrajudicial killing was done by the security forces and intelligence services. Yasin Muhammad Shahi Baloch held a news conference at the Quetta Press Club in July 2010 and said he would kill himself in front of the high court if his missing brother was not found. Mujeeb Baloch was let out of jail in Quetta on December 24, 2010.

Faqir Mohammad Baloch was a poet and the Mastung zone supervisor for Voice for Baloch Missing Persons. His body was found on October 21, 2010, in the district of Mastung, along with the body of Zahoor Baloch, who had been taken by the BSO-A on August 23, 2010. According to news sources, a single bullet fired at point blank range hit both of their heads, and their bodies showed signs of torture.

A month earlier, on September 23, 2010, Faqir Mohammad Baloch, who didn't belong to any party, and Abdul Rehman rode a motorcycle to the Cadet College Mastung, where Faqir Mohammad Baloch worked. They were stopped at the FC checkpoint by people in plain clothes, who took Faqir Mohammad Baloch away.

The Baloch. Abdul Rehman told the head of Cadet College right away, but Faqir Mohammad Baloch's fate and whereabouts were unknown until his dead body was found in October 2010.

Saba Dashtiari, a well-known Baloch scholar and professor of Islamic studies at the University of Balochistan, was one of the people who helped the Voice for Baloch Missing Persons the most. On June 1, 2011, in the Sariab neighborhood of Quetta, unidentified guys on a motorcycle shot and killed him. He fought for the Baloch language, supported new ideas, and spoke out against the abuse of Baloch people's human rights. During the last three years of his life, he worked hard to stop the forced disappearance of hundreds of Baloch people. He took part in hunger strike camps, showed his support for the families of the "disappeared," and spoke at several seminars about the problem. At his funeral, a former student remembered that Dashtiari had said a few months earlier, "I know this (heart problem) can't kill me. My guess is that I will be shot and found dead on the side of a road." Most observers did, in fact, link Dashtiari's death to his work for the release of "disappeared" Baloch people. The murder was blamed on a man who called the Quetta Press Club and said he was a spokesman for a group called Ansarul Islam. But many people were still suspicious and saw this as an attempt to keep people from asking who was really behind the murder. Zohra Yusuf, who is the head of the HRCP, said in an article that "the chances of this being a "front" organization seem high, since Islamic groups have little reason to kill a university professor who is known for his nationalist views." So far, no one has been caught.

The latest person to be killed on purpose was a human rights worker in Balochistan who worked to protect people who had been forced to move.

Mir Rustam Marri was shot and killed by people on a motorcycle on June 23, 2011, as he stood outside his home in the Dera Allahyar neighborhood of Jaffarabad. The attackers were unknown. Marri used to be a part of the BNP-Mengal, but he hasn't done any political work in the last five years. Instead, he has helped Baloch people who have moved within their own country. He is said to have put together a secret database about Baloch internally displaced persons (IDPs), shared it with national and foreign media, and helped anyone who wanted to learn more about the Baloch IDP crisis. Police said that they couldn't figure out what happened and that an investigation had been started. No one has said they did the killing, and no one has been caught in connection with it.

When family members and friends of victims of human rights abuses talk about it in public, they often get hurt themselves. In fact, some people have died because they spoke out about lost family members.

Asim Karim Baloch, a student at Multan Polytechnic College and the head of the BSO-A's Multan zone, went back to Balochistan when he heard that his brother, also a BSO-A activist, Tariq Kareem Baloch, had been taken by Military Intelligence in Karachi on October 21, 2010. Asim Karim Baloch spoke at a press meeting in Quetta on October 26, 2010, to bring attention to his brother's case. He then went back to his home in Besima town. On October 30, after going to a wedding, security forces apparently shot at him, and some people saw it happen. He was then taken away. On November 1, 2010, his dead body was found in the Khanozia area of Balochistan. Tariq Karim Baloch's fate and whereabouts were unknown until May 2011, when his body, which had been shot, was found in Quetta.

People who were just trying to get in touch with a family member who had their rights violated in a serious way and were fighting for justice have also been abused. Mehran Baloch, a human rights campaigner, said, "Pakistani security forces not only kill Baloch youth, but they also scare the families of people who have gone missing."

On March 29, 2010, Yar Khan Marri, Sikandar Marri, Bhawal Marri, and Abdul Majeed Marri, who were all related to Murad Khan Marri, were taken by security guards while they were on their way back to look for Murad Khan Marri, who had been taken.

Murad Khan Marri and his brother Sikander were taken into custody in Hub on June 29, 2009. Sikander was released the next day. Murad Khan Marri was first held in a local police station, then moved to an unknown place. After Murad Khan Marri went missing for nine months, an FC colonel said in public on March 27, 2010, that Marri had just been caught near Chaman in connection with the killing of Chinese engineers and for having Indian money and explosives. "We arrested BLA commander Haji Murad Khan Marri after a gunfight and found explosives, radios, and Indian and Afghan money on him," said Commandant Frontier Corps (FC) Pishin, who said that Marri had driven into Pakistan from Afghanistan on March 27, 2010, in a car.

But the evidence for his arrest in June 2009 and against the FC claim was overwhelming. Newspapers had reported his arrest in the middle of 2009, and his mother, Nazi Marri, had filed a habeas corpus petition against the FC and intelligence agencies on August 17, 2009. On December 8, 2009, the inspector general of FC went to the Balochistan High Court and said that Murad Khan Marri had not been arrested or held. Again, Nazi Marri filed a FIR at the Hub police station on February 10, 2010. Marri's name also showed up on several lists of people who "disappeared," including one put out by the government's National Crisis Management Cell. Marri told the High Court on May 25, 2010, during a hearing about the constitutional case, that he had been arrested on May 25 and had been missing for nine months. He was also said to have said that he had been tortured in different places where he was being held.

After Murad Khan Marri showed up at a news conference held by the FC on March 27, 2010 and looked weak, scared, and unable to walk properly, his four relatives went to see him in Chaman on March 28, 2010, but they were not allowed to. Instead, they were stopped by the FC at the Baleli check post on their way back to Quetta. All four of them were taken to an unknown place. Other family members said that they had been taken by intelligence agents. Murad Khan Marri was then moved to the ATF jail in Quetta, but to this day, we still don't know what happened to his four cousins or where they are. Some news stories say that Murad Khan Marri went missing again on April 13, 2010, while he was in the hands of FC.

In the same way, security forces often harass or threaten family who have taken part in public hunger strikes or demonstrations. For example, in October 2010, when relatives of the "disappeared" held a demonstration in front of the Quetta Press Club, the sisters of three "disappeared" people, Safeer Baloch, Din Mohammad Marri, and Wadood Raisani, said that they had been threatened by some people to stop their three-month hunger strike for their recovery.

The sister of "disappeared" Vice Chairman of Baloch Students Organization (BSO) Zakir Majeed Baloch, who was taken by intelligence agencies at Mastung on June 8, 2009, said the same thing: "The goal of our protests is to get my brother back, free him, and get justice, but the agents of Pakistan's intelligence agencies have started to warn us of bad things that will happen to us; they are threatening to hurt us." Zakir Majeed Baloch's family said that the main reason he was taken away by Pakistani authorities was because he supported "disappeared" Baloch activists and the release of UNHRC representative John Solecki. They didn't want Solecki to be freed because they didn't want the Baloch movement to be seen as a terrorist movement by Pakistan.

In 2009, three important Baloch politicians were first kidnapped by security forces and then killed without a trial. Many observers say this was because they were on a committee set up to find "disappeared" people and negotiate the release of John Solecki, a UNHRC representative who had just been taken hostage. Witnesses to the kidnapping were told that if they went after the cases, "dire consequences" would happen.

On April 3, 2009, Mir Ghulam Muhammad Baloch, president of the Baloch National Movement (BNM), Lala Munir Baloch, a member of the BNM's central committee, and Sher Muhammad Baloch, general secretary of the Baloch Republican Party (BRP), were taken from the office of their lawyer, Kachkol Ali Baloch, a former leader of the opposition in the Balochistan Assembly and member of the National Party, in Turbat town. Even though these nationalist leaders supported the Baloch resistance movement, it was said that none of the men were involved in any kind of armed action. An assistant lawyer in the office of Kachkol Ali Baloch was also picked up at first, but he was let go when his name was found out.

All three men and some of their family members had been kidnapped and held in secret custody for a while. They had also been charged with crimes under the anti-terrorism act. In April 2009, they went to Turbat to go to the district and sessions court about this. The court gave them bail before they were taken into custody. Obeidullah said that his brother, Ghulam Muhammad Baloch, had been told to stop doing political work by people in the intelligence services. The last time this happened was just 10 days before he died.

The bodies of the three "disappeared" Baloch leaders were found on April 8, 2009, near Murghab Pasni Road, about 18 km from Turbat city. The bodies were in bad shape and had been there for a long time. The medical staff thought that the guys had died on the day they were arrested. A medical report says that gunshots were the cause of death, but since there was no blood where the bodies were found, it was not clear where and how they died. There were no tests done after the person died. Most Baloch nationalist groups agree with eyewitness accounts of the kidnapping that security and/or intelligence personnel were behind the kidnapping and killing of the three Baloch leaders. Lawyer Kachkol Ali Baloch, who represented the three politicians, saw them being taken away. He told an HRCP fact-finding team that on April 3, while he and his clients were talking about the case, his assistant Hassan came into the office to tell them that security forces and secret agencies were outside. Six people came into his office almost right away and arrested Lala Munir, Ghulam Muhammad Baloch, and Sher Muhammad Baloch. At first, they also caught a junior lawyer, but when they found out who he was, they let him go. The men were blinded and taken away in cars. Two vehicles from the Frontier Corps, which had been waiting a bit away from Kachkol Ali Baloch's office, followed closely behind. "They were people from the agencies," Kachkol is said to have said. "They were in plain clothes, but from their hairstyles and the way they talked, we knew who they were." Nisar Ahmed, who owns a shop next to the lawyer's office where the three men were taken, saw them being pushed into a truck, which was followed by a second vehicle with 10 more armed men in plain clothes who appeared to be Frontier Corps members. When the HRCP team asked him how he knew the people who took him were from security or intelligence forces, he said, "It's not new to me. Twice or three times a week, they come and stand over here. On the day of the incident, I thought it might be routine." Nisar Ahmed said that after he told his witness story in public, members of the FC and security forces came to him several times and told him he shouldn't talk about what happened.

On April 9, 2009, the HRCP said that it had "credible information" that the violations were done by the security forces. It said, "The facts strongly suggest that members of state security picked up the three victims, tortured and killed them, and then dumped their bodies, which were found mutilated and rotting." The organization's fact-finding mission confirmed these initial findings and listed several accounts of witnesses to the abduction.

Officials denied that the state had anything to do with the kidnapping and killing. On April 9, 2009, the Director General of the Inter-Service Public Relations department released a statement in which he strongly condemned the killing of the Baloch leaders and denied that the intelligence agencies had anything to do with it. He also asked the public to wait for the results of the judicial investigation before making accusations against the intelligence and security services. At the same news gathering in Quetta, Interior Minister Rehman Malik said, "The killing of the Baloch leaders was a plot against Pakistan." How can these things be done with the help of secret agencies?"

As with other serious violations of human rights in Balochistan, the people who did it were not punished. On April 4, lawyer Kachkol Ali Baloch made a complaint with the Turbat police, saying that people from Military Intelligence (M.I.) and Inter Services Intelligence (I.S.I.) were behind the kidnappings. The application made it clear that the men who had been taken could be tortured or killed in prison. But the police didn't file a First Information Report (FIR), which is the first report that should start a police probe. Instead, they just wrote down the complaint in the police daily diary (roznamcha). Then, Kachkol Ali Baloch asked for a court order called habeas corpus. But the judge of the Turbat session court said he couldn't take it because it wasn't his job. He told him to file it with the Balochistan High Court. This happened. After that, a major from

Military Intelligence called Kachkol Ali Baloch, but he wouldn't go to their office because he was afraid for his safety, the safety of his family, and the safety of his coworkers. The Commissioner of the Makran Division told the HRCP team that the police couldn't protect people from threats made by the federal security forces because "they are not under our control, so we can't stop them or tell them what to do." However, the police are doing their best to protect eyewitnesses.

On April 16, 2009, the Balochistan High Court took notice of the killings on its own and called the provincial Home Secretary and the officers in charge. The provincial government put together a team of Balochistan High Court judges to look into what happened. The central government also asked for an investigation. But the families of the three people who died and a number of Baloch nationalists have turned down these inquiries. Instead, they want an investigation to be done by the UN.

The three men were probably taken and killed because they were part of a group of 10 people called the Baloch Qaum Dost Committee, which was set up by Nawab Khair Bakhsh Marri in mid-March 2009. Its goal was to help find hundreds of "disappeared" Baloch and free John Solecki, the head of the UN High Commission for Refugees (UNHCR) in Quetta. Solecki was taken from Quetta on February 2, 2009, by a group called the Baloch Liberation United Front (BLUF), which was unknown at the time. In exchange for Solecki's freedom, this group had asked for the return of all "disappeared" Baloch and an answer to the "problem" of the Baloch. Only two days before they were taken, the three political leaders met with a UN team at the home of Nawab Khair Bakhsh Marri to help negotiate John Solecki's release.

Recommendations to the State of Pakistan and Balochistan Govt.

Human rights activists in Balochistan say that the government has broken a wide range of their rights. Some of these rights are the right to life, the right to freedom and security, and the right not to be tortured, arrested or detained without a reason, or made to disappear. People in Pakistan have all of these rights because of the Constitution of Pakistan and other laws. Pakistan has also made international promises by ratifying the International Covenant on Civil and Political Rights (ICCPR) and the UN Convention against Torture and Other Cruel, Inhuman, and Degrading Treatment and Punishment (CAT). Pakistan signed both of these foreign agreements in 2010, and they are now law. Some of the most important rights that the ICCPR protects are the right to life (Article 6), the right not to be tortured or treated in a cruel, barbaric, or degrading way (Article 7), and the right not to be arrested or detained without a reason (Article 9). The Convention against Torture says that torture is always wrong.

When the UN General Assembly, where Pakistan has a seat, passed the Declaration on Human Rights Defenders in 1998, Pakistan also promised to protect and support the rights of people who fight for human rights. It's clear that the state hasn't kept the promises it made back then.

It has also not done what it was supposed to do to make sure that private people don't hurt people who fight for human rights. In recent years, the world view of state responsibility for human rights abuses has changed a lot. It now includes not only abuses by state agents but also abuses by private actors that the state doesn't care about. International human rights law says that the state is just as responsible as the abusers if it doesn't do enough to stop, investigate, and punish abuses like harassment, beatings, and killings of human rights advocates by private actors. The governments of Pakistan and Balochistan haven't done anything to stop and stop killing people who work for human rights. It hasn't tried to stop the abuse of people who fight for human rights, even when threats were made in public or brought to its attention. It also hasn't tried to stop the abusers from getting away with it.

Human rights defenders have been abused by state agents or private people or groups, but the police and courts have often ignored victims' or relatives' attempts to get justice. This is against the law, because the police and courts are supposed to take action to bring the abusers to justice. Because of this, abuses have continued to go unpunished, which encourages more abuses.

The federal and provincial governments of Pakistan, as well as all of its agencies, are asked to keep their promises to protect human rights activists in Balochistan and to acknowledge the value and legitimacy of their work. This means telling law enforcement and security forces in Balochistan to follow the law in everything they do. When state officials violate the rights of people who fight for human rights, the crimes must be looked into quickly so that the people responsible can be brought to justice. At the same time, the state must take the right steps to protect human rights advocates from abuses committed by non-state actors.

The Vigor of Baloch Rebellion Resilience

Balochistan's past since 1948 is summed up by the way it is described geographically: as a "dark and sad place." Its past with the Pakistani government is full of lies and contradictions. It is the biggest and most resource-rich state in Pakistan, but it has the fewest people and is the least developed. Even though the state has always repressed the Baloch nationalist movement harshly, it has always come back stronger than before and outlasted other resistance groups. The insurgency began when the Khan of Kalat was made to sign the instrument of accession in 1948. Since then, it has mostly happened during five different times. The fifth and current period began in 2004 and is still going on. It is the longest and most violent time. In order to do this, the paper tries to figure out the main reasons why the uprising started and why it is still going on. The paper also looks at the reasons why the rebellion got weaker after 2015 and then got stronger again in 2020.

It is important to remember that the reasons for the present insurgency are not unique to the past. Instead, they are the result of decades of unresolved problems that keep getting worse. So, to help the paper reach its goal, it is split into three main parts. In the first part, the past of Balochistan and its people is explained so that you can understand why there is an uprising. The second part explains why the current insurgency is happening by talking about political alienation and marginalization, economic poverty and underdevelopment, megaprojects in the province, and the state's military reaction. The second-to-last part is about what happened after 2015, when rivalries between Baloch groups caused the insurgency to weaken, and what happened in 2020, when it started up again.

Region and the Habitants

Before the British came to the area, Balochistan, which used to be the state of Kalat, was ruled by Khan of Kalat and was made up of four provinces: Kalat, Lasbela, Makran, and Kharan. The Khanate of Kalat covered what is now Iran and Afghanistan. The Khan of Kalat told the Afghan and British envoys that "all the regions where the Baloch live are a part and parcel of our state."

After losing the First and Second Afghan Wars, the British began to take over and unite big parts of the area near where Pakistan and Afghanistan meet today. Devasher also says that to stop the Russians from moving into British India, "the British marked their border with Iran (then called Persia) and Afghanistan by giving large parts of the princely state of Kalat to these two countries." This was done to make the rulers of these countries happy and to act as a buffer zone to stop the Russians from moving in.

"We will respect Kalat's independence as long as it acts in subordinate coordination," the British government said. They basically split the Khanate into two administrative regions. The first was the state of Kalat, and the second was directly under British rule. It included areas "leased by the British from Kalat and the Marri and Bugti tribal areas," as well as areas that were mostly Pashtun. So, the second unit was also a part of British India, but the first unit was not.

In Baloch affairs, the Marri and Bugti tribes have also been very powerful. The Marris are the biggest tribe in Balochistan in terms of population, and they "think of themselves as Balochistan's master tribe." The two groups are part of a larger group called the Eastern or Sulaiman Baloch. This group is also the largest of the 17 groups and 400 subgroups that make up the Baloch. The Western Baloch, also called Makran Baloch, are the other major group. They have always been seen as the "original core" of the Baloch people.

Also, in the 1901 census, the British made a distinction between the Baloch and the Brahvis, even though the Brahvis are just another group of Baloch. The British called the Brahvis a "ethnic group of Dravidian origin based in central Balochistan," while most of the other groups lived in the south and south-west parts of the state. There are three groups of Brahvis: the Brahvi core, the Sarawan, and the Jhalawan. The Khan of Kalat is from a subgroup of the Brahvi core, while the Mengals, a Jhalawan tribe, have become the most influential group in Balochistan politics.

Balochistan's geography and the fact that its people are spread out helped them build strong tribal identities or walls that kept them apart from each other and kept outsiders out. This changed a lot when the British took over. In his book Baloch Nationalism: Its Origin and Development, Taj Mohammad Breseeg says that Baloch resistance to the British was caused by different clan chiefs with their own ideas. "The lack of communication between the Baloch tribes and contact with the Indian people, the fact that the enemy had more weapons and resources, and the lack of a proper political organization to rally the masses" were all reasons why a national struggle didn't happen.

According to Devasher, the establishment of the Anjuman-e-Ittehad-e-Balochistan in 1929 marked the emergence of a "secular, non-tribal nationalist movement" . Most of the members and leaders of the group "were from the urban bourgeoisie, large and small, educated youth, and nationalist-minded members of the clergy and tribal aristocracy" . Finally, as also stated by Breseeg , it is pertinent to list the demands made by them:

1. Reform in the Khanate.
2. Unification of the traditional Baloch lands which were divided between different administrative units (and countries).
3. Establishment of a sovereign, independent and united Balochistan.

Accession to Pakistan

Baloch nationalism and rebellion got worse when India and Pakistan were split up in 1947, just like many other problems that have always been a part of South Asia. As the British left and it became clear that India and Pakistan would be split up, the state of Kalat chose to stay independent and not join either India or Pakistan. In 1946, M.A. Jinnah, the founder of Pakistan and the legal advisor to the Khan of Kalat at the time, sent a memorandum to the Cabinet Mission arguing that "Geographically, Kalat does not fall within the territorial limits of India" and "ethnographically, the people of Kalat and of the territories under its suzerainty, have no affinities with the people of India."

After that, a new Parliament, a new constitution, and a new flag were made and used to set up the government of Kalat. In late August of 1947, there were also elections for the two parts of Parliament. Pakistan at first agreed to let Kalat be independent, but "Jinnah had second thoughts... and now wanted to get its accession in the same way that other rulers who joined Pakistan had agreed to" So, when talks between the two countries broke down, Pakistan invaded Kalat and "the Khan was forced to sign the merger document," and Kalat became part of Pakistan. In 1948, the Khan's brother led the first armed uprising against the government.

After the first time the Baloch rebelled against the government, and before 2004, they did it three more times: in 1958, 1963–69, and 1973–77. Devasher is right when he says that "every Baloch rebellion has lasted longer than the one before it, covered a larger area than the one before it, and involved more Baloch than the one before it." For example, the first two periods were pretty small, but in 1973, "55,000 insurgents faced 80,000 Pakistani troops who were backed by both the Pakistani Air Force and the Iranian Air Force." In the uprising that lasted until 1977, more than 5,000 rebels and more than 3,300 soldiers were killed.

Pakistan's constant and harsh reaction has led to a "psychological alienation from Islamabad" among the Baloch, which has made many of them want independence from the state rather than provincial autonomy. Tension and violence had been building up for a few years, but the current time of conflict began in 2005 when a female doctor, Shazia Khalid, was raped in the small Baloch town of Sui in the Dera Bugti Area. "The captain and three members of the Defence Security Guards are said to have done it," the BBC said. The government's handling of the situation afterward and its obvious attempts to hide the crime and protect the people who did it caused a lot of anger.

With the rise of Baloch nationalist groups like the Balochistan National Party (BNP) in the 1990s, there was hope for political peace. However, Pervez Musharraf's coup in 1999 and his aggressive stance helped start the insurgency. The state said that the conflict was caused by the tribal chiefs (Sardars), but the tense relationships had been going on for decades and were "centered on grievances related to provincial sovereignty, the allocation of resources, interprovincial migrations, and the protection of local language and culture."

Primary Factors behind the Insurgency

Political Isolation

One of the main reasons for the rebellion is that the dominant Punjabis have taken over the Baloch and many other ethnic groups. The Punjabis control not only the federal (central) government, but also all of the state's institutions and machinery. The Baloch have been totally cut off from the rest of the state because their population is so small. Only about 6% of the state's people live in the province, but it takes up almost 44% of the state. Also, there aren't enough Baloch in all of the "organs of the Pakistani State," and even most of the province jobs are filled by people from outside of Pakistan. Because of this, it's hard for people to connect with the government. So, the government and its institutions are seen as foreigners ruling over Baloch land.

The problem of not having enough people in politics is made worse by the "belief that the Punjabi establishment did not let the Baloch governments finish their terms." For example, until the 1990s, provincial governments run by people of Baloch ethnicity only lasted for a total of three years. The first was fired after ten months by Zulfikar Ali Bhutto in 1972–73. The second government was led by Nawab Akbar Bugti and ended when Benazir Bhutto's first government took over. In the end, Akhtar Mengal led the third government for about fifteen months in 1997 and 1998. Also, "only 4 of the 179 people who joined the Pakistani cabinet at different times during the first 30 years of the country's existence were ethnic Baloch." Before the 1970s, only Akbar Bugti was a federal minister. He also led the fifth wave of rebellion until he was killed in 2006. Pervez Musharraf made Zafarullah Khan Jamali, a Baloch, Prime Minister in 2002, but he had to quit after only nineteen months, making him one of the Prime Ministers who served the shortest amount of time.

Frederic Grare also says that Baloch nationalist parties were able to get support and form the government in the late 1990s by working with major parties or joining them. But in the elections of 2002, "the military rigged the elections and renewed its long-standing alliance with the region's mullahs," which helped the union of religious Islamic parties called Muttahida Majlis-e-Amal (MMA) win power. Also, the Election Commission of Pakistan worked with the establishment to disqualify some qualified candidates, like Akbar Bugti, while accepting madrassa diplomas as acceptable in an attempt to Islamize the mostly secular Baloch province and movement.

Even when Baloch leaders were put in charge, they had no say in what decisions were made. For example, Mohammad Jam Yusaf was named Chief Minister in 2002, but his government was run by the Jamaat-Ulema-u-Islam, a conservative Islamist party. Musharraf also started a plan called "devolution," which was meant to make local governments "entirely dependent on the central government for their survival" and make provincial councils seem like they didn't matter. Even though it was a form of decentralization, "all provinces except Punjab saw it as imposing a centralized form of government and taking away provincial autonomy." This made Baloch nationalists angry.

Setting up the boundaries of Balochistan's voting districts is another interesting problem. The NA-272 Gwadar-cum-Lasbela district includes all 750 km of Balochistan's coastline, from Karachi to Iran. In the same way, the NA-270 is made up of the four central Balochistan districts and covers a total area of 94,452 square kilometers, which is about half the size of Punjab province and bigger than Khyber Pakhtunkhwa province. In fact, Balochistan has ten times more people in each provincial constituency and 12.8 times more people in each national constituency than the other three provinces.

In a piece called "Obfuscating Balochistan," which is a good name for it, Tahir Mehdi (2018) says that "numerical equality of constituencies does not always lead to equal suffrage." If it is taken too seriously, it can be used to push people away and make them feel less important. Mehdi points out that it is interesting that the state "legally allowed the population number in FATA (Federally Administered Tribal Areas) constituencies to be half that of the national average to make up for 'the representation deficit' that it suffers from not being part of a provincial assembly." So, it is clear that neither a politician's campaign nor the people of Balochistan can use their most important political rights. So, not only do they risk losing all political value, but this also makes them feel even more disconnected from the state.

In addition to not having enough political power, the Baloch have a small role in the bureaucracy and, by extension, in government and governing. Zia-ul-Haq promised after the fourth period of insurgency that Baloch people would have the same number of jobs in the government as their part of the population. However, this never happened. "The fake domicile certificate racket has been going on systematically and on purpose to keep the Baloch people from moving up the economic ladder," which makes the problem even worse. Since the reservations are based on provinces rather than ethnic groups, Pashtuns, who are the second biggest ethnic group in Balochistan, also get to use the quotas. But the trouble is not just with the bureaucracy. In 2002, for example, only four of the fourteen provincial government secretaries in Quetta were Baloch. Less than 500 of the 3,200 students at Balochistan University were Baloch, and only thirty of the 180 staff members were Baloch.

The previous leader of Balochistan said that Islamabad acts "like the East India Company," and he was right. Even in the army, most recruits have come from the Punjab area, while the number of Baloch recruits only went from 0.6% during British rule to 5% in the 1970s. In 1972, the leader of Balochistan said, "There aren't more than a few hundred Baloch in the whole Pakistan Army." "There are no Baloch in the famous Baloch Regiment." "The officers of the Kalat Scouts and Sibi Scouts are from Punjab, and the soldiers are from the Frontier." The problem of underrepresentation is shown by the fact that "there were only 3,753 ex-servicemen from Balochistan from 1995 to 2003, while there were 1,335,339 and 229,856 ex-servicemen from North Punjab and NWFP during the same time period." Even though the state has a 750-kilometer-long coastline, there are no Baloch in the Navy.

Like in the Bureaucracy, Pashtuns from Balochistan rather than ethnic Baloch fill the Army limits. The Pashtuns now make up about 35% of the people living in Balochistan, and most of them live in the northern areas. The Baloch are always worried that the growing number of Pakhtoon and other Pakistanis will push them to the side in their own state. Since the Soviet invasion of Afghanistan in 1979, there has been a big influx of Afghan refugees of Pashtun origin. This has made this fear worse, and "Pashtun claims of equal or even majority population in Balochistan" have made the Baloch a minority in their own country.

Economic Hardship and Lack of Progress

Balochistan is Pakistan's poorest region, and its rich natural resources are still being used to make money. This makes people feel even more left out of politics and like they are being colonized by the state. Selig Harrison said in 1981 that "the belief that Baluchistan has a lot of natural resources that haven't been used is central to the separatist creed." One of the most important reasons why the province is an important part of Pakistan is because of its economic potential. The insurgency, on the other hand, is caused by the lack of local ownership and benefits.

In a speech to the Kalat State Assembly on December 12, 1947, the governor at the time, Baksh Bizenjo, said, "Officials in Pakistan say that Balochistan should join Pakistan because it couldn't survive on its own economically." We have a lot of materials, oil, and ports. Where would Pakistan be if we weren't there?" Even though Balochistan only adds about 4% to Pakistan's GDP, it gives almost 40% of the country's energy needs through natural gas, coal, and electricity. Large amounts of uranium, coal, platinum, gold, silver, copper, and aluminum are also found in the area. Many of these deposits haven't been looked into yet, and the government wants to start new projects and grow old ones to meet the needs.

On the other hand, "more than 50 years after the first Sui gas was found, 70% of the provincial population of Balochistan still doesn't have access to this resource, and 78% don't have electricity." Grare also says that Balochistan only uses about 17% of its own resources, while the other 83% "is sent to the rest of the country." Also, the central government charges a much lower price for Baluch gas than it does for gas from Sind and Punjab. Also, the gas fields were not connected to the town of Dera Bugti until the middle of the 1990s, when a militia camp was set up in the area. Even in 2014, 59% of the urban population did not have access to gas, but in Punjab, 97% of the people did.

The central government has never put money into building up the region's basic infrastructure. "Over the period from 1989-90 to 2015-16, the average allocation for development projects through the Public Sector Development Plan (PSDP) was less than 6% of the total federal PSDP allocations and just 0.19 % of the national GDP." However, the actual amount spent on development projects is still less than the allocations.

Also, after the rule for the seventh National Financial Commission (NFC) in 2009 was changed to take poverty and underdevelopment into account in addition to population, Balochistan's share went from 5% to 9%, while it went down slightly in other provinces. However, "most of these funds have been used up by the increase in development funds for legislators and payments to federal security agencies on "internal security" duty in the province."

Social and Economic Problems

According to the Human Development Index, most of the Balochistan areas are among the worst in the country, with Dera Bugti, which has a lot of gas, being the worst. According to a 2008 World Bank report, Balochistan has the "weakest long-term growth, the worst quality of employment, and the weakest social development" of all provinces. The province grew by an average of 2.8%, which is less than the 4% it grew by in the 1980s and 1990s. Other provinces grew by an average of 4.5–5.5% between 2000 and 2011. The province also "gets the lowest scores in the 10 key indicators for health, water, sanitation, and education for 2007-2008." Also, a report from the United Nations Development Programme in 2003 said that about 62% of the population didn't have access to safe drinking water. In 2015, another report said that "roughly 60% to 70% of the population is expected to be directly or indirectly at risk from droughts in the area." Even though the province's part of the country's total population is only 6%, it has nearly 20% of the country's unemployed. This, of course, makes other problems worse or creates new ones.

A report from 2016 said that "two out of three households in Balochistan cannot afford a proper meal," and that "83.4% of children in the province are severely malnourished." This led the provincial health minister to declare a nutritional emergency in 2018. In terms of social indicators like death rate and infant mortality rate, the report makes a clear comparison between Balochistan and Punjab. It also compares Balochistan to war-torn countries like Somalia and Liberia. According to Ali, Pakistan needs to: Invest in taking care of its people, especially in the health and education sectors. Balochistan and other rural parts of Pakistan have a hard time getting ahead economically because resources aren't shared fairly and there aren't enough health care facilities. Balochistan needs a health, education, and development corridor in addition to the CPEC.

Infrastructure

The big infrastructure projects, like the Gwadar International port, the China-Pakistan Economic Corridor (CPEC), the Saindak copper-gold project, and the Reko Diq project, are another big point of disagreement between the Baloch and the state. As was said in the last part, the Baloch see these projects as tools of colonization because they serve the state's strategic needs but don't help the people of the province in any way.

The province only gets a small amount of money from the natural resources in the area, because it is only entitled to 12.4% of the royalties for providing gas. For example, the province brings in nearly $1.4 billion USD a year from gas sales, but the government only gives it $116 million USD in royalties. In the same way, the Chinese run the Saindak project, but only give 2% of the total earnings to the Baloch. Instead, they take 80% and give 18% to the Pakistani federal government.

Interestingly, "the federal government violates the right of Baloch province (and the constitution of Pakistan), and only Islamabad and Lahore have had the power to make any decisions" about giving land to both foreign and domestic players. Also, in 2013, the Chief Minister of Balochistan said, "We don't know how much gold and other minerals the Chinese company is digging out of the Saindak project." The fact that the provincial government has no power over either the land or the resources of the province is also a big part of the problem.

Even though "the Baluch are determined to stop further exploration and development without their consent," the federal government regularly gives contracts or leases for the extraction of "19 trillion cubic feet of gas and 6 trillion barrels of oil reserves in Baluchistan." In the last few years, for example, "nearly six new exploration concessions were signed with Pakistani and foreign companies, but the province had no say in the matter."

The two Chinese megaprojects, the Gwadar port and the CPEC, are at the heart of the insurgency. They can't be separated because the success of one rests on the other. The building of the Gwadar port began in 2002. Since then, the people of Balochistan have been very critical of it for many different reasons. The Baloch were not involved in any way in the planning of the project. As part of the deal, Gwadar was leased to the Chinese for forty years. Also, fifty percent of the wealth will go to Pakistan and forty-eight percent will go to China, leaving only two percent for the province.

Many fishers, who make up about 80% of the local population, had to leave their homes because of the project. They were never given any money to make up for this. According to the former Chief Secretary of Balochistan, the government of the province lost trillions of rupees because "land grabbing became one of the most controversial issues when Punjabi elites took land from locals who didn't have proof of ownership." Aslam noticed something important:

Most of the technical jobs at the port were taken by Punjabis and other non-Baloch workers. The central government hasn't done anything to train local people. The Baloch also worry that once the government's plans for the port are finished, the population of Gwadar and the surrounding districts will grow from about 70,000 to about 2 million. This will change the ethnic makeup of the area dramatically as more Punjabis, Sindhis, and other workers move there to work.

There is also a growing fear that Pakistan and China are trying to turn Gwadar into a naval camp because of the port's strategic location. This would make the area even more militarized and pose a constant threat to the Baloch. As part of the port and the CPEC, the Chinese plan to settle nearly 500,000 Chinese. This will have major effects on the national, economic, and historical rights of the Baloch. Since so many Chinese are going to move to Balochistan, the Baloch are worried that the population will change in a way that can't be changed back and that they will be left out even more.

Even as the insurgency got worse, CPEC became a more important problem in the country. In 2013, the government, which was run by a Punjabi named Nawaz Sharif, changed the project's original (and shortest) route from Balochistan and KPK to Sindh and Punjab. People in Balochistan liked the first path and the idea of investment, but when the route was changed, people from all walks of life protested. By connecting Gwadar to Karachi, the Baloch fear that "they are being turned into a landlocked province even though they have the longest coastline in the country."

In 2015, the President of the Balochistan National Party (BNP) said, "All they are doing is building a modern Punjab with all the facilities it needs and boosting its economy." Another report from the Federation of Pakistan Chambers of

Commerce and Industry (FPCCI) confirmed what everyone in Balochistan had been afraid of. It said that "at the current rate of influx of Chinese nationals into Balochistan and after completion of the China Pakistan Economic Corridor (CPEC), the native population of the area will be outnumbered by 2048".

Since 2004, Baloch insurgents have repeatedly attacked Chinese workers in Pakistan. This shows that they are very unhappy with these projects and their future chances. Most of the killings in Gwadar were done to Chinese workers. In August 2018, the BLA (Balochistan Liberation Army) carried out the first-ever suicide attack by a Baloch Nationalist. The attack was on a bus with Chinese workers and guards from the Frontier Corps. The goal was to "warm China to leave Balochistan and stop stealing its resources."

In November, the 3 BLA attackers tried again to use suicide bombs to get into the Chinese embassy in Karachi (Hassan, 2018). In fact, Baloch nationalists often attack energy infrastructure, especially transnational gas pipes and other ways of getting gas to people, because, like Chinese workers, they are seen as helping Pakistan's colonial projects and making money from them. Baloch(s) are always making the war more expensive for the Pakistani government by systematically attacking economic infrastructure and often cutting off energy supplies.

Government Oppression

Baloch rebellion has been going on for a long time because there hasn't been a clear political solution yet. Instead, most of the time, the Baloch and the state have dealt with each other in a harsh and military way. Grare says that "the state's repressive response radicalized most of the 'nationalist' movement," and that the possibility of a political solution "disappeared, or at least became much less likely, as soon as it became clear that the military regime wanted to get rid of the nationalist leadership." So, the rebellion has been kept going in large part because the military is violent and the government doesn't do enough to stop it.

Balochistan had "four existing cantonments at Quetta, Sibi, Loralai, and Khuzdar, three naval bases, four testing sites, two nuclear development sites, and fifty-nine paramilitary facilities" before the start of the fifth period. "35,000 FC, 12,000 Coast Guards, 1,150 Levis, 6,000 Balochistan Reserve police, 2,000 marines, and four army brigades are deployed in Balochistan," said the Human Rights Commission of Pakistan. When people won't sell their land, the military has been taking it over by force more and more. Devasher says that the cantonments have become their own kind of parallel government, where the provincial government (and sometimes even the central government) does not have authority.

After a series of attacks on security forces in 2005, both the Inspector General of Frontier Corps and President Musharraf said that they "rejected any political compromise and went to Military Intelligence, who told him to crush the opposition." Musharraf also thought that Nawab Akbar Bugti was in charge of the Baloch, so he went on TV and told the Baloch, "Don't push us. We are not in the 1970s. They won't even know what's going on."

In August 2006, Bugti and sixty other people were killed in the mountain hideout where they had been living. The rebellion got a lot worse after Bugti was killed. Musharraf made sure that "not only the Baloch rebels, but also the rest of the Baloch population, who didn't believe in taking up arms but were still angry at Islamabad for not developing the province, were against him." In 2006, the war had spread from 6% of the province to almost half of it. In September, the Khan of Kalat called a meeting of all the tribal chiefs, called a Grand Jirga. The International Crisis Group gives a good explanation of what happened at the meeting:

It was attended by 380 leaders, including 85 sardars. This disproved Musharraf's claim that all but three sardars supported him. The jirga protested Bugti's death and asked the International Court of Justice (ICJ) in The Hague to stop the "violation of territorial integrity, exploitation of Balochistan's natural resources, denial of the Baloch right to ownership of their resources, and military operation in the province." Baloch separatists say that the jirga achieved both of its goals: to bring attention to the Baloch cause around the world and to bring together the different Baloch tribes and groups.

Musharraf's reaction to Baloch nationalists and militants was to set up more military cantonments and outposts all over the province. The government started a full-scale military operation against the Baloch militants and even attacked civilians in Baluchistan with Cobra helicopters and F-16s. Also, the military "launched major security operations" in the Marri Bugti areas, which caused 200,000 people to leave their homes. Twenty to thirty thousand of these people found refuge in Afghanistan.

Between 2006 and 2010, there were more than 1,600 deaths in a total of 1,850 events. Almost half of the deaths were citizens, 23% were militants, and 22% were security forces. Some of the people are also well-known Baloch leaders, like Balach Marri, who was the boss of the BLA and was killed by the Army during an operation near the Afghan border. In April 2009, three well-known Baloch nationalist leaders from the middle class were taken from their lawyer's office in broad daylight and their abused bodies were found in Turbat.

Because of this, the extremists have slowly moved from attacking and bombing government buildings and pipelines to attacking Punjabi settlers and security forces. Killings of Punjabis and people of other nationalities became more common. For example, "well-known non-Baloch teachers and professors at universities, schools, and colleges have been killed, and as a result, many schools have stopped working." The state's use of too much violence and repression also led to a trans-tribal Baloch nationalism, which Lieven explains further:

Due to the growth of a Baloch urban society in Quetta over the past few decades, and especially the rise of a trans-tribal Baloch "intelligentsia" that is only partially trained by Balochistan's poor higher education system and can't find work in the province's poor economy. This class naturally shares a lot of Baloch anger about how non-Baloch have taken over the Baloch economy. This part of the population doesn't see a future for itself in Pakistan. Because of this, it is a very important part of the nationalist movement.

Still, the 'kill-and-dump' operations or 'forcing disappearances' have been the military's most well-known way to control people. Baloch students, doctors, nationalists, lawyers, and journalists have been intimidated, arrested at random, tortured, disappeared, and killed without due process since 2006. All of these people were held, but none of them were tried in a court of law. Most of the time, people are kidnapped only to be added to the list of missing people, which is always growing. Many times, their bodies are found badly disfigured by the side of the road or their bones are found in mass graves."

The exact number of people who were kidnapped or killed is still unknown because they are kept very secret. However, during the Musharraf administration, which ended in August 2008, "Baloch nationalists claim that the number is in the thousands," while the provincial and federal governments say it is between 1,000 and 1,100. Bashir Azeem, the Secretary-General of the Baloch Republican Party (BRA), who was taken into custody in 2010, says that he was told, "Even if the president or chief justice tells us to let you go, we won't. We can kill you, abuse you, or hold you for years if we want to. We only listen to the Army chief and the chief." After the Supreme Court set up an inquiry commission to look into the case, the commission's head said that "the government seems helpless in the face of the spy agencies."

Decline of the Rebellion

As both sides kept up their cycle of violence, a few things happened that made the rebellion stop moving forward for a while. The Armed Conflict Location & Event Data Project (ACLED) says that the Baloch insurgency hit its peak in 2015, with 96 violent events and 383 reported deaths. This is up from almost 80 violent events and 300 reported deaths in 2014. But "from 2017 to 2019, ACLED records 38 events with a total of 110 reported deaths."

In 2015, the Pakistani government started a program to help Baloch rebels give up their weapons and get back on their feet. The government says that over the past few years, almost 2,000 Baloch rebels have turned themselves in to the security forces. As part of the amnesty plan, the rebels who turned themselves in were to get money and jobs with the government. But the identities of the militants who turned themselves in are still unknown, which makes it hard to believe that the story is true. In fact, in 2017 "Baloch separatist and leader of the Baloch Liberation Army Abdul Rasool and his group turned themselves in to the security forces."

Through Islamization of the region, both the military and the government have tried to stop the secular, ethnic, and tribal movements and identities. Most Baloch have turned down the process of Islamization. Along with supporting anti-nationalists and bribing rival tribe leaders, the state actively supports Deobandi madrassas and groups like Jamaat-ud-Dawa, Lashkar-e-Taiba, and Lashkar-e-Janghvi, which often recruits young Baloch people. This has made things harder for the Baloch rebels because they now have to fight both the government and its troops, as well as extremists who are backed by the government.

Still, the main reason why the rebellion is getting weaker is because of the insurgents. After the insurgents started attacking Baloch lawmakers and settlers who weren't Baloch, they "turned off the moderate Baloch political parties that were against violence by questioning their patriotism and dedication to the 'national cause.'" The attacks also break the Baloch code of behavior, called "Balochmayar," and "alienate Baloch supporters who live outside the province and the country."

This group, along with the political elite, "who talk nationalist talk but are usually close to Pakistan," has also hurt the movement's reputation. For example, Obaidullah, a Lashkar-e-Balochistan captain who gave up, said, "Our leaders led us into a trap by saying they were fighting for the rights of the Baloch, but we found out later that they were living lavishly abroad while sending us and our families to fight here."

Rivalries between the Baloch and a lack of leadership have also been major flaws of the uprising. According to the ACLED study, the insurgency lost a leader when Nawab Khair Bakhsh Marri died in 2014. He gave Baloch armed movements an ideological base and was credited by many for starting the most recent wave of Baloch militancy. This made his two sons unhappy about who should take over, and they finally split into two different groups. Separatist groups in Balochistan are split into two different groups. The first group is made up of BLA, BNLF, and UBA. The second group is made up of BLA and BNLF.

In the past, Baloch groups were able to strengthen their control over different areas and work together to attack a shared enemy. But after 2014, the groups were busy attacking each other, sometimes even their own members. This led to a lot of deaths and a steady game of who was to blame. The military was happy about this, and they were able to make progress in parts of the district that had been called "no-go areas" before. Last but not least, the nationalists haven't been able to come up with a clear plan or a good option for Balochistan's future because they are divided.

Lastly, as of July 31, 2020, 30 planned violent events involving Baloch separatists and 95 deaths have happened this year, with 75 percent of the deaths involving security forces. This is because the two biggest militant groups, BLA and BLF, have come together to make a new alliance called the Baloch Raaji Ajoi Sangar (BRAS). This alliance is made up of the two groups that used to fight each other. In July 2020, BRAS and the Sindhudesh Revolutionary Army (SRA) worked together to attack the Karachi Stock Exchange. BRAS later announced a formal operational alliance with the "Sindh-based militant group that wants to create an independent homeland for Sindhis, the people who live in Sindh province and are the province's native ethnic group." Both groups have also been trying to hurt the Chinese.

The partnership was also made because the military was making life harder in Baloch villages, so it is likely that they want to get back at the military. The group has carried out "26 attacks in the province during the first three months of 2020" with "a degree of technical sophistication in making bombs and in the availability of human intelligence needed to track security forces' communications in the province." As the military started a campaign against the groups along the border with Iran, the Baloch spoke out more about the growing number of people who are being taken away against their will.

Conclusion

The Baloch have been fighting against the Pakistani government for almost 72 years. Even though the Baloch's problems have mostly stayed the same, they keep getting worse. It goes from one phase to the next, just like the uprising. Balochistan is a sign of the bigger problems that Pakistan is having as a country. The state stays a Punjabi nation that is ruled by people from other countries. Pakistan's tendency to become more centralized and authoritarian has led it to try to use violence and the military to solve a problem that is mostly political and economic. This again brings up the problem of the military-intelligence complex going too far against its own people and the poor state of the country's minorities.

Lastly, through different times of insurgency, the Baloch show that they are strong and able to give a grassroots cause momentum that won't go away even if they don't win. Pakistan needs to rethink how it treats Balochistan and other provinces, nations, and minorities because of this. The rebels should do the same with their own violations of human rights and weaknesses if they want to be taken seriously and get a lot of support. The best way for the state to make peace with Balochistan is to put the Baloch people, not their riches, at the center. Even if the military is able to control the insurgents, the Baloch will still be there, and there is a chance that there will be a sixth time of insurgency. So, the Pakistani government is actively reliving the past.

Chapter 6
Government Apathy and State Collaboration

Introduction

Pakistan is a scary place for religious, ethnic, and ideological minorities. Minority groups have been pushed into ghettos and driven to leave because of violence, both direct and indirect, and because it happens so often. The Hazaras in the Balochistan area are the only people who are facing violence that could kill them. Hazaras are an ethnic group that lives mostly in Afghanistan, but there are also between 650,000 and 900,000 of them in Pakistan, according to figures. Most Hazara people in Pakistan live in Quetta, which is the capital city of Balochistan. Even though some Hazaras are Sunni, most of them are Shia.

In Pakistan, sectarian violence has been a problem for decades, but in Balochistan, it is a relatively new problem. In 2003, gunmen went into a mosque during Friday prayers and killed more than 50 Hazaras. This was the first big attack on the Hazaras. Lashkar-e-Jhangvi (LeJ), a group of Sunni fundamentalists, has led the fight against the Hazaras in Pakistan. In 2011, LeJ sent out a letter that was widely shared in Quetta. It said, "We will make Pakistan the graveyard of the Shi'ite Hazaras, and bombs and suicide bombers will destroy their homes. Jihad against the Shi'ite Hazaras has now become our duty." A website that keeps track of human rights violations against Hazaras says that the group has been attacked more than 200 times since 1999. The fact that LeJ can attack Hazaras with no consequences shows that they are working with some people in the government. The people in charge of security don't see ethnic groups as a major threat to the state's stability. In fact, it has often used them as important strategic assets in its security strategy for both its own country and the countries around it. So, the state has not been as determined to get rid of religiously motivated extremist groups as it has been to get rid of other types of insurgent groups in the area.

The Situation

The explosion on April 12, 2019, which killed 19 people, including eight Hazaras, is just one more warning of how vulnerable the Hazaras are. The shooting happened in Hazarganji, in a market for fruits and vegetables on the edge of Quetta. The Hazara people come to this market to buy fruits and veggies to sell in their own shops. After a series of deadly attacks in the past, the cops started going to the market with them. On this day, a suicide bomber blew himself up in the veggie market, according to the police and the Balochistan Home Minister, Zia Langove. His vest was full of explosives.

It was the community's first big attack in more than a year. In the past few years, some of the worst killings that have happened in the country have been against the Hazaras. There have been attacks on funerals, religious processions, mosques, and culture events. More than 100 people were killed and more than 250 were hurt in the attack on Yaum-al-Quds in December 2010. As a result, hundreds of Hazara students at Balochistan University stopped going to class out of fear. In another case of killing people on purpose, armed men stopped a bus bringing about 40 Hazaras from Quetta to Iran at the border post in Mastung. The bus was on its way to Iran from Quetta. The Sunnis on the bus were let go, but 26 Hazara men and boys were lined up and shot while the women and children on the bus were forced to watch. Later that day, three of the Hazara survivors were killed by shooters as they tried to get the injured to a hospital in Quetta. At least 180 Hazara people were killed when bombs went off in Quetta in January and February 2013.In its 2018 report, the National Commission on Human Rights (NCHR) says that since 1999, suicide bombings and targeted strikes have killed more than 2,000 Hazaras. In the last five years, more than 500 people died and more than 600 were hurt.

Their physical room has shrunk because of the constant security risks. They now live in two ghettos, one in the east (Marriabad) and one in the west (Hazara Town) of the city. In response, the government has built stronger walls and limited traffic on streets that lead to the twin areas. Because of this, attacks inside Hazara districts have gone down, but attacks outside of these areas have gone up. This has forced the Hazaras to stay in these two townships, making them feel like a caged community. Some Hazaras try to hide their faces so they can't be identified by covering their heads or wearing sunglasses or traditional Baloch caps. But most of the time, these strategies haven't worked. Because they can't move around as much, they are having a hard time financially and can't get to school or other places of interest as easily. Many have gone to other countries, mostly Australia, to get away from dangerous situations. People say that more than 70,000 Hazaras have left Quetta, and thousands are stuck in Indonesia. Hundreds of people have died because the boats turned over in Indonesian seas on their way to Australia.

Identity of Hazaras

Sunni terrorist groups see the Shia sect that Hazaras belong to as heretical. Sectarian groups think that Shia heterodoxy is like leaving the faith and should be punished with death. Even though Shias in different parts of the country have been attacked on occasion, the fact that Hazaras are easy to spot makes things worse. A well-known Pakistani writer named Mohammed Hanif says, "The cursed fate of the Hazara is staring them in the face." Their unique looks, which make them look like Central Asian Turks and Mongolians, make them easy to catch. About 600,000 of the 2.3 million people who live in Quetta are Hazaras.

The past of the Hazaras is a painful story of losing their race, killing their own people, and staying strong. The Hazaras are a large group in Afghanistan. They are mostly Shia and make up 9 percent of the country's population. The Hazara people have moved into Pakistan on and off over the ages. They first moved to Balochistan from Bamiyan, which is in central Afghanistan and is a Hazara area. Under the rule of Pashtun Emir Abdul Rehman Khan at the end of the 19th century, they were treated very badly. Scholars think that more than half of the Hazara people were killed or forced to leave their homes. Many people were able to escape to Balochistan, where they settled in and around Quetta. During the end of the British era, some people came to Quetta to work on the Indian Railways.

But the Hazaras did not stop moving from Afghanistan to Quetta after Rehman Khan's rule ended. Thousands of people have left Afghanistan both during the Afghan war (1979–1989) and since the Taliban became the most powerful group in the country. Sunni fundamentalists in the Taliban see Shia Muslims as people who say bad things about God. They have killed people, burned down villages, and taken hostages from the Shia community, which is mostly made up of Hazaras, the country's third biggest ethnic group. The fact that the Hazaras are seen as friends of the Northern Alliance, the Taliban's rivals, is another reason why they dislike them.

In August of 1998, the Taliban killed many Hazara Shia people in Mazar-i-Sharif. One story said that Hazaras were shot in front of their families or had their throats cut, just like Muslims kill goats for holiday meals. After the Taliban took over Mazar-i-Sharif, women from Hazara neighborhoods were kidnapped and raped. But as the world's politics have changed and the Taliban's relationship with Iran has warmed up, it seems likely that the Taliban has also changed its mind about the Hazaras. In 2015, it even spoke out against an attack by the Islamic State in which 13 Hazaras were killed. Even though relations between the Taliban and the Hazaras may have gotten better in Afghanistan, the Hazaras of Balochistan are still being hurt by ethnic violence in Pakistan.

Intolerance and Disregard

The problems of religious minorities in general and the Hazaras in particular are made worse by the shocking disregard of the ruling elites and law enforcement agencies to the repeated attacks by sectarian groups inside the country. The people in power seem to have either gotten used to the violence against the Hazara or are too afraid to work with them to stop the violence. Also, protests by Hazaras don't get much support or unity from other ethnic groups in Pakistan or elsewhere. Even though Imran Khan, the current Prime Minister of Pakistan, had criticized Nawaz Sharif for not caring about the troubled community, he did not go to Hazarganj to show his own sorrow after the terrible attack. After backlash from the public, he didn't go to a university in Quetta for more than a week. When he did, he mixed up his official job of opening a new housing scheme with a quick meeting with the families of the victims. The fact that he didn't want to go to the Hazara town at first and then thought it would be a good idea to take the grieving families to a local university for a consolation meeting was unbecoming of a leader who had claimed to make politics more fair and compassionate.

The comments made by the then-Chief Minister Nawab Aslam Raisani after Hazara travelers were killed on purpose in the Mastung district in 2012 were perhaps the clearest example of political apathy. When asked how he would stop the Hazaras from crying, the minister said, "Of the millions of people who live in Balochistan, 40 dead in Mastung isn't a big deal." I will send a stack of tissues to the families who have lost someone. If I wasn't a politician, I'd send tobacco.' There is more to people's indifference to the situation of Hazaras than a few rude comments here and there. In the security system, there is a lot of discrimination against the Hazara people. They are seen as "agents of Iran" and "untrustworthy," and their claims of being persecuted are seen as "exaggerated" in order to "gain financial and political support from Iran to carry out its agenda in Pakistan." Worse, even the previous Chief Minister Abdul Malik Baloch, who is a doctor by trade, thinks that the Hazaras are partly to blame for their own plight because they don't marry into other groups like the Baloch and Pashtuns have.

Conspiracy

The Qari Husain group of the Tehrik-e-Taliban Pakistan (TTP) and the Islamic State (IS) both said they were behind the attack on April 12. LeJ and TTP are said to have worked together to plan and carry out the attack. LeJ has been at the front of a genocidal war against the Hazaras. They are very sectarian and hate Shias and Iran very much. It wants to get rid of Shias so that Pakistan can become a Sunni state. It is said to have operational links with other terrorist groups in Afghanistan and Kashmir, like Harkat-ul-Mujahideen and Jaish-e-Muhammad, as well as with the Taliban and al-Qaeda. People also say that LeJ has joined forces with the IS.

Scholars, people who work for human rights, and victims all point the finger at the government for not doing anything, helping radicals, or giving them covert support. The people who do the killings do so in broad daylight and don't do much to hide their identities. The fact that militants are able to do their jobs so easily and with such bravado makes me wonder if the cops are so weak that they can't catch or stop them, or if there is some kind of unspoken agreement between them. People often say that the problem with religious extremism in Pakistan is that the government isn't sure what to do about it. This could be because different governments have used fanatics to achieve their strategic goals in neighboring countries.

Scholars at well-known think tanks in the West, like the United States Institute of Peace (USIP), have criticized Pakistan for having "a complex and contradictory but close historical relationship between the state and the LeJ both in Balochistan and elsewhere." Human Rights Commission of Pakistan (HRCP) and Human Rights Watch (HRW) use a number of cases to back up their claims that the state supports radical groups.

For example, HRCP points to the case of Saifullah Kurd and Shafeeq Rind, two well-known criminals who admitted to killing dozens of Hazaras after they were caught. But they somehow got out of a very well-guarded Anti-Terrorist Force (ATF) jail in Quetta Cantonment, where HRCP says that no one can enter or leave without a pass, suggesting that the ATF helped them get out. It also says that people who were caught and sentenced by the courts lived a comfortable life in bars, where they were treated like VIPs and had access to things like TVs and cell phones. The panel says that there were times when prisoners led prayers and policemen prayed behind them. Some police officers have already been put on trial for working with LeJ, which shows how far sectarianism has reached into Pakistan's security system.

The government has banned the LeJ, its predecessor Sipahi-e-Sahaba Pakistan (SSP), and its current incarnation Ahle Sunnat Wal Jamaat (ASWJ). However, they still hold rallies with both armed and unarmed supporters in places where the Frontier Corps (FC) is present in large numbers. This means that "the police and the courts don't have the power to investigate, prosecute, and convict sectarian killers," or, more likely, that the intelligence services stop them from doing so. In fact, some people say that the military and intelligence services often help these militants escape or get out of jail if the police catch them. After an attack on Hazaras, the FC is known to go after rebels and round up Baloch youth instead of the real attackers. Malik Ishaq, the feared leader of LeJ, was arrested several times by the police, but in 40 terrorism-related cases, he was found not guilty because there wasn't enough proof and all witnesses refused to testify. He planned some of the most horrible acts, like the bombings in Quetta in 2013 that killed almost 200 Hazaras. In 2014, the US Department of State called him a "Specially Designated Global Terrorist."

Ishaq was killed for good in 2015 in Punjab province, along with his two kids and 11 other militants. There is so much doubt about this kind of action that many people in Pakistan thought that the meeting had been "staged," since he was likely to be freed again. Some people still liked that he was killed because it showed the government's new determination to get rid of anti-Shia militants. However, the "extra-judicial" way he was killed throws doubt on Pakistan's legal and justice system. Some critics pointed out that Ishaq was killed not because the State cut ties with extremist groups for good, but because he got in trouble with the military system. Ishaq had been a big help to the Pakistani military and spy agencies up until this point. In 2009, he was taken from Lahore to Rawalpindi on a military plane to help free some high-ranking military officers who had been taken hostage by armed people. But by 2015, he might have gone bad or become a problem for the agencies, which would have led to his encounter killing. It could have been because the deep state was getting more worried about the LeJ as an organization that had gotten out of hand and was becoming a major threat to it.

Usman Saifullah Kurd, who was the leader of the LeJ group in Balochistan, was killed by police in Quetta in 2015. After Ishaq and Kurd were killed, ethnic violence against Hazaras dropped sharply. Dawood Badini was Saifullah Kurd's second-in-command. He was not as ambitious as Saifullah Kurd and dodged large-scale attacks in favor of killing smaller targets. The explosion at Hazarganji on April 12 of this year broke the "lull" and marked a return to the old ways of doing the most damage. Even though the attack was blamed on a part of the TTP and not the LeJ as a whole, the fact remains that both the LeJ and the TTP have created a kind of mutually beneficial relationship, and it is thought that there is a link between the operations of different Sunni sectarian groups in the province.

The April 2019 attack brought to light two things: that the infrastructure of extremism is still in place, even though the leaders of LeJ were killed, and that despite what the military said, the deep state has not cut its secret links with those who spread sectarian violence. Ramzan Mengal, the head of the province for the illegal ASWJ and a well-known preacher of sectarian hate against

Shias, was released two days before the Hazarganji attack. Mengal is said to have admitted to killing many Hazaras. In the 2018 election for the National Assembly, Mengal was allowed to run. Even though he didn't win, there were a lot of sectarian chants on the campaign trail.

Importantly, after this attack, the Hazaras stopped the road in bad weather to ask for better security and action against extremists. After another round of weak assurances from the government, the Hazaras stopped their angry and sad sitins, which they did after every attack. But Hazaras are not going to get better, at least not in the near future. The Hazaras know this, but they have no choice but to seek safety from the state's security managers, who seem to be friendly with the people who hurt them. For real and long-lasting change to happen, Pakistan's security strategy must be changed from the ground up. The strategy of using extremists for short- or long-term strategic purposes needs to be thrown out. Maybe the military can use the same "zero tolerance" policy against Sunni sectarians who are attacking Hazaras as it does against Baloch insurgents. This is an option that the security system has not been willing to consider until now. But there are no signs of a major change in state policy, with the focus on moving away from the current strategy of openly supporting terrorists and radical groups to use them as strategic pawns against neighboring states. Without this, it would be impossible to stop the extremists who are attacking Hazaras with no consequences.

Chapter 7
Unexplained Vanishings in Balochistan

In Pakistan's southwestern province of Balochistan, students, activists, journalists, and people who fight for human rights are still being pushed to disappear. People are taken away from their families by state officials or other people working on their behalf. This takes them out of the protection of the law. The police then deny that they have the person in custody or won't say where they are. Families of those who have gone missing are in a lot of pain and are trying to hold on to hope even though they are afraid of the worst. A lot of people have been in this state for years.

The people who have been taken away could be tortured or even killed. If they are set free, they will always have physical and mental scars. If they die, the family will never be the same again. Disappearances are a form of terror that affects not just people or families, but also whole societies. Because of this, they are against international law, and if they are part of a large-scale or systematic attack on a civilian community, they are a crime against humanity.

Forced disappearances break many human rights, such as the right to be recognized as a person in the eyes of the law, the right to freedom and security of the person, the right not to be tortured or treated badly, the right to life when a person who has disappeared is killed, the right to an identity, the right to a fair trial, the right to an effective remedy, and the right to know the truth about how a person disappeared. Forced disappearances are also a "continuous violation" because the violation happens and keeps happening until the person who went missing can be found.

In a 2014 decision, Pakistan's Supreme Court said that even though Pakistan hasn't signed the International Convention for the Protection of All Persons from Enforced Disappearance, "the Supreme Court could use the Convention to get justice done." "Forced disappearances of people," the Supreme Court said, "were a crime against humanity and a clear violation of Article 10 of the Constitution, which gave direct protection against such disappearances."

They also go against the rights of the family. Most of the people who have gone missing in Pakistan are guys, and they are often the only ones who bring money into the home. Disappearances violate the economic and social rights of the family, such as the right to protection and help for the family, the right to a decent standard of living, the right to health care, and the right to education if a child can't go to school after a parent has gone missing.

Families are often pushed to take on political roles because they have to start showing up in public as part of their desperate efforts to get their loved ones back. They have to learn how a complicated criminal justice system works, and they don't have many legal options because forced disappearances are still not illegal in Pakistan.

The United Nations (UN) Working Group on Enforced or Involuntary Disappearances also recognizes that "women and girls are victims of enforced disappearance as disappeared persons, as relatives of someone who has disappeared, or as any other person suffering harm as a result of an enforced disappearance. Women and girls experience and deal with enforced disappearances in different ways because of gender roles, which are deeply rooted in history, tradition, religion, and culture."

WGEID has until the end of 2019 to figure out what happened to 731 people who went missing in Pakistan. Pakistan's Commission of Inquiry on Forced Disappearances received 23 new cases in August 2020, bringing the overall number of cases received since March 2011 to 6,752. This is according to the monthly progress report from October 2020.

Dr Deen Mohammad

On June 28, 2009, Dr. Deen Mohammad was taken away against his will, the day after his daughter had surgery. His wife, girls, and son have been trying to get him back for more than 11 years, going to the police, courts, media, human rights groups, and even the United Nations to ask for help. Even though judges and government leaders have said many times that he would be back soon, nothing has happened in his case. They haven't heard from him, so they're worried about the worst. Because they don't know what happened to their father, they have been in pain for a long time and it has broken them mentally and financially. They protest often, and people bother them because of it. His daughter Sammi Baloch, who was only 10 years old when her father was taken, also took part in the 3,000 km long march put on by the Voice of Missing Baloch Persons. Also, they've lost their home.

Dr. Mohammad's wife has a lot of health problems, and her children spend all of their already very limited money on her care. Sammi says that they have spent their whole lives trying to get their father back. In an article for Dawn.com, she said, "I don't know why my father was arrested, but I've always said that if he did something wrong, he should be brought to court and punished after a trial. Think of him and us as equal citizens and apply the same rule to us both as you would to anyone else. Don't just get rid of him like this. Don't make us suffer."

Hani Gul and Mohammed Naseem Baloch

Hani Gul and Mohammed Naseem were getting married, but in April 2019, they were both taken by force from Karachi. Both are from the Balochistan city of Gwadar. Hani was a student at a medical school when she was taken away. Hani says she was tortured during the three months she was missing or detained, and she says that the one time she saw her boyfriend, he looked like he had been beaten.

Hani was freed in August of this year. Mohammed is still being held. No one has been blamed for taking her away. Hani says that she was kicked out of her university after she came back. This happened after she went missing.

Hassan Qambrani

Hassan Qambrani went grocery shopping on February 14, 2020, but he never came back. Hassan's family kept waiting for him to call, putting off dinner and leaving messages. Finally, a neighbor told them that they had seen Hassan get into a police car and drive away. This happened a few days after he took part in a sit-in protest in Quetta against people being taken away against their will.

Hassan's absence is not the first time someone in the family has gone missing. In 2016, their bodies, which had been cut up, were found. Hassan's sister Haseeba and his mother have been pushing hard for him to come home so that he doesn't end up like his father. At a protest, Haseeba gave a speech in which she said, "We don't party; we only mourn. We have no idea what to do next. Just be kind and give our brothers back."

Rashid Hussain Brohi

Rashid Hussain Brohi is a 24-year-old Pakistani from the city of Shahdadkot in Sindh province. He is of Baloch tribe and is of that group. He had been a member of the Baloch National Movement while he was in Pakistan. Rashid went to the United Arab Emirates in 2017 because he was afraid for his life after some of his family members and fellow activists were taken and killed for no clear reason.

But on the morning of December 26, 2018, Rashid Hussain was on his way to work with three coworkers when he was stopped by Emirati security forces.

Rashid Brohi was sent back to Noshki, Balochistan, against his will on June 22, 2019. According to the news, he was caught as soon as he got back.

Rashid hasn't been in court or been able to talk to his family or lawyer since he was sent back. On April 16, 2020, a Pakistani anti-terrorism court said that Rashid was a fugitive, even though news reports said that Pakistani officials were holding him. This means that they no longer have him in custody. Amnesty International hasn't been able to confirm this through court records, but if it's true, it's a very big deal because it means no one knows where he is, which gives the government an out if something bad happens to him.

Rashid's mother wrote in a letter to Amnesty International on June 23, 2020, "Since Rashid was sent to Pakistan, I have been protesting in different towns of Pakistan. I have been to all of Pakistan's courts and paid lawyers to defend him if he is charged with anything. No one heard how sad I was, and no one could answer my questions.

Shabbir Baloch

Shabbir was 24 years old when he went missing on October 4, 2016. His wife and he were staying with friends when, between 5 and 6 a.m., armed and uniformed Pakistani soldiers broke into their home and surrounded it. He was tied to a chair, blinded, and taken away. The family says that the police didn't make a report when he went missing. Shabbir, like Zahid, was the Information Secretary for BSOA.

Zahid Baloch

On March 18, 2014, Zahid Baloch, the leader of the Baloch Student Organization-Azad (BSOA), was taken from Quetta. Still, no one in his family knows where he is or what happened to him. Witnesses say that he was taken by force, with a gun. BSOA is a student group that wants the region of Balochistan to break away from the country of Pakistan. It was banned by the Pakistani government in March 2013 because they said it was "involved in terrorism." In an interview with the BBC six months before he went missing, Zahid claimed that his group's fight for self-determination was a peaceful one.

Pakistan's International human rights obligations

2010 was the first year that the International Convention for the Protection of All Persons from Enforced Disappearance took effect. Its goal is to stop forced disappearances, find out what really happened when they do happen, and make sure that survivors and the families of those who were hurt get justice, the truth, and compensation.

The Committee on Enforced Disappearances (CED) keeps an eye on how the Convention is carried out. A state can say that it recognizes CED's ability to receive and review communications from or on behalf of victims or other states parties when it ratifies or joins the Convention, or even later. The CED also gives official explanations of what the Convention means.

Pakistan has neither signed nor approved the Convention, even though it agreed at its 2017 Universal Periodic Review that forced disappearance should be a crime. The government has also turned down suggestions to bring the people who do these kinds of kidnappings to justice.

As a newly re-elected member of the UN Human Rights Council, Pakistan has a responsibility to "uphold the highest standards in promoting and protecting human rights." This means that Pakistan needs to do more than just admit that human rights have been broken; it also needs to take steps to stop people from getting away with it.

In March 2011, the Pakistani government set up the Commission of Inquiry into Enforced Disappearances. Its job is to "find out where allegedly enforced disappeared people are" and "name the people or groups responsible." Even though it may have found some cases, it still doesn't know where and what happened to a large number of them. Critics have also said that the Commission made many mistakes, such as using a bad meaning of "forced disappearance," limiting the scope of its investigation, not doing enough to protect victims and witnesses, and not holding the people who did wrong to account.

No one in Pakistan has been punished for the forced disappearances of people. There is nothing in the law that lets families get money back for what they went through.

Counsel

- Amnesty International calls on the Pakistani authorities to:
- Ensure that all measures are taken to immediately end the practice of enforced disappearance
- Immediately disclose the fate or whereabouts of victims of enforced disappearance to their families
- Either immediately release the victims of enforced disappearance or ensure that they are brought promptly before a judge in a civilian court to rule on the lawfulness of their arrest or detention and whether they should be released
- If people continue to be detained, ensure that they are charged with

an internationally recognizable offence and that their rights, including to a fair trial are fully respected

- Consult civil society and families of the disappeared on the draft bill to criminalize enforced disappearance and ensure that the offence is defined in accordance with international law and standards
- Ratify and implement into national law the International Convention for Protection of All Persons from Enforced Disappearance, including making declarations, pursuant to Articles 31 and 32 of the Convention, recognizing the competence of the Committee on Enforced Disappearance to receive and consider communications from individuals and states parties
- Ensure that all allegations of enforced disappearance are promptly, thoroughly, effectively, independently and impartially investigated and, where sufficient admissible evidence exists, prosecute those suspected of criminal conduct irrespective of their rank and status or the security agency they are affiliated with through fair trials
- Ensure that the victim families are free to associate with groups working on resolving the issue of enforced disappearances and to peacefully protest in public with fear of reprisal
- Ensure all victims, including family members are provided with full and effective reparation to address the harm that they have suffered

Chapter 8
CPEC- Future Scenarios and Complexities for Balochistan and Pakistan

Introduction

Balochistan has a lot of natural resources, but in the past, these resources couldn't be used as well as they could have been because of the country's hard geography and lack of infrastructure, such as roads, energy, and water. With the start of the China-Pakistan Economic Corridor (C-PEC), there are many chances to use these resources, which are expected to lead to economic actions in Balochistan that have never been seen before. From the point of view of natural resources, these activities include, but are not limited to, the development and management of water resources, the mining of coal and minerals, the exploration of unexplored hydrocarbons, the use of dimension stones and building materials, and the creation of related and subsidiary industries. All of these things require the development of human resources, better health, and educational facilities, especially institutions for the technical and skill development of the people, and, most importantly, the sustainable development of water resources and reservoirs for drinking, municipal, and industrial uses. In this study, the most important natural resources in Balochistan are listed in terms of how they can be used in a sustainable way as part of C-PEC-driven development projects. Some of these are water, minerals, fuels, shalegas, and coal. There are ideas for how to make the most of these resources to make money and help the people of Balochistan in the long run. As part of the C-PEC, a lot of big projects are already happening, like building a deep-sea port in Gwadar, building power plants, building highways, and setting up special economic zones. But it looks like small and medium-sized neighborhood businesses and production units have not gotten the attention they deserve. In this paper, it is suggested that local people and their Chinese peers could be found through local bodies and paired up to start joint ventures. Most of the production and growth areas listed in this paper are already sending goods to China through the Karachi port. So, it's clear that people in China want these goods, and there's no need to do a survey to prove it. All kinds of transportation for C-PEC will go through a big part of Balochistan, where these resources already exist, so the products suggested in this paper are likely to work.

In Pakistan's 70-year past, starting and launching the China-Pakistan Economic Corridor (C-PEC) is a major economic event that has been called a "game-changer." Since the fall of Dhaka in 1971, which led to the birth of Bangladesh, Pakistan has been trying hard to get back on track economically. Pakistan has had to deal with a number of internal and external conflicts and problems, such as the Soviet invasion of Afghanistan, the Iran-Iraq War, the Kuwait War, and the Iraq War. There has also been a lot of trouble in Afghanistan for the past 40 years, and tensions with India have gone up and down over the Kashmir issue. Both India and Pakistan have also done nuclear tests, and Pakistan's government has been unstable because of the military's control.

The One Belt One Road (OBOR) Initiative and the start of C-PEC in 2013, when China and Pakistan signed the official MoU, have given Pakistan a good chance to get its economy back on track. The goal of the C-PEC was to link the western parts of China and Pakistan by investing in energy, trade, and transportation all at once. The C-PEC will improve trade between China and the Middle East, Africa, and Central Asia through Pakistan. The corridor will be a strategic game-changer in the area, and it will definitely help Pakistan's economy grow and get stronger over the long run. This paper gives a review of the chances for Pakistan's economy to grow now and in the future, especially in Balochistan, where long-term planning is urgently and very much needed. The paper also talks about the areas to focus on for successful economic development and the natural resources in Balochistan that can help a business make money. People from Balochistan and Chinese companies should work together to start these kinds of businesses, so that the real benefits of growth reach the poorest communities.

Key Technological Domains in Pakistan

According to the latest annual report from the US National Science Foundation and the National Science Board, China is now the second-largest country in the world when it comes to spending on research and development. China spends 21% of the roughly $2 trillion that is spent on R&D, which is less than the US (26%). The amount of growth in R&D spending is what people are most interested in. Between 2000 and 2015, China's R&D budget grew at a rate of 18% per year, which is more than four times faster than the US rate of 4%. China will almost certainly spend the most on research and development by the end of 2018. This should be of interest not only to the leaders of Pakistan, but also to the leaders of China's neighbors. Pakistan needs to teach as many of its young people, especially, as it can. It can do this by using both domestic and international institutions. In light of the recent rise in anti-immigrant and anti-Muslim feelings in the U.S., China may be a good option for young Pakistanis.

The Chinese government has put more money into research and development, which has led to a rise in the number of trained technical workers. This, in turn, has led to a huge rise in technical output. Table 8.1 shows that the number of science and engineering graduates in China went from 359,000 in 2000 to 1.65 million in 2014. This is a rise of almost five times. Chinese scholars are publishing more and more study papers on technology at a rate that has never been seen before. Chinese scientists and engineers work hard to improve technology. They have made important advances in artificial intelligence, telecommunications, robots, electric cars, and renewable energy, among other areas. With help from China, Pakistan also needs to get better at these things and build up its people resources.

Table 8.1 Analyzing Research and Development Expenditures and Technical Workforce between China and the USA

	USA	**China**
R&D Expenditure in 2017	$520 Billion	$420 Billion
R&D Global share in 2017	26%	21%
R&D Rate of Increase	4% per year	18% per year
R&D Expected expenditure in 2019	$562 Billion	$588 Billion
Technical Workforce 2000	4,83,000	3,95,000
Technical Workforce 2014	7,42,000	1.65 Million
Technical Workforce 2017 (Estimated)	-800,000	-2.1 Million

Most people in Pakistan think that most C-PEC projects are related to energy or roads. In practice, though, most C-PEC projects are about technology. The C-PEC projects will almost certainly use new technologies. With the speed at which technology is changing, it is clear that only technologically strong countries will be able to survive in the near future. The future economic growth of a country will rest on how big data, artificial intelligence, and connectivity are used and applied together. Pakistan needs to take action in these areas. So, Pakistan needs to start academic and study programs with the help of Chinese institutions to train as many Pakistani youths as possible in the five areas of focus: 1) artificial intelligence, 2) robotics, 3) renewable energy, 4) agriculture, and 5) biotechnology.

Major CPEC Touchpoints in Pakistan

At present a major portion of the funds under C-PEC are allocated to the projects in the following seven areas;

1. Construction of highways and railway tracks
2. Development of Gwadar port
3. Energy generation projects
4. Establishment of industrial zones along the C-PEC route (Fig. 1)
5. Laying down of pipelines for oil and gas transmission
6. Cyber networking and telecommunication
7. Water supply projects for industrial and municipal use (mostly in Balochistan)

Figure 8.1 Map showing major projects of China-Pakistan Economic Corridor.

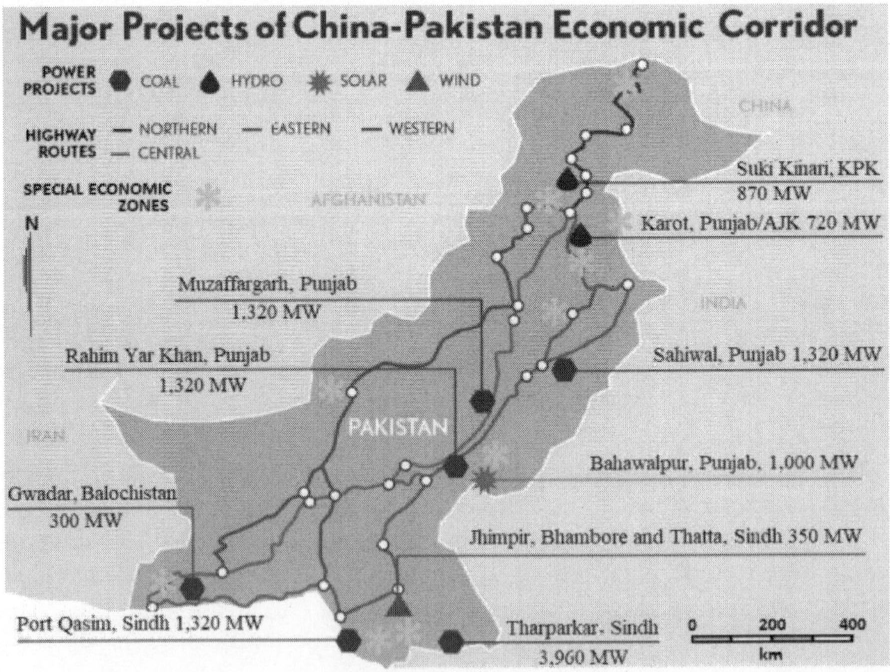

All projects require technology development and human resource development. Therefore, it is imperative for Pakistan to create and strengthen proper infrastructure and facilities at R&D organizations and universities in

Pakistan so that the future demand of technologies technologists, scientists and engineers are met. The list of C-PEC projects and their current statuses are tabulated in tables 8.2 to 8.6, . The energy and power generation sector comprised of 18 projects, the overall progress varies from 15 to 75% while a few are completed, table 8.2. The transportation and communication infrastructure including eight projects, the overall progress varies between 15-70%, table 8.3. Six projects are related to industrial cooperation and ten projects to Gwadar Port with nominal progress on all of them, table 8.4 and 8.5. There are ten Special Economic Zones have been planned to establish in different parts of the country, the feasibility studies and technical evaluation is under progress on all the projects, table 8.6.

Considering the present rate of development work under C-PEC, it has been estimated that the GDP of Pakistan is expected to experience an annual increase of about 2.5 percent by the year 2030 whereas ca.700,000 jobs are expected to be created in next 10 years. Most of the jobs shall be in the Energy, Communication (Highways and Railways) and Port Development sectors .

CPEC Influence on Balochistan's Local Residents

The people who live in the countryside of Balochistan are proud of their customs, culture, and natural surroundings. They are aware of the province's natural resources, agriculture, forests, rangelands, watersheds, biodiversity, and mineral deposits. However, harsh living conditions like aridity, depleting groundwater resources, periodic droughts, overgrazed and degraded rangelands, low-yielding livestock, and rugged terrain make it hard for them to move forward. The provincial and federal governments haven't been able to do much to stop desertification, deforestation, the loss of vegetation on rangelands, and the depletion of groundwater supplies.

To get the most out of C-PEC for community development, the province needs an integrated development plan that brings together all stakeholders, such as government offices, politicians, civil society leaders, community elders, and local NGOs. There is a lot of opportunity for development projects along the western route of the C-PEC. For sustainable development that works well with local communities, development efforts should involve local communities through a consultative process. It's important to bring rural areas into the center by changing them and giving them more power in making decisions. Communities can be given more control over development projects from the time they are planned to the time they are run and maintained, and even when they own the projects.

The people who live in rural areas rely on the environment and natural resources around them. Small-scale farming, orchards, grazing cattle, limited mining, and fishing along the coast may help the economy of the area. In some cases, the natural climate and the availability of surface and groundwater supplies have already shaped these economic activities and jobs. It is important for the physical, social, and economic health of rural areas that water resources are managed, saved, and protected in a way that is sustainable.

The effects of climate change on Balochistan are clear, but scientists don't fully understand them. Through C-PEC, the appropriate government departments, research and development groups, and universities may be able to use the Chinese experience to help them deal with and solve these problems. Protecting and preserving groundwater supplies is one of the most important things to do.

Principles Concerns for Balochistan

Despite being resource-rich, contributing more than 40 percent to the country's energy requirement in the form of electricity, natural gas, and coal, Balochistan is still the most underdeveloped province of Pakistan. There are multiple reasons and justifications for the slow development of Balochistan and each one has counter-arguments . But the bottom line fact remains unchanged that people of Balochistan are lagging behind in the race towards better socioeconomic conditions and lifestyle.

After a long wait of more than seventy years, the C-PEC is the first ray of hope for the people of Balochistan to prosper. In order to take advantage of this unique opportunity, it is necessary to move forward without indulging into the unending discussions on the background and history of the political, geographical, tribal and social conflicts that kept Balochistan away from the mainstream of development path in the past. With this context, five major focus areas of natural resources are proposed here for initiating new projects table 8.7.

The focus areas projects are comprised of minerals, coal deposits, and construction materials, which are widely exposed along the new trade corridor. The proved oil and gas reserves are present in many parts of the province, even oil and gas seeps at the surface are known from a long time. The renewable energy resources including solar, wind and geothermal potential are extensively present. New projects are required to initiate the development of these natural resources.

The management of the water resources is the sweltering issue of the province. The climate change has deteriorated the surface and groundwater balance. The different categories of droughts have become a permanent feature in one or the other part of the province. The groundwater table is depleting at an alarming rate in most of the river basins. The development of new water resources and management techniques are needed to apply for a sustainable supply of water.

Table 8.2 Energy Projects and Initiatives

No	Project Name	Status
1	Two 660MW Coal-Fired Power Plants at Port Qasim	Under construction
2	Two 660MW Coal-Fired Power Plants at Sahiwal	Two units inaugurated
3	Four 330MW Engro Thar Coal-fired Power Plant	Under construction
4	50MW (Dawood) Wind Farm, Gharo	Ready for operation
5	900MW Solar Power Park Bahawalpur	Energization achieved
6	100MW Jhimpir Wind Energy Farm Jhimpir	Under construction
7	50MW Sachal Wind Energy Farm, Sachal	Under construction
8	720MW Karot Hydro-Power Project,	Financial close achieved
9	873MW Suki Kinari Hydropower Project	Under construction
10	Two 60MW Coal-Fired Power Plant Rahimyar Khan	Feasibility stage
11	Two 660MW Coal-Fired Power Plant Hub (Habco)	Under construction
12	300 MW Power Plant Gwadar	Feasibility stage
13	Faisalabad-Matiari-Lahore Transmission Line	Negotiation in process
14	Two 660MW Power Plants Gadani Lasbela,	Feasibility stage
15	1100MW Hydro-Power Station Kohala	Negotiation in process
16	300MW Power Plant at Salt Range Mine	Feasibility stage
17	Two 660MW Coal-Fired Power Plants, Thar Coal Mine	Feasibility stage
18	Two 660MW Coal-Fired Power Plants Muzaffargarh	Feasibility stage

Table 8.3 Logistics, Communication and Infrastructures.

No	Project Name	Status (April 2018)
1	120 km KKH Phase-II, Havelian- Thakot:	Under construction
2	392 km Karachi-Lahore Motorway (S-M-S)	Under construction
3	Establishment of Havelian Dry port	Feasibility completed
4	Upgradation of Multan-Lahore Section, 339 km; Hyderabad-Multan Section, 749 km; and Kemari-Hyderabad Section, 182 km.	Agreement under discussion
5	Construction of New Havelian Dry Port	Feasibility completed.
6	110 km Khuzdar-Basima Highway (N-30)	Feasibility completed.
7	280 km KKH Phase III (Raikot-Thakot Section)	Feasibility completed. Procedural formalities to be completed soon
8	533 km D.I.Khan-Quetta Highway (N-50)	Feasibility stage

Table 8.4 Industrial Projects

No	Project Name	Status
1	700 km Gwadar-Nawabshah LNG Terminal and Pipeline	Ready to be inaugurated
2	Haier & Ruba Economic Zone Phase-II	Feasibility stage
3	Laying of Optical Fiber Cable Rawalpindi to Khunjrab	Under construction, Expected Completion by Dec 2018
4	DTMB Demonstration Project	MOU Signed
5	Lahore Orange Line Metro Train	Under construction
6	Promotion and commercialization of TD-LTE in Pakistan	Feasibility stage

Table 8.5 Gwadar Port and Projects in Proximity

No	Project Name	Status
1	19 km Gwadar Eastbay Expressway	Framework Agreement Signed
2	New International Airport Gwadar	Framework Agreement Signed

3	Free Economic Zone Gwadar	1st phase completed
4	Smart Port City Master Plan Gwadar	Contract negotiations underway
5	Expansion of Multi-purpose Terminal	Feasibility stage
6	Fresh Water Supply, Wastewater Treatment Plants for Gwadar City	Feasibility stage
8	China-Pakistan Faqeer Primary School Gwadar	Completed.
9	Pak-China Friendship Hospital Gwadar	Feasibility study underway
10	Pak-China Friendship Technical and Vocational College Gwadar	Feasibility study underway

Table 8.6 Special Economic Zones

No	Name	Type of Industry
1	Rashkai Economic Zone, M-1, Nowshera, KPK	Fruit/Food/Packaging/Textile Stitching/ Knitting
2	Special Economic Zone Dhabeji Sindh	To be determined during feasibility stage
3	Bostan Industrial Zone Balochistan	Fruit Processing, Agriculture machinery, Pharmaceutical, Motor Bikes Assembly, Chromite /Ceramic, Ice and Cold storage, Electric Appliance
4	Allama Iqbal Industrial City (M3), Faisalabad, Punjab	Textile, Steel, Pharmaceuticals, Engineering, Chemicals / Plastics, Food Processing, Agriculture Implements
5	ICT Model Industrial Zone, Islamabad	Steel, Food Processing, Pharmaceutical & Chemicals, Printing and Packaging, Light Engineering etc.
7	Industrial Park at Port Qasim, Sindh	Steel, Auto & allied industries, Pharmaceutical, Chemical, Printing and Packaging, Garments.
8	Special Economic Zone at Mirpur, AJK	Mix industry
9	Mohmand Marble City FATA-KPK	Marble / Granite, Mineral Processing Industry
10	Moqpondass Special Economic Zone, Gilgit-Baltistan	Marble / Granite, precious stones, Fruit Processing, Steel Industry, Mineral Processing and Leather Industry

Talent Development

Education and training for the people who live there are important parts of all development work. For C-PEC projects in Balochistan, people with skills in engineering, medicine, computer science, social sciences, business, and natural sciences will be needed. Higher Education Institutions (HEIs) in Balochistan will be given extra money to build cutting-edge labs on their own or with the help of Chinese universities.

About 6% of all the people who work in Pakistan are skilled workers. In a bigger picture of C-PEC, the professional and vocational trade schools are not nearly as good at meeting current and future needs. The situation at Balochistan's primary, intermediate, technical, and vocational schools and colleges is very bad. Compared to other provinces of Pakistan, the number of technical schools, the number of students who can join, and the number of people who graduate from those schools are all very low. To meet the needs of different technical and professional skills now and in the future, technical and vocational schools need to be set up as soon as possible. Institutions for teaching Chinese must also be set up so that trained workers can learn the language and communicate better with their Chinese coworkers on the job.

Prospects for Collaborative Projects in Balochistan

A lot of expensive projects, such as Industrial Zones, Power Generation Plants, Road and Highway Construction, Special Economic Zones, etc., are already underway as part of the C-PEC. But small production units and businesses need more attention because they have the ability to make a big difference. When business transport on C-PEC starts, it is likely that a lot of heavy-duty trucks and trawlers will bring goods from China to Gwadar port. When the things are unloaded, these trucks and trawlers won't have much or anything to take back to China. Large cars that aren't carrying anything will waste a lot of time, gas, and equipment when they drive around. To avoid these losses, local industrial and production units could be built up by making it easier for local people and their Chinese peers to work together. Here, it is suggested that the local people could be found and put in touch with their Chinese peers in order to start joint ventures. Most of the production and growth areas mentioned in this paper are already sending goods to China through Karachi Port. So, it's clear that there is already a market for these products in China, and there's no need to do a survey there.

Balochistan hasn't done much to help connect local business owners with potential Chinese partners who want to start joint projects in the country. The

Ministry of Industries and Production in Islamabad set up a meeting on August 22, 2016, to which business people from the Quetta Chamber of Commerce and Industry (QCCI) were called. The final result of this meeting hasn't been decided yet, but people here think that the QCCI business community doesn't have much to offer at this point. This is because Quetta is on the Western Route of the C-PEC, while most of the development work on the C-PEC is currently being done on the Eastern Route, according to the latest news in the press and media.

The Balochistan part of the Eastern Route starts in Sindh at Shahdad Kot, crosses the Kirther Mountains to the west, and goes through the towns of Karkh, Khuzdar, Basima, Nag, Panjgoor, Turbat, and Gwadar before ending at Gwadar. Figure 1: A different route goes from Khuzdar to Wadh, Bela, and Winder, then links to the Coastal Highway, which leads to Ormara, Pasni, and finally Gwadar. In either case, both paths pass through the town of Khuzdar. Since all C-PEC transportation will go through Khuzdar, the items suggested in this paper are thought to be a good idea. Also, the goods that have been found are made either along the C-PEC route in Balochistan or very close to it.

Table 8.7 Significant Regional Resources for Balochistan's Development Schemes

No	Natural Resource	Types of deposits	Location in Balochistan
1	Minerals and Coal deposits	• Iron Copper and Gold • Barite, Lead, and Zinc • Chromium and Iron • Iron, copper, chromium gold, Rare Elements • Coal deposits	Chaghi Mountains. Khuzdar and Bela districts. Muslim Bagh and Zhob districts, and Raskoh. Raskoh Mountains. Quetta, Bolan, Kohlu, Barkhan (Chamalang).
2	Construction Material	• Aggregates • Limestone and sand-stone • Dimension stones: • Granite, Limestone, Onyx Marble and sand-stone	All districts of Balochistan. Sulaiman and Kirther Mountains. Sulaiman and, Kirther Mountains, Chaghi Mountains and Raskoh Moun-tains.
3	Oil and Gas Reserves	• Petroleum • Gas • Shale Gas	Kharan Basin and Offshore Makran. Offshore Makran. Coastal Makran Ranges and Offshore Makran.

4	Energy Resources	• Solar Energy • Geothermal Energy • Bioenergy • Ocean Energy • Hydrogen Energy	All Balochistan. Murri-Bugt Hills, Chaghi Hills, Bolan district and Makran Coast (mud volcanoes). All Balochistan. Coastal Makran. All Balochistan.
5	Water Resources	• Surface Water (perennial) • Rain Water (nonperennial) • Groundwater • Seawater	Nag, Hoshab, Panjgoor (Rakhshan River), Bolan, Harnai, Zarghoon, and Zhob. All Balochistan; Natural dam sites are available where rainwater can be stored both for groundwater recharge and water supply. Fractured hard rocks, conglomerates and alluvium available all along the C-PEC route in Balochistan; Specific aquifers are a) rocks of Binga and Diz units of Khojak Formation in Central Balochistan (Panjgur and Turbat districts) and b) rocks of Talar and Hinglaj units of Makran Group in Makran Coastal Range between Ormara and Jiwani. Along Makran Coast; desalination of sea water

Structural Stones

In Balochistan, there are huge amounts of dimension stones of international grade. Some examples of these stones are limestone, granite, marble, sandstone, and onyx. From a geographical point of view, Kirther and the Sulaiman Mountains in Balochistan are natural places where there are many different kinds of high-quality natural stones. Because of strong geological activity (tectonically compressed), most rocks in the northern parts of Pakistan and even the Tibbet Plateau in western China are very crushed or broken. Most of the time, places where rocks have been compressed hard don't have large, unbroken dimension stones of the same color, texture, and strength that are needed in business. Some of these dimension stones are already being mined or cut in the area and then shipped to China through Karachi Seaport. Some of the places in Balochistan where these stones are made, most of which are along the C-PEC road, are:

1. Saruna, District Khuzdar

2. Karkh, District Khuzdar
3. Nal, District Khuzdar
4. Basima, District Qalat.
5. Duraji, District Lasbela
6. Loi, District Lasbela
7. Gajri, District Lasbela
8. Shah-e-Noorani, District Lasbela
9. Yak Mach, District Chaghi
10. Dalbandin, District Chaghi
11. Nokundi, District Chaghi
12. Different localities in District Loralai, Ziarat, Quetta and Zhob

In these places, the mines and structures are very basic, and the equipment is old. Adding more machines to their mines is an easy way to boost their output. Chinese mining companies can do a lot of good by working with local miners to increase output through joint ventures.

Minerals and Mining

Balochistan is a host of large deposits of metallic and nonmetallic minerals. These include ores of Gold, Copper, Iron, Chromium, Barium, Magnesium. Aluminum, Tungsten, Lead, Zinc, Antimony and many more. The minerals named Chromite, Pyrite, Barite, Magnesite, Galena, and Sphalerite, are already being mined in various localities of Khuzdar, Bela, Chaghi and Muslim Bagh areas of Balochistan. With the exceptions of few, all these ores are being exported to China through Karachi port for further refining and processing. The transport of these ores may be diverted to C-PEC and the production may be enhanced with the help of Chinese mining companies. Some of the major mineral deposits and their locations are listed below for ready reference;

1. Copper-molybdenum deposits of Dasht-e-kain, Chaghi.
2. Copper deposits of other areas of Chaghi District.
3. Iron Ore reserves of Dalbandin and Nokundi District Chaghi.
4. Sulphur reserves of Koh-i-Sultan Nokundi.
5. Chromite deposits of Wad, District Khuzdar.
6. Chromite deposits of Kharan.
7. Laterite deposits of Ziarat District.

8. Antimony deposits of Arambi Village District Qila Abdullah.
9. Chromite deposits of Muslim Bagh District Qilla Saifullah.
10. Magnesite deposits of Muslim Bagh.
11. Chromite deposits of Zhob District.
12. Lead-Zinc Deposits of Lasbela District.
13. Quartzite deposit of Gajri village Lasbela

Agriculture

Balochistan has a climate that is either desert or semi-desert. Since water is scarce, it may not be possible to grow a lot of crops. But between Khuzdar and Gwadar, a large area with a lot of land, there are a lot of different kinds of high-quality "dates" that grow in deserts. These dates are easy to process and store so that they can be sent to China or countries in Central Asia (through C-PEC) where dates don't naturally grow.

Cement Manufacturing Plant

From Mughal Kot (Zhob) in the north to Surab (near Khuzdar) in the south, there are many places to get the raw materials for a cement factory. Calcium, Silicon, Aluminum, and Iron are the four main ingredients in cement. These can be taken from limestone and shales, which are rich in the rocks along the road between Quetta and Zhob. The best place for the cement plant is the Bostan Industrial Zone, which is near Quetta. It is about halfway between Zhob and Gwadar on the western road of C-PEC, so it is easy to get to both northern and southern parts of Balochistan.

Ferro-Chrome Beneficiation

Chromium is an important part of the process of making steel. Muslim Bagh has the world's second biggest chromite (chromium ore) deposit, which has been mined for the past 100 years. At the moment, raw chromite rock from Muslim Bagh is being sent all the way to Karachi so that it can be shipped to China for a very low price. This raw Chromite ore is processed in China to make Ferro-Chrome, which is then shipped back to Pakistan at a very high cost for use in the iron and steel business, mostly in Pakistan Steel Mills. A Ferro-Chrome plant will not only cut down on the cost of transportation, but it will also save a lot of foreign currency. All of the factories in the C-PEC Projects will need iron and steel in one way or another, which the Ferro-chrome plant can provide. The best place for this business to be is close to Muslim Bagh.

Fisheries/Fish Farming

Makran Coast and its seas are thought to be one of the cleanest natural places because they are not affected by pollution from factories. So, it is home to the most healthy and clean sea life. Along the Makran Coast, fish farming has a lot of promise, especially in the towns of Gwadar, Pasni, and Ormara. People who live along the coast already fish in traditional ways, even though they don't have many tools or training. With the help of local people and their Chinese peers, places to process and store fish and sea food could be built. Then, these fish and other kinds of raw seafood can be sent to China through C-PEC.

Livestock

Balochistan has a lot of room for animals to grow, especially sheep, lamb, and goat. People in the area already do traditional livestock business, but they don't have the tools to do animal farming with machines. Small and medium-sized processing plants could be set up along C-PEC or near Khuzdar to take care of killed cattle and process them to keep them fresh so they can be shipped to China via C-PEC.

Conclusion

The China Pakistan Economic Corridor (C-PEC) has given Pakistan a lot of chances to improve its social and economic life. Pakistan needs to focus on developing its people resource in key areas like artificial intelligence, robotics, renewable energy, agriculture, and biotechnology. With Chinese investment, a sustainable growth will depend on having trained technical people in these areas. In the same way, Balochistan, which has a lot of natural resources but is very poor and underdeveloped, needs to focus on seven key areas to get the most out of the trade and transportation projects that C-PEC will bring about. Minerals and coal exploration, buildieng materials, oil and gas exploration, energy production, including sustainable energy, water, including surface water, groundwater, and seawater, and human resource development. Balochistan could also work with Chinese companies to make and sell dimension stones, mine mineral deposits, raise fish, make livestock, make cement, and make ferro-chrome.

Bibliography

1972 (H. Van Skyhawk, Trans.). Oxford: Oxford University Press.

A. Floyer, Unexplored Baluchistan. A Survey with Observations Astronomical, Geographical, Botanical, etc., of a Route through Mekran, Bashkurd, Persia, Kurdistan and Turkey, London, 1882.

A. Rooman, The Brahuis of Quetta-Kalat Region, Pakistan Historical

A. T. Embree, ed., Pakistan's Western Borderlands, Durham, 1977.

A. W. Hughes, The Country of Baluchistan, its Geography, Topography, Ethnology and History. 1877, London : George Bell and Sons. Reprinted by Indus Publications, Karachi (1977).

Ahmad Salim, Pakistan of Jinnah: The Hidden Face, 1993, Lahore: Brothers Publishers

Ainslie T. Embree (Ed.), Pakistan's Western Borderlands: The Transformation of a Political Order, 1977, New Delhi: Vikas Publishing House Pvt. Ltd.

Ali, Dr Sadia. "The Poor Daughter of Balochistan." The News International, 16 Aug. 2016, www.thenews.com.pk/print/142987-The-poor-daughter-of-Balochistan.

Ali, Tariq. Can Pakistan Survive? The Death of a State. Suffolk: Penguin Books, 1983. Amin, A.H. 'The Six Steps to Get Out of the Balochistan's Quicksand'. South Asia Tribune. Washington DC, 25 February 2005.

Amin, Tahir. Ethno National Movements of Pakistan. Islamabad: Institute of Policy Studies, 1988.

Amnesty International. (n.d.). Conflict diamonds: Did someone die for that diamond? Retrieved November 6, 2013, from http://www.amnestyusa.org/our-work/issues/ business-and-human-rights/oil-gas-and-mining-industries/conflict-diamonds

Appadurai, A. (1990). Disjuncture and difference in the global cultural economy. In M. Featherstone (Ed.), Global culture: Nationalism, globalization and modernity (pp. 295-310). London: Sage.

Asian Human Rights Commission. (2006). A statement by the Asian Human Rights Commission, Pakistan: UN Human Rights Council must Respond to the Bombing in Baluchistan, August 28.

Asian Human Rights Commission. (2012). Pakistan: Army creates an organization to kill intellectuals and activists in Balochistan, in the name of peace. Retrieved May 2, 2012, from http://www.humanrights.asia/news/ahrc-news/AHRC-STM-005-2012

Aslam, Rabia. "Greed, Creed, and Governance in Civil Conflicts: a Case Study of Balochistan."Contemporary South Asia, vol. 19, no. 2, 2011, pp. 189-203., do i:10.1080/09584935.2011.560654.

Axmann, M. (2009). Back to the future: The Khanate of Kalat and the genesis of Baluch Nationalism, 1915-55. Karachi: Oxford University Press.

B. D. Clark, "Harappan Outposts on the Makran Coast," Antiquity 36/ 142, 1962, pp. 86-93.

B. Spooner, Religious and Political Leadership in Persian Baluchistan, Ph.D. thesis, Oxford University, 1967.

Babar, Farhatullah. 'Nibbling away at autonomy'. The Dawn, Karachi, 21 October 2004. Bakhtiar, Idrees. 'Mega-projects are a Conspiracy to turn the Balochis into a Minority in their Homeland'. Interview with Sardar Ataullah Mengal. The Herald (August 2004): 50-53.

Bajoria, J. (2009). India-Afghanistan relations. Council on Foreign Relations. Retrieved February 24,2014, fromhttp://www.cfr.org/india/india-afghanistan-relations/p17474#p2

Baloch, Abdul Hakim. 'Bringing development to Balochistan'. Dawn, Karachi, 13 December 2004.

Baloch, S. (2012). Retrieved May 2, 2012, from http://www.thenews.com.pk/Todays- News-9-99303-The-real-Balochistan

Balochistan govt decides to quash cases against Brahamdagh. (2012, March 16). Dawn. Retrieved March 16, 2012, from http://dawn.com/2012/03/16/balochistan-govt- decides-to-quash-cases-against-brahamdagh/

Baluch, Mir Ahmad Yar Khan. Inside Balochistan - A Political Autobiography of His Highness Baiglar Bagi: Khan-e-Azam XIII. Karachi: Royal Book Company, 1975.

Baluchistan: List of Leading Personages in Baluchistan, Government of India Central Publication Branch, Calcutta, 1932.

Bangash, Y. K. (2013). Subjects to citizens: Accession and integration of the princely states of Pakistan (Chapter 3). Karachi: Oxford University Press.

Bano, Masooda. 'Dialogue is the only Solution'. The International News, Internet Edition, 21 January 2005.

Bansal, A. (2006). Balochistan: Continuing violence and its implications. Strategic Analysis, 30(1), 46-63.

Bansal, A. (2010). Balochistan in Turmoil: Pakistan at the crossroads. New Delhi: Manas. BBC News. (2006, September 1). Lonely burial for Baloch leader. Retrieved November 6, 2013, from http://news.bbc.co.uk/1/hi/5304594.stm

Bansal, Alok, 'Balochistan: Continuing Violence and Its Implications'. Strategic Analysis 30 no. 1, (January-March 2006): 46-63.

Bansal, Alok, 'Iran: America's Options'. Available from http://in.rediff.com/news/2005/ oct/07guest.htm (accessed on 15 July 2006).

Bansal, Alok. 'The Revival of Insurgency in Balochistan'. Strategic Analysis 29 no. 2, (April-June 2005): 250-68.

Bansal, Alok. "Factors Leading to Insurgency in Balochistan." Small Wars & Insurgencies, vol. 19, no. 2, 2008, pp. 182-200., doi:10.1080/09592310802061356.

Bansal, Alok. "The Revival of Insurgency in Balochistan." Strategic Analysis, vol. 29, no. 2, 2005, pp. 250-268., doi:10.1080/09700161.2005.12049805.

Baren Ray, "Pakhtun National Movement and the Transfer of Power in India" in Myth and Reality, Edited by A. K. Gupta, Introduction by Ravinder Kumar, 1986, Manohar for NMML "A Unique Leader of a Unique Movement" in Abdul Ghaffar Khan: A Centennial Tribute, 1995, Har Anand for NMML.

Bhutta, Z. (2012). Pakistan should think about Reko Diq carefully. The Express Tribune. Retrieved June 29, 2012, from http://tribune.com.pk/story/400703/pakistan-should- think-about-reko-diq-carefully-thomson/

Breseeg, T. M. (2004). Baloch nationalism: Its origins and development (p. 353). Karachi: Royal Book.

Breseeg, Taj Mohammad. Baloch Nationalism: Its Origin and Development. Karachi: Royal Book Company, 2004.

Breseeg, Taj Mohammad. Baloch Nationalism Its Origin and Development. Royal Book Company, 2004.

Brubaker, R. (2005). The 'diaspora' diaspora. Ethnic and Racial Studies, 28(1), 1-19. Bull, H. (1977). The anarchical society: A study of order in world politics. New York: Columbia University Press.

Buzan, B. (1991). People, states and fear: National security problem in international relations (2nd revised ed.). New York: Prentice Hall.

C. E. Bosworth, Sistan under the Arabs, from the Islamic Conquest to Bray, Life-History of a Brahui, London, 1913. Idem, The Jat of Baluchistan," Indian Antiquary 54, 1925, pp. 30-33.

C. Masson, Narrative of Various Journeys in Balochistan, Afghanistan and the Panjab, London, 1842.

C. McC. Pastner and S. Pastner, "Agriculture, Kinship and Politics in Southern Baluchistan," Man 7/1, 1972, pp. 128-36.

C. P. Skrine, "The Highlands of Persian Baluchistan," Geographical Journal 78, 1931, pp. 321-40.

Central Intelligence Agency. (1992, September). Report on heroin in Pakistan: Sowing the wind.

Centre for Research and Security Studies. (2011). Balochistan's maze of violence. Islamabad: Author.

Chinapage.com. (n.d.). Proposed Qatar-Pakistan gas pipeline. Retrieved July 25, 2012, from http://www.chinapage.com/transportation/pipeline/pipeline-qatar.html

Cohen, A., Curtis, L., & Graham, O. (2008). The proposed Iran-Pakistan-India gas pipeline: An unacceptable risk to regional security (No. 2139). The Heritage Foundation. Retrieved from http://www.heritage.org/research/reports/2008/05/the- proposed-iran-pakistan-india-gas-pipeline-an-unacceptable-risk-to-regional-security

Cohen, Stephen Philip. The Idea of Pakistan. New Delhi: Oxford University Press, 2005. Duncan, Emma, Breaking the Curfew - A Political Journey through Pakistan. London: Penguin Books, 1989.

Collier, P., Hoeffler, A., & Sambanis, N. (2005). The Collier-Hoeffler model of civil war onset and the case study project research design. In Collier & Sambanis (Eds.), Understanding civil war: Evidence and analysis. 1: Africa (Vol. 1, pp. 1-33). Washington, DC: The World Bank.

Davidson. 'Pakistan: Unravelling the Mystery of Balochistan Insurgency'. Available from website http://www.newscentralasia.com/ (accessed on 17 March 2005).

DefenceNow. (2011, October 7). India decides to train Afghanistan's army and signs other bilateral agreements with Afghanistan. Retrieved October 7, 2011, from http://www.defencenow.com/news/322/india-decides-to-train-afghanistans-army-and- signs-other-bilateral-agreements-with-afghanistan.html

Devasher, Tilak. Pakistan: the Balochistan Conundrum. Harper India, 2019.

Dunne, J. S. (2006). Crisis in Balochistan: A historical analysis of the Baluch nationalist movement in Pakistan. Monterey, CA: Naval Postgraduate School.

Dunne, Justin S. "Crisis in Baluchistan a Historical Analysis of the Baluch Nationalist Movement in Pakistan." Calhoun NPS, Dudley Knox Library, Naval Postgraduate School, 1 June 2006, calhoun.nps.edu/handle/10945/2755.

E. Blatter and P. F. Halberg, "Flora of Persian Baluchistan and Makran," Journal of the Bombay Natural Historical Society 24, 1910.

E. C. Ross, "Memorandum of Notes on Mekran, together with Report on a Visit to Kej and J. P. Rumsey, "Some Notes on Leadership in Marri Baloch Society," Anthropology Tomorrow (University of Chicago) 5, 1957, pp. 122-26. J. Saldanha, Official History of the Mekran Telegraph Line from Karachi to Jask, n.p., 1895.

E. W. Vredenburg, "A Geographical Sketch of the Baluchistan Desert and Parts of Eastern Persia," Memoirs of the Geological Survey of India 31/2, 1901, pp. 179-302.

E. W. Vredenburg, "Geology of Sarawan, Jhalawan, Mekran and the State of Las Bela," Records of the Geological Survey of India 38, 1909, pp. 189-215.

Editorial: Abolishing sardari system or Baloch nationalism? (2006, August 26). Daily Times. Retrieved July 18, 2013, from http://www.dailytimes.com.pk/default.asp? page=2006%5C08%5C26%5Cstory_26-8-2006_pg3_1

Editorial: Mengal's stance. (2013, July 12). The News International. Retrieved July 25, 2013, from http://www.thenews.com.pk/Todays-News-8-189429-Mengals-stance

Effendi, Aslam. 'Balochistan: A Victim of its Geography'. The International News Internet Edition, 4 March 2005.

F. Barth, "Ethnic Processes on the Pathan-Baluch Boundary," in Indo- Iranica. Mejanges pre,sente,s aa G. Morgenstierne, Wiesbaden, 1964, pp. 13-20.

Fair, C. (2010). India in Afghanistan and beyond: Opportunities and constraints (A Century Foundation Report). New York.

FerePta, tr. Briggs. J. P. Ferrier, Caravan Journeys and Wanderings in Persia, Afghanistan, Turkestan and Beloochistan, London, 1857.

Frontier and Overseas Expedition from India (in 7 vols.). Compiled in the Intelligence Branch, Army Headquarters, India. Vol. III entitled Baluchistan and the First Afghan War. Reprinted by Mittal Publications, Delhi (1983).

Gazdar, H. (2007). Balochistan economic report, background paper on social structures and migration. Karachi: Collective for Social Science Research.

Girdhari Lal Puri, Oral Transcript (Senior Activist in the Red Shirt movement, MLA and Deputy Speaker in NWFP Legislative Assembly, also journalist (Hindustan Times). Later appointed by Nehru in the External Affairs Ministry. Entrusted with very senior responsibility on sensitive questions for over 20 years. The interview runs to some 400 pages. Held at the Nehru Memorial Museum (Manuscript Section).

Government of Balochistan. (2006). Mines and minerals department (Presentation). Retrieved December 28, 2006, from www.balochistan.gov.pk

Government of Pakistan. (2009). Aghaaz-e-Huqook Balochistan. Islamabad: Author.

Government of Pakistan. (2010). Amendment XVIII of the Constitution of Pakistan. Islamabad: Author.

Grare, F. (2006). The resurgence of Baluch nationalism (Carnegie Papers No. 65).

Grare, Frederic. "Balochistan: The State Versus the Nation." Carnegie Endowment for International Peace, 11 Apr. 2013, carnegieendowment.org/2013/04/11/balochistan-state-versus-nation-pub-51488.

Grare, Frederic. "Pakistan: The Resurgence of Baluch Nationalism." Carnegie Endowment for International Peace, 26 Jan. 2006, carnegieendowment.org/2006/01/26/pakistan-resurgence-of-baluch-nationalism-event-848.

H. Field, An Anthropological Reconnaissance in West Pakistan 1955, Peabody Museum, New York, 1959.

H. G. Raverty, Notes on Afghanistan and Baluchistan, Lahore, 1878.

H. Pottinger, Travels in Beloochistan and Sinde; Accompanied by a Geographical and Historical Account of Those Countries with a Map, London, 1816 (repr. Westmead, 1972).

Harrison, S. (1981). In Afghanistan's shadow. New York: Carnegie Endowment for International Peace.

Harrison, Selig S. In Afghanistan's Shadow: Baloch Nationalism. New York: Carnegie Endowment of International Peace, 1981.

Harrison, Selig S. In Afghanistan's Shadow: Baluch Nationalism and Soviet Temptations. Carnegie Endowment for International Peace, 1981.

Hasnat, S. F. (2011). Global security watch - Pakistan. Santa Barbara: Praeger.

Hassan, Syed Raza. "Three Bombers, Two Policemen Killed During Attack on Chinese Consulate in Karachi." The Wire, 23 Nov. 2018, thewire.in/south-asia/gunmen-attack-chinese-consulate-in-karachi-two-policemen-killed.

Human Rights Commission of Pakistan. (2006). Conflict in Balochistan: Report ofHRC fact-finding mission, December 2005-January 2006. Lahore: Author.

Human Rights Commission of Pakistan. (2009). Pushed to the wall: Report of the HRCP fact-finding mission to Balochistan (5-11 October 2009). Lahore: Author.

Human Rights Commission of Pakistan. (2011). Balochistan: Blinkered slide into chaos. Lahore: Author.

Human Rights Commission of Pakistan. Conflict in Balochistan: report of HRCP fact, finding missions December 2005-January 2006 / Human Rights

Commission of Pakistan Human Rights Commissions of Pakistan ; Centre for Democratic Development Lahore : Islamabad 2006

Human Rights Watch. (2011). 'We can torture, kill, or keep you for years'. Enforced Disappearances by Pakistan Security Forces in Balochistan. Retrieved May 2, 2012, from www.hrw.org/sites/default/files/reports/pakistan0711WebInside.pdf

Hussain, Irfan. 'Out of Time, Out of Place'. Dawn, Karachi, 24 December 2005. Hussain, Zahid. 'Gathering Storm'. Newsline, February 2005, 21-25.

Idem, The Political Structure of a Tribal Federation: The Brahui of Baluchistan, Ph.D. dissertation, Columbia University, New York, 1969.

Idris, Kunwar. 'Is the federation at risk?'. Dawn, Karachi, 8 January 2006.

Ikelegbe, A. (2005). The economy of conflict in the oil rich Niger delta region of Nigeria. Nordic Journal of African Studies, 14(2), 208-234.

Inayatullah Baloch, The Problem of Greater Balochistan: A Study of Baloch Nationalism, 1987, Steiner Verlag Wiesbaden GMBH, Stuttgart, for South Asian Institute, University of Heidelberg.

J. Elfenbein, "Baluchistan," in Marc-Edouard u. Enay and Siawosch Azadi, Einhundert Jahre Orientteppich-Literatur, Hanover, 1977.

J. Goldsmid and W.T. Blandford, ed., Eastern Persia. An Account of the Persian Boundary Commission 1870-1872 (Two Vols.), Macmillan, London, 1876.

Jamali, H. (2012, November 17-20). Shorelines of memory, sediments of history: Britain, Oman and the shifting geographies of trade on the Mekran Coast. Paper presented at the 46th Annual Meeting of Middle East Studies Association (MESA), Denver.

Jamali, H. (2013, August 2). Interview with anthropologist who has conducted fieldwork in Oman and has completed a PhD thesis on Gwadar.

James, A. (2012). Foreign policy magazine Laura Rozen and Christine Fair of Rand Corp. confirmed that India (RAW) were neck deep in supporting terrorists (TTP) against Pakistan. Retrieved July 28, 2012, from http://www.fourwinds10.net/ siterun_data/government/war/afghan_war/pakistan_war/news.php?q= 1337959875

Joan L. G. Baart and Ghulam Hyder Sindhi (eds.), Pakistani languages and society: problems and prospects ,121-131. Islamabad and Horsleys Green: National Institute of Pakistan Studies, Quaid-i-Azam University and Summer Institute of Linguistics.

Joshua Project. (n.d.). The Baloch. Retrieved July 15, 2012, from http://www.joshuaproject.net/people-profile.php

K. Ferdinand, "The Baluchistan Barrel-Vaulted Tent," Folk 2, 1960, pp. 33-50.

Khan, M. Ilyas. 'Back to the Hills'. The Herald, Karachi, September 2004, 50-59. Khan, M. Ilyas. 'Money, Money, Money'. The Herald, Karachi, September 2004, 52-53. Kukreja, Veena. Contemporary Pakistan: Political Processes, Conflicts and Crises. New Delhi: Sage Publications, 2003.

Khurshid, Haris. "Is Balochistan Insurgency Dying?" Foreign Policy News, 14Aug.2015,foreignpolicynews.org/2015/08/14/is-balochistan-insurgency-dying/.

Kiani, K. (2006, December 11). Balochistan wants 20pc share in PPL. Dawn.

Kumar, T. (2012). Testimony by Amnesty International on Human Rights in Balochistan to the Committee on Foreign Affairs, United States House of Representatives. T. Kumar - House Committee on Foreign Affairs. Retrieved May 2, 2012, from foreignaffairs. house.gov/.. ,/HHRG-112-FA-WState-TKumar-201202

Lieven, Anatol. "Counter-Insurgency in Pakistan: The Role of Legitimacy." Small Wars & Insurgencies, vol. 28, no. 1, 2017, pp. 166-190., doi:10.1080/09592318.2016.1266128.

Lockhart, Nadir Shah. A Critical Study Based Mainly upon Contemporary Sources, London, 1938.

Lustick, I. (1979). Stability in deeply divided societies: Consociationalism versus control. World Politics, XXXVI, vol. 31, April, pp. 325-344.

M. L. Dames, Popular Poetry of the Baloches, 2 vols., London 1904a.

M. L. Dames, The Baloche Race, London, 1904. A. C. Edwards, The Persian Carpet, London, 1953, l960, 1975.

Mahmood, Shafqat. 'Centre does not hold'. The International News Internet Edition, 21 January 2005.

Malik plans APC on Balochistan issue. (2013). Dawn, 19 October 2013. Retrieved November 6, 2013, from http://dawn.com/news/1050518/malik-plans-apc-on- balochistan-issue

Matheson, S. (2009). The tigers of Baluchistan. Karachi: Oxford University Press.

Matheson, Sylvia. The Tigers of Baluchistan. Karachi: Oxford University Press, 1998.

Mazari, S. (2005, February 2). Balochistan and the 'Great Power Games'. The News International.

Mazari, Shireen. 'Balochistan and the "Great Power Games"'. The International News Internet Edition, 2 February 2005.

McGarry, J., & O'Leary, B. (1993). The politics of ethnic regulation: Case studies of protracted ethnic conflicts. London: Routledge.

Mehdi, Tahir. "Obfuscating Balochistan." Dawn, 30 Mar. 2018, www.dawn.com/news/1398427.

Mendez, Zeus Hans. "Repression and Revolt in Balochistan: The Uncertainty and Survival of a People's National." Air University (AU), Journal of Indo-Pacific Affairs, Air University Press, 31 Aug. 2020, www.airuniversity.af.edu/JIPA /Display/Article/2331243/repression-and-revolt-in-balochistan-the-uncertainty-and-survival-of-a-peoples/.

Mir, H. (2009). Pakistan has proof of '3 Indian Kasabs' in Baluchistan'. Rediff.com. Retrieved from http://news.rediff.com/report/2009/jul/28/hamid-mir-on-the-real- reason-why-india-agreed-to-discuss-baluchistan.htm

Mir, Nazir Ahmad. "Abysmal Human Rights Situation in Balochistan."Manohar Parrikar Institute for Defence Studies and Analyses, 2020, idsa.in/idsacomments/abysmal-human-rights-balochistan-nazir-300520.

Mir Ahmad Yar Khan Baluch, Inside Baluchistan: A Political Autobiography of His Highness Baigi: Khan-e-Azam-XIII, Karachi, 1975.

Mir Khudabux Bijarani Marri Baloch, Searchlights on Baloches and Balochistan, Karachi, 1974.

Mir Khudabux Bijarani Marri Baloch, The Balochis through Centuries. History versus Legend, Quetta, 1965.

Mohsin, Attaul. 'NA Debates Baluchistan Situation; MPs call for Political Solution'. Pakistan Times 1 March 2005.

Mountstuart Elphistone, An Account of the Kingdom of Caubul, London, 1815.

Muhammad Sardar Khan Baluch, History of Baluch Race and Baluchistan,1958, Post Box 32, Quetta

Muhammad Sardar Khan Baluch, History of the Baluch Race and Baluchistan, Quetta, 1962 (repr. 1977).

Mustikhan, A. (2011, June 30). Gulf Baloch army officers say Paki soldiers are cannibals. Examiner.com. Retrieved June 30, 2011, from http://www.examiner.com/ article/gulf-baloch-army-officers-say-paki-soldiers-are-cannibals

Mustikhan, A. (2012, January 2). Some Baloch happy over bomb attack on 'I.S.I. safehouse' in Quetta. Retrieved from http://www.examiner.com/article/some-baloch- happy-over-bomb-attack-on-i-s-i-safehouse-quetta

Muzaffar, Muhammad et al. "Balochistan Insurgency: Causes and Prospects." Orient Research Journal of Social Sciences, vol.3, no. 1, 2018, pp. 111-127., https://gcwus.edu.pk/wp-content/uploads/8.-Balochistan-Insurgency.pdf

N. B. Swidler, "Brahui Political Organization and the National State," in Embree, 1977, pp. 108-25.

Nabeel, Fahad. "Factionalism in the Balochistan Insurgency - An Overview." Stratagem, 7 Feb. 2017, stratagem.pk/armed-dangerous/factionalism-balochistan-insurgency-overview/.

National Commission on Terrorist Attacks upon the United States. (2004). 9/11 commission report: Final report of the National Commission on Terrorist Attacks upon the United States. Washington, DC: Author. Retrieved from http://www.9-11 commission.gov/report/911Report.pdf

Nawaz, S. (2009). Crossed swords: Pakistan, its army, and the wars within. Karachi: Oxford University Press.

Niazi, T. (2008). Globalization, resource conflicts and social violence in South Asia. International Journal of Contemporary Sociology, 5(1), 184-208.

O'Leary, B. (2001). Introduction. In B. O'Leary, I. Lustick, &T. Callaghy (Eds.), Right-sizing the state: The politics of moving borders (pp. 1-14). Oxford: Oxford University Press.

P. C. Salzman, "Adaptation and Political Organization in Iranian Baluchistan," Ethnology 10/4, 1971, pp. 433-44.

Pakistan: The Forgotten Conflict in Balochistan. International Crisis Group, 2007.

Pakistan: The Worsening Conflict in Balochistan. International Crisis Group, 2006.

Pandey, G. (2007). India: Mainstreams and minorities. In G. Pandey & Y. Samad (Eds.), Faultines of nationhood (pp. 13-66). New Delhi: Roli.

Panhwar, S. H. (n.d.). Sardari system abolished by Prime Minister Zulfikar Ali Bhutto in 1976. A historical document. Retrieved July 18, 2013, from http://www.pppusa.org/ Acrobat/Sardari_System.pdf

Pantucci, Raffaello. "Lesson of the Pakistan Suicide Attack: China Will Pay a High Price for Infrastructure."South China Morning Post, 26 Aug. 2018, www.scmp.com/news/china/diplomacy-defence/article/2160918/lesson-pakistan-suicide-attack-china-will-have-pay-high.

Participant observation. (2012-2013). Baloch meetings in London.

Patnaik, Smruti S. 'Pakistan's North West Frontier: Under a New Name'. Strategic Analysis 22 no. 5 (August 1998): 761-81.

Paul Titus (Ed.), Marginality and Modernity: Ethnicity and Change in Post Colonial Balochistan, 1996, Karachi: Oxford University Press.

Paul Titus, "Routes to ethnicity: roads, buses, and differential ethnic relations in Pakistani Balochistan", in Paul Titus, ed., Marginality and Modernity: Ethnicity and Change in Post-Colonial Balochistan, Karachi, Oxford University Press, 1996

Peterson, J. E. (2004). Oman's diverse society: Northern Oman. Middle East Journal, 8(1), 31-51.

Phadnis, Urmila 'Ethnic Movements in Pakistan'. In Pakistan: Society and Politics South Asian Studies Series, 6, ed. Nayak Pandav, 182-211. New Delhi: South Asian Publishers Pvt Ltd, 1984.

Qayyum, D. (2009). ISI summons RAW chief over terrorism in Pakistan, July 22, 2009. Retrieved July 22, 2009, from http://pakistankakhudahafiz.wordpress.com/tag/ christine-fair/

R. B. Diwan Jamiat Rai, The Domiciled Hindus, ed. Denys Bray, Delhi, 1913.

R. E. H. Dyer, Raiders of the Sarhad, Being an Account of a Campaign of Arms and Bluff against the Brigands of the Persian-Baluchi Border, London,1921.

R. G. Wirsing, The Baluchis and Pathans, London, 1981.

R. L. Raikes, "The Ancient Ghabarbands of Baluchistan," East and West, N.S. 15/1-2, 1964-65, pp. 26-35.

R. Leech, "Brief History of Kalat Brought down to the Disposition and Death of Nawab Khan Braho-ee," JASB 12, 1843, pp. 473-512.

R. N. Pehrson, The Social Organization of the Marri Baluch, ed. F. Barth, Viking Fund Publications in Anthropology 43, New York, 1966.

Rahman, Mir Jamilur. 'Balochistan in Turmoil'. The International News Internet Edition, 15 January 2005.

Rashid, A. (2006, September 1). Rebel killing raises stakes in Pakistan. BBC News. Retrieved November 6, 2013, from http://news.bbc.co.uk/1/hi/world/south_asia/ 5290966.stm

Raza, Syed Irfan and Sharif, Arshad. 'Troops to Protect Sui Plant: Sherapo, - Operation in the Offing - ISPR'. Dawn Karachi, 13 January 2005.

Reddy, B. Muralidhar. "Jamali's Exit." Frontline, 29 July 2004, frontline.thehindu.com/world-affairs/article30223654.ece.

Reeve, S. (1999). The new jackals - Ramzi Yousef, Osama Bin Laden and the future of terrorism. London: Andre Deutsch.

Rehman, I.A. 'The Rise and Fall of Democracy', Newsline August 1997, 31-34. Rizvi, Hasan-Askari. Military, State and Society in Pakistan. London: Macmillan, 2000. Saedi, Tariq, Sergi Pyatkov, Ali Nasimzadeh, Qasim Jan, S.M. Kasi, Rupa Kival and Mark

S. B. Miles, The Countries and Tribes of the Persian Gulf, London, 1919 (repr. 1966). V. Minorsky, "Mongol Placenames in Mukri Kurdistan (Mongolica 4)," BSOAS 19, 1957, p. 81.

S. S. Harrison, In Afghanistan's Shadow: Baluch Nationalism and Soviet Temptations, Carnegie Endowment for International Peace, New York, 1981.

Saeedi, T., Pyatakov, S., Nasimzadeh, A., Jan, Q., Kasi, S. M., Kival, R., & Davidson, M. (2011, July 18). Pakistan: Unveiling the mystery of Balochistan insurgency

- Part One. News Central Asia. Retrieved July 26, 2013, from http://newscentralasia.net/2011/07/18/archive-material-pakistan-unveiling-the-mystery- of-balochistan-insurgency-part-one/

Sahadevan, P. Coping with Disorder - Strategies to End Internal Wars in South Asia. RCSS Policy Studies 17. Colombo: Regional Centre for Strategic Studies, 2000.

Saleem, Farrukh. 'Balochistan: an objective assessment'. The International News, Internet Edition, 22 January 2006.

Samad, Y. (1995). Pakistan or Punjabistan: Crisis of national identity. International Journal of Punjab Studies, 2(1), 23-42.

Samad, Y. (2002). In and out of power but not down and out: Mohajir identity politics. In C. Jaffrelot (Ed.), Pakistan - nationalism without a nation? (pp. 63-83). Delhi: Manohar.

Samad, Y. (2007). Minority rights to majoritarian discourse. In G. Pandey & Y. Samad (Eds.), Faultines of nationhood (pp. 67-138). New Delhi: Roli.

Samad, Y. (2011). The Pakistan-US conundrum: Jihadists, the military and the people, the struggle for control. London: Hurst.

Samad, Yunas. "Understanding the Insurgency in Balochistan." Commonwealth & Comparative Politics, vol. 52, no. 2, 2014, pp. 293-320., doi:10.1080/14662043.2014.894280.

Scholz, F. (2002). Nomadism and colonialism: A hundred years of Baluchistan 1872

Scraping the barrel, the trade in surplus ammunition. (2011, April). Small arms survey (Issue Brief, No. 2).

Selected Writing of Jawaharlal Nehru, Vol. 15, Old Series and Vols. 1 , 2 and 5 of New Series

Senate Sub-Committee on Balochistan. (n.d.). Final report headed by Senator Mushahid Hussain Sayed.

Sethi, Najam. 'Balochistan's Volcanic Eruption', Editorial. The Friday Times, Lahore (January 2005): 14-20.

Shah, A. H. (2007). The volatile situation of Balochistan - options to bring it into streamline (Master's thesis). Naval Postgraduate School, Monterey, CA.

Siddiqa, A. (2007). Military Inc. inside Pakistan's military economy. London: Pluto. Stanley, M., Koryukin, E., & Maraboli, L. (2006). Balochistan economic report - mining sector development (Presentation). The World Bank Group.

Siddiqa, Dr Ayesha. 'The Cost of Conflict in Balochistan', The Friday Times January (2005): 21-26.

Siddiqi, Farhan Hanif. "Security Dynamics in Pakistani Balochistan: Religious Activism and Ethnic Conflict in the War on Terror." Asian Affairs: An American Review, vol. 39, no. 3, 2012, pp. 157-175., doi:10.1080/00927678.2012.704834

Sinha, Aditya. 'Battlefield Balochistan', Hindustan Times New Delhi, 15 January (2006). Weaver, Mary Anne, Pakistan in the Shadow of Jihad and Afghanistan. New York: Farrar, Straus and Giroux, 2002.

Supreme Court declares Reko Diq agreement void. (2013). Dawn. 13 January 2013. Retrieved February 22, 2013, from http://dawn.com/2013/01/07/supreme-court- declares-reko-diq-agreement-unlawful/

Syed, B. S. (2011, September 11). Pakistan seeks Bramdagh's extradition. Dawn. Retrieved September 11, 2011, from http://dawn.com/2011/09/11/pakistan-seeks- bramdaghs-extradition/

T. C. Coen, The Indian Political Service: A Study in Indirect Rule, 1971, London: Chatto and Windus and Allied Publishers, New Delhi.

T. H. Thornton, Colonel Sir Robert Sandeman: His Life and Work on Our Indian Frontier, London, 1895 (Quetta, 1977).

Talbot, I. (2002). The Punjabization of Pakistan: Myth or reality? In C. Jaffrelot (Ed.), Pakistan - nationalism without a nation? (pp. 51-62). Delhi: Manohar and Zed Press.

Talpur, Mir Mohammad Ali. "Not the Brinjals' Servant." Daily Times, 12 Sept. 2015, dailytimes.com.pk/98543/not-the- brinjals-servant/.

Temple, D. (2007). The Iran-Pakistan-India pipeline: The intersection of energy and politics. New Delhi: The Institute of Peace and Conflict Studies.

Titus, P. (Ed.). (1997). Marginality and modernity: Ethnicity and change in post-colonial Balochistan. Karachi: Oxford University Press.

Transfer of Power (in 12 Vols.) specially Vols. VI and VII and X-XII about British official records, Directives to Mountbatten, Correspondence between Listowell (Secretary of State) and Mountbatten regarding Baluchistan, All the details of negotiations between the three sides, Kalat, League and the British.

U. Aitchison, A Collection of Treaties, Agreements and Sanads Relating to India and Neighbouring Countries XI, XIII, Calcutta, 1933

US bill seeks Balochistan sovereignty. (2012, February 18). Dawn.

US State Department. (2006a). 06ISLAMABAD5596, Ryan Crocker, Government's charm offensive leaves many Baloch unimpressed. Embassy Islamabad, April 3. Retrieved July 25, 2012, from http://wikileaks.org/cable/2006/04/06ISLAMABAD5596.html#

US State Department. (2006b). Islamabad 017547, Peter Bodde, 'Balochistan (6): The Nationalist Insurgency', Embassy Islamabad, September 4. Retrieved May 2, 2012, from http://wikileaks.org/cable/2006/09/06ISLAMABAD17547.html#

US State Department. (2006c). Islamabad 16994, Peter Bodde, Balochistan (4): Who's who - the Baloch tribes. Embassy Islamabad, August 29. Retrieved November 15, 2013, from http://wikileaks.org/cable/2006/08/06ISLAMABAD16994.html

US State Department. (2007). 07ISLAMABAD2782, Peter Bodde, Boucher visits Balochistan. Embassy Islamabad, June 22. Retrieved July 25, 2012, from http:// wikileaks.org/cable/2007/06/07ISLAMABAD2782.html#

US State Department. (2008). 08ISLAMABAD3533, Anne W. Patterson, Zardari reaches out to Balochistan. Embassy Islamabad, November 10. Retrieved July 25, 2012, from http://wikileaks.org/cable/2008/11/08ISLAMABAD3533.html#

US State Department. (2009a). 09ISLAMABAD42, Anne W. Patterson, Pakistan political roundup. Embassy Islamabad, January 8. Retrieved July 25, 2012, from http:// wikileaks.org/cable/2009/01/09ISLAMABAD42.html#

US State Department. (2009b). 09ISLAMABAD1840, Pakistan media reaction. Embassy Islamabad, August 7. Retrieved July 25, 2009, from http://wikileaks.org/cable/2009/08/09ISLAMABAD1840.html#

US State Department. (2009c). 09ISLAMABAD3037, Anne W. Patterson, 'Baloch request UNCHR facilitate movement of Brahmdagh Bugti to Ireland'. Embassy Islamabad, December 18. Retrieved July 25, 2012, from http:// wikileaks.org/ cable/2009/12/09ISLAMABAD3037.html

US State Department. (2009d). 09RIYADH716, Saudi interior ministry briefs Special Advisor Holbrooke and Treasury Das Glaser on Terrorism Finance, Embassy Riyadh, May 25. Retrieved August 5, 2013, from http://wikileaks. org/cable/2009/ 05/09RIYADH716.html

US State Department. (2009e). 09ISLAMABAD1840, Pakistan media reaction: August 07, 2009. Retrieved August 5, 2013, from http://wikileaks.org/ cable/2009/08/ 09ISLAMABAD1840.html

US State Department. (2010a). 10NEWDELHI387, Uzra Zeya, more on Feb 25 Indo- Pak talks: 'No breakdown but no breakthrough', February 25. Retrieved from http://wikileaks.org/cable/2010/02/10NEWDELHI387.html#

US State Department. (2010b). 10ABUDHABI33, UAE FM discusses Taliban financial flows and reintegration with Amb. Holbrooke and Treasury A/S Cohen, January 25. Retrieved August 5, 2013, from http://wikileaks.org/ cable/2010/01/10ABUDHABI33. html

W. A. Fairservis, Preliminary Report on the Pre-Historic Archaeology of the Afghan Baluchi Areas, American Museum Novitates, American Museum of Natural History, New York, 1952.

W.A. Wilcox, Pakistan: The Consolidation of a Nation, 1963, Columbia University Press, New York and London. (Detailed account of the absorption of the Princely states into Pakistan.)

W. T. Blanford, Note on the Geological Formations Seen Along the Coasts of Baluchistan, etc., Records of the Geological Survey of India, Calcutta, 1872.

Wani, Shakoor Ahmad. "The Changing Dynamics of the Baloch Nationalist Movement in Pakistan." Asian Survey, vol. 56, no. 5, 2016, pp. 807-832., doi:10.1525/as.2016.56.5.807.

Wani, Shakoor Ahmad. "The Changing Dynamics of the Baloch Nationalist Movement in Pakistan: From Autonomy toward Secession." Asian Survey, vol. 56, no. 5, 2016, pp. 807-832. JSTOR, www.jstor.org/stable/26364389. Accessed 25 Nov. 2020.

Weaver, Mary Anne. Pakistan: Deep inside the World's Most Frightening State. Farrar, Straus and Giroux, 2010.

Werbner, P. (2004). Theorising complex diasporas: Purity and hybridity in the South Asian public sphere in Britain. Journal of Ethnic and Migration studies, 30(5), 895-911.

Wirsing, R. (2008). Baloch nationalism and the geopolitics of energy resources: The changing context of separatism in Pakistan. Carlisle, PA: Strategic Studies Institute, U.S. Army War College.World Bank. (2008). Pakistan: Balochistan economic report from periphery to core, Volume II: Full report (Report No. 40345-PK). Document of the World Bank. Retrieved from https://openknowledge.worldbank. org/handle/10986/8094

World Bank. (2008). Pakistan: Balochistan economic report from periphery to core, Volume II: Full report (Report No. 40345-PK). Document of the World Bank. Retrieved from https://openknowledge.worldbank.org/handle/10986/8094

Y. Gankowsky, "Social Structure of Pakistan's Brahui-Baluchi Population," Journal of South Asian and Middle Eastern Studies 5/4, 1982, pp. 57-73.

Yusuf, Moed. 'Use of Force will Worsen the Situation in Balochistan'. The Friday Times, January (2005): 21-26.

Zulfiqar, Shahzada. 'Land-Mine'. Newsline, August (2004), 58-60.

"Baloch Seek Answers from Pakistan as More Disappear in Conflict." Al Jazeera, 20 July 2020, www.aljazeera.com/news/2020/7/20/baloch-seek-answers-from-pakistan-as-more-disappear-in-conflict.

"Chinese to Outnumber Balochistan Natives by 2048: FPCCI Report." The Financial Express, 29 Dec. 2016, www.financialexpress.com/world-news/chinese-to-outnumber-balochistan-natives-by-2048-fpcci-report/490203/.

"Growing Regional Disparity in Incomes." Dawn, 14 Feb. 2005, www.dawn.com/news/382393/growing-regional- disparity-in-incomes.

"Health Minister Declares Nutrition Emergency in Balochistan." Dawn, 26 Nov. 2018, www.dawn.com/news/1447706/health-minister-declares-nutrition-emergency-in-balochistan.

"Mr. Musharraf's Other War." The New York Times, 23 Feb. 2006, www.nytimes.com/2006/02/23/opinion/mr- musharrafs-other-war.html.

"Projects without Public Consent Not Acceptable, Says Mengal." Dawn, 25 Feb. 2015, www.dawn.com/news/1165770.

"Rising Organized Political Violence in Balochistan: A Resurgence of Baloch Separatism?" ACLED, 5 Sept. 2020, acleddata.com/2020/09/04/rising-organized-political-violence-in-balochistan-a-resurgence-of-baloch-separatism/.

"Wavering Baloch Resistance?" The Nation, 28 June 2017, nation.com.pk/29-Jun-2017/wavering-baloch-resistance. "WHITE PAPER BUDGET 2015-16." Balochistan.Gov.Pk, Finance Department-Government of Balochistan, 2015, balochistan.gov.pk/wp-content/uploads/2019/07/White-Paper-Budget-2015-16.pdf.

"World Bank. 2008. Pakistan - Balochistan Economic Report : From Periphery to Core, Volume 1. Summary Report. Washington, DC. © World Bank. https://openknowledge.worldbank.org/handle/10986/8082 License: CC BY 3.0 IGO."

"'We Can Torture, Kill, or Keep You for Years.'" Human Rights Watch, 28 July 2011, www.hrw.org/report/2011/07/28/we-can-torture-kill-or-keep-you-years/enforced-disappearances-pakistan-security.

Index

H

I

J

K

L

M

N

O

P

Q

R

S

T